You Are My Happy Ending

You Are My Happy Ending

SCHITT'S CREEK AND THE LEGACY OF QUEER TELEVISION

EMILY GARSIDE

APPLAUSE
THEATRE & CINEMA BOOKS

Essex, Connecticut

APPLAUSE
THEATRE & CINEMA BOOKS

An imprint of Globe Pequot, the trade division of
The Rowman & Littlefield Publishing Group, Inc.
4501 Forbes Blvd., Ste. 200
Lanham, MD 20706
www.rowman.com

Distributed by NATIONAL BOOK NETWORK

Library of Congress Cataloging-in-Publication Data

Names: Garside, Emily, author.
Title: You are my happy ending : Schitt's Creek and the legacy of queer television / Emily Garside.
Description: Essex, Connecticut : Applause Cinema & Theatre Books, 2024. | Includes bibliographical references and index. | Summary: "From its modest beginnings to its massive Emmy sweep, You Are My Happy Ending tells the story of how Schitt's Creek became the surprise hit that changed the way we think about LGBTQ relationships" —Provided by publisher.
Identifiers: LCCN 2023033590 (print) | LCCN 2023033591 (ebook) | ISBN 9781493067978 (paperback) | ISBN 9781493067985 (epub)
Subjects: LCSH: Schitt$ Creek (Television program) | Gay men on television. | LCGFT: Television comedies.
Classification: LCC PN1992.77.S347 C37 2024 (print) | LCC PN1992.77.S347 (ebook) | DDC 791.45/72—dc23/eng/20231001
LC record available at https://lccn.loc.gov/2023033590
LC ebook record available at https://lccn.loc.gov/2023033591

∞™ The paper used in this publication meets the minimum requirements of American National Standard for Information Sciences—Permanence of Paper for Printed Library Materials, ANSI/NISO Z39.48-1992.

For my Mum, Beverley Slee,
who is the Moira and Johnny to my David Rose.

Contents

Acknowledgments

Thank you to 404Ink, who generously allowed me to take the work on this show I created with them and grow it.

Thank you to the fans who generously shared their stories of *Schitt's Creek* with me. Who told me over and over what this show meant, and reminded me why I wanted to write this book. I'm sorry I didn't have space for all your stories, but I'll forever treasure having heard them. To everyone in the fandom who has been a friend near or far, of which there are wonderfully too many to mention, I appreciate you.

To everyone who read my fanfiction, who let me tell my stories through David and Patrick, you helped me write this book too. (Sooner or later, someone will figure out who I am too.)

Thank you to Mads Misani for always being my ally in this fandom and to you along with Rebecca Humphreys-Lamford for being part of my journey with Patrick Brewer and feeling "right."

As ever "The Grown Ups" who weather every book with me. And Jon Rainford who learned more about fanfiction than he bargained for when he supported this book.

Thanks to the Bishopsgate Institute for allowing me to try out some of the ideas in this book in my teaching.

Thank you Eugene and Dan Levy, for creating a world where all of us fit in.

Introduction
"It's Called Schitt's Creek, and It's Where We Live"

"It's called Schitt's Creek, and it's where we live," Johnny Rose declares at the end of season 2 of the CBC hit. By the end of season 6 in 2020, many people wanted to call Schitt's Creek home. As the world became a very different place overnight, many people found refuge in the fictional town they could escape to for twenty-two minutes of their day. It's unusual for the final season to be the point where everybody suddenly discovers your show, but that seemed to be the case for the creation of Eugene and Dan Levy; social media was awash with gifs, TikTok with Moira Rose impressions, and numerous "quarantine pets" got christened David, Patrick, or Moira.

But while the show had a "moment" culminating in an Emmy sweep in 2021, the slow burn and, indeed, the deeper impact of the show is far more significant. It had been a "slow burn" hit on CBC, gathering fans' loyal following before it exploded when Netflix bought the rights. Wrapped up in this renewed interest was the introduction of Patrick Brewer as a love interest for David in season 3. Their romance blossoming in season 4 quickly became an iconic queer love story that fans prayed would end well. Dan Levy delivered, giving queer viewers and himself as a gay man the "happy ending" he longed to see.

"Ew David": Discovering the Hottest New Best-Kept Secret

By the summer of 2020, everyone had visited *Schitt's Creek*, a quirky town in Nowheresville, Canada. Sounds of "Ew David" could be heard far and wide, and the show's stars, particularly co-creator Dan Levy, were riding high on the wave of its success. David Rose briefly went viral with his "wine, not the label" speech; until then, *Schitt's Creek* had felt like the best-kept TV secret. And then in 2020, with the world on pause, and just before it swept the board at the Emmys, it was the show everyone was talking about. The show occupied a space of both slow-burn hit and overnight success simultaneously. With the impact of 2020 and much of the world stuck at home, there's no doubt that the happy, safe world of *Schitt's Creek* became a tonic of sorts to the world's reality. While the pandemic and politics seemed to tear the world apart, the quiet acceptance of Schitt's Creek the town and *Schitt's Creek* the show became an important part of its success. And in a politically and socially fraught year, what better time for the show that sought to "lead by example" to get its time in the spotlight finally?

Suddenly the world discovered that "the mom from *Home Alone*" was Moira Rose, and somehow Eugene Levy had gone from "the dad from *American Pie*" to everyone's new adopted father figure. And wrapped up in that, the audience was rooting for a gay love story as the central "endgame" love affair in a sitcom for the first time. And all from a small Canadian TV show.

For many, the show and its creators had come seemingly from nowhere. Daniel Levy had not followed directly in his father's footsteps. While he had several small acting credits, he began presenting early in his career. He is known in Canada for his time as an MTV Canada presenter, hosting various shows, including covering various red-carpet events. He then became known for The Great Canadian Baking Show, hosting the show's first two seasons alongside Julia Chan (2017–2018). These seasons overlapped with the first seasons of *Schitt's Creek* and so for audiences, depending on which you saw first. By comparison, Eugene Levy has worked consistently but often in the background for several decades. Despite being well known to many—in particular, by the loyal fans of Christopher Guest's films, many of which Levy co-wrote and starred in. Or, for a generation being a face of *Second City Television*, again with a cult following. To a younger generation—specifically the generation around his son's age—he was best known as Jim's dad from the *American Pie* movies. As with most great character actors, Eugene Levy was probably known to most as "that guy from that thing" with a quick look to IMDB to remind viewers exactly what they were remembering.

But in the autumn of 2020, *Schitt's Creek* was sweeping the board at the Emmys. After taking five seasons even to get one nomination, they won eleven in 2020, including for all the leading cast members and Outstanding

Comedy Series. For a show that ended by placing a gay wedding and a gay romantic "happy ending" at its core, this was a huge moment in inclusive, progressive television. On Emmy night, the CN Tower lit gold to celebrate its homegrown hit. But the importance of *Schitt's Creek* extended far beyond the critical and commercial successes at the end of 2020.

But queerness in *Schitt's Creek* is not just limited to the central romance. At the same time, Patrick and David's story is iconic, groundbreaking, and hugely important to many people. The show is a "queer" one in the broader sense, not just a "gay story." Taking the notion of "queerness" in its truest form in that it breaks down existing expectations and structures and blows them open. The show subverts expectations from previous TV comedy-drama, and in showing the idyllic world of Schitt's Creek, the town, *Schitt's Creek*, the show, asks us to question how we look at the world.

The queerness of *Schitt's Creek* will be looked at not through the lens of just David and Patrick and their relationship (though that is, of course, central) but more through the broader definition of "queerness" and "queering." Because first, queerness is not just who you love or have sex with (as much as that is an element). Queerness is also a way of being. It is fundamentally also at odds with the status quo. It's about creating spaces where people can see themselves authentically. And if that isn't the town of Schitt's Creek, what is?

Though the conversation here is about *Schitt's Creek* and its power as a revolutionary queer text, this aspect highlights the idea that spaces where people can be their authentic selves benefit everyone. As queer people, we see it all the time—in the places we can be our authentic selves, everything from romantic relationships to work, we live and thrive. The show is a marker of that, with a culture of inclusivity fostered from the top down. And in the world of the show, then, we see what happens when you take away the fear of prejudice and replace it with support—everyone elevates one another to be their best selves, and it also snowballs: one person feeling supported and able to be their best self will help other people to do the same. Moira is as ever right, "When one of us shines, all of us shine."

Looking at how the town looks at life, the idea of the town as a queer safe space and what that means in the broader context is reflected. The town allows the Roses to thrive. It offers a message of support to bring out the best in people through tolerance beyond gay identities to take in Jewish identity, mental health support, and neurodivergence in the Roses. Beyond that, how the show treats women, and the solid feminist

The Rose Family, Episode 1 "Our Cup Runneth Over."
Pop TV Network/Photofest © Pop TV Network

perspective, its offers are explored before looking at the Roses and the notion of a "chosen family" within the show. Looking at how queering the idea of family is presented in the show, what the characters learn from queer culture, and what viewers might learn in return.

The book begins with a look at the queer characters, their various "coming out" moments, and why these are all important. The book reflects on specific queer narratives, from including *Cabaret* in the show's storylines to David and Patrick's romance and what it means for queer love stories on screen. Wrapped up in this is a reflection on queer affection and sexuality on screen and how the show contributes to the conversation and activism in that area. The discussion considers what the queer stories do for activism, representation, and furthering the representation of queer people. Then, the book moves on to consider the role of activism beyond the show, in terms of its promotion, visibility of queer creators, and adjacent activism. We end with a reflection on Dan Levy's commitment to activism and how he has taken his notion of "lead by example" with the show and embodied that personally and politically moving forward.

Fans were integral in supporting the show through the early seasons when it was a hidden gem, and they continue to be necessary even after the show ends. In two chapters, we look at how fans embraced, responded to, and were impacted by the show. Then, we look at how fanfiction and fans expressing their love for (and occasional lust for) David and Patrick in stories has been essential and how in a show where the ending is already happy, the conversation in fanfiction and fandom, more broadly, has changed.

In pushing the boundaries of queer representation on TV, Levy also showed that he "knows his history" in both TV and queer representation. And within the world of the show, and in reading it as viewers, in its "town without prejudice" Schitt's Creek the town and *Schitt's Creek* the show is aware of that. And it becomes a powerful tool.

1 A (Canadian) Family Show

Schitt's Creek was a slow burn in terms of ratings and fan popularity. It first aired in January 2015 on the Canadian Broadcasting Corporation (CBC), and while the Levys pitched the show to various networks in the United States and Canada, it was ultimately the "homegrown" element that found it an unlikely home with CBC, which is not a network known for comedy output. When *Schitt's Creek* was pitched to them in 2014, it was as Eugene Levy remembered a case of an opportune moment. The CBC was intent on rebranding itself. "When we came in, we were at the right place at the right time" (Wong, January 12, 2015). Eugene Levy's experience working in film and TV for several decades no doubt helped steer the network discussions—he recalls responding to CBC nervously saying they "couldn't wait to get their hands on it" (Jung, January 16, 2019). It also wasn't a fit for many networks; again Eugene Levy recalled that other networks, including HBO and Showtime, did not respond well to the idea. Finding a home on CBC then seemed an almost fatalistic stroke of luck that ultimately allowed the show freedom and understanding to tell the stories they wanted to.

In part, they were ahead of what CBC planned as a new curve for their output. "In 2014, we decided to prioritize half-hour, single-camera comedies with a unique point of view and authentic, character-driven storytelling," said Sally Catto, general manager for programming at CBC, in 2019. In a case of the right show at the right time, CBC was able to get behind the show but also allow them relative freedom that likely more established US counterparts would not. Similarly, the network's new direction and support of a new comedy-drama show also meant they got on board for the long haul; the show wasn't an out-of-the-box hit in the first season. It did steady numbers of around the one million viewers mark on first airing (some episodes seeing half that). This held steady across season two, which the network greenlit before the first season even aired, in another bold and supportive move. But it wasn't until the fourth season that the show broke two million viewers an episode. On another network, the same grace period probably wouldn't have been offered. And neither would perhaps the boldness of support for both their ideas, from the title that some US broadcasters even struggled to say on air in promotional slots to the inclusive and groundbreaking LGBTQ+ content that would also characterize it.

The idea itself was also an out-there and quirky one. The format is not quite a "cookie cutter" for comedy or drama. It falls into the "sitcom" format in terms of run time and uses many conventions and influences of the genre. However, it can't be strictly termed one in TV terms: it's a single-camera show (multi-camera filming style being a hallmark of sitcom style). While not all sitcoms utilize the live studio audience, *Schitt's Creek* also eschews this being part studio-filmed and part location-based. Technical television definitions aside, the dramatic style also defies some traditional conventions. It is a character-driven comedy-drama that, despite seeming an outlandish concept on the surface, has its characters' emotional journey at its heart.

In the United Kingdom, the show found a home on E4, a traditional home for North American imported sitcoms. Usually, a space and timeslot (the Friday evening slot previously occupied by *The Big Bang Theory* and *How I Met Your Mother*) that does well for sitcoms, *Schitt's Creek* did equally quietly well in the United Kingdom. That is until they ran into controversy during the fourth season for allegedly censoring a kiss between David and Patrick. The network responded that it was a "human error" edit for timings that would be rectified in future broadcasts. Not alone in this issue with edits in international markets, Comedy Central India also came under fire for similar censorship. Though there are minor blips in an otherwise successful export, the ongoing discussion around content illustrates the show's importance and its depictions of queer relationships.

Around these minor controversies, the real boost to the show came in 2017 when Netflix bought it. With seasons 1 and 2 initially dropping on Netflix, the third season came to the streaming service shortly after its initial broadcast. Following this pattern with seasons 4 to 6, with international markets including the United Kingdom and season 6 coming to Netflix before cable networks, it was Netflix that allowed the show to leap in popularity by its final two seasons. The unprecedented twist came in 2020 when the show began airing as planned on January 7, and by the time the finale (in the United States and Canada) came around in April, the whole world had stopped, and *Schitt's Creek* had become a worldwide "lockdown hit."

CBC and the Origins of *Schitt's Creek*

The CBC is a public broadcasting service over AM and FM radio networks and television networks in English and French, two national cable television channels, and shortwave radio, among other media in Canada. Advertising sales and annual appropriations from Parliament finance the CBC's operations. It is especially noted for the high quality of its news and public affairs programs. CBC's headquarters are in Ottawa, Ontario. It would become the home of *Schitt's Creek*, a network that at once didn't know what to do with it but didn't interfere. This was to be intrinsic in the success of the show—a slow burn of a show that on a more cut-throat network would have ended before it began.

The CBC was created as a radio service by the Canadian Parliament in the Broadcasting Act of 1936. It presented various news, documentaries, dramas, classical music, entertainment, and educational programs on English and French networks. The CBC began offering television programs in French and English in Montreal, Quebec, and Toronto, Ontario, in 1952. Among its most popular programs, *Hockey Night in Canada* was the weekly broadcast of National Hockey League games. Montreal is the network's principal source for programming in French, and Toronto is its primary source for programming in English; Vancouver, British Columbia, and Winnipeg, Manitoba, are other important sources of English-language programming. Programs in both languages originate in Ottawa. Apart from its networks, the CBC has a full-time news channel on national cable television. With the Canadian Department of National Defence, the CBC operates an armed force broadcasting service; the CBC also operates an international shortwave radio service.

It is a public broadcaster in three senses, as David Taras and Christopher Waddell outline in their book on the broadcaster (2020). First through public funding, second through its mandate to the public and national interest, and finally through free TV/news services (Taras and Waddall, 2020, p. 1). The CBC fulfills the critical role of public broadcasters worldwide, a mediation between state and media and a bubble away from commercial media production. It fulfills an essential social function, like the BBC in the United Kingdom, RTE in Ireland, or the Australian

Broadcasting Corporation in Australia. Indeed, the CBC has high aims in that area; in the 1991 Broadcasting Act, it was set out that the public broadcaster was expected to be "predominantly and distinctly Canadian," as well as reflect the country and its regions while contributing to "national consciousness and identity while participating in the flow and exchange of cultural expression," while having the remit to reflect Canada's multicultural and multiracial character. As Taras and Waddall say, it was expected to be all things to all people (2020, p. 5).

Toronto, where *Schitt's Creek* was filmed, ranks third as an exporter of television programming in North America, behind only Los Angeles and New York City. Among North American cities in total industry production (Film and Television Industry Review 2011), CAD $903.5 million were spent by production companies on 209 major film and television projects in 2010 in Toronto, according to a 2011 report from the Toronto Film and Television Office. In 2011, the film industry contributed CAD $1.13 billion from 244 on-location film and television projects to Toronto, the largest figure since 2002; this increase in revenue over the past years was attributed to a film tax credit offered by the provincial government in 2009. A 47 percent increase in Hollywood productions in 2011 over 2010 was mainly attributed to this tax credit. In 2012, film and television production increased again to CAD $1.2 billion generated. Leading up to the production of *Schitt's Creek* in 2015, Toronto, where presentations were based, was already a world leader in film production.

However, its status outside the US-based Los Angeles and New York bases had advantages for homegrown talent, away from the circus or pressure cooker environments of these "industry towns." Because Toronto (and its West Coast sibling Vancouver) generate income from outside productions, there is a certain element of breathing space for homegrown shows among them. This film economy also subsidizes homegrown work, but it needs to be improved comparatively. Liz Czach, in her work on the lack of Canadian "stars" in a homegrown sense, states that the relatively low number of feature films produced yearly doesn't allow Canadian actors to build up a substantial body of work in feature films needed to become a "star" in the bigger sense (quoted in Bredin, Henderson, and Matheson, 2012, p. 64).

From its inception, the CBC intended to convey Canadian culture and be an instrument of national unity. Given the popularity and proliferation of competing programs in the United States, these objectives have been difficult to achieve. Therefore, quotas mandate the percentages of CBC programming that must be of Canadian origin—and so entered *Schitt's Creek* when they were looking for original programming.

As Eugene Levy recalled, it was good timing for the network and the show: "The CBC was intent on rebranding themselves. When we came in, we were at the right place at the right time. . . . We set out to make a show we wanted to watch. And the CBC, fortunately, latched on to it in a big way and said, 'This is what we want to do'" (Wong, January 12, 2015).

However, as Taras and Waddall point out in their analysis of the CBC, finding audiences and producing programs in a purely "Canadian" setting is difficult, especially when competing with star-studded American counterparts (2020, p. 7). In the infancy of funding such drama-comedy output, CBC needed help to back the entire series. What it became was a co-production between three funding networks/distributors. Eventually, they cobbled together funding—first, they made a deal with the CBC. Europe's ITV Studios came on as a distributor, and, finally, Pop rounded out the budget. The arrangement left the Levys with an unusual degree of creative control. *Schitt's Creek* became a co-production in part for these reasons. While the original offers from bigger US networks likely came with a larger budget, they also came with a loss of creative control for the Levys (the show was supported, too, it's of note, by Fred Levy, Eugene's experienced producer brother).

The co-production also put the show as a network buddy with *Coronation Street,* one of Canada's international programs supported by the CBC/ITV collaboration. *The Great British Bake Off* was known to fans for Dan Levy's two-season stint on the Canadian version of the show. It also housed many significant contributions to Canadian TV, including *Franklin the Turtle,* which Noah Reid voiced for several seasons. Or, of course, *Degrassi,* in which a guest spot on is a rite of passage for any actor in Canada, from Drake to Dan Levy and Noah Reid. The network was home to *Second City Television,* the show on which Eugene Levy and Catherine O'Hara met and got their comedy start (the show continued, just broadcast on another network).

This formed the logistical backdrop of *Schitt's Creek* finding a truly Canadian home. But how, then, thematically, did it fit into Canadian TV? What, indeed, is Canadian TV as a landscape? John Doyle maintains two strands of Canadian TV, the first being "generic," which follows the formulaic American approach: good-looking characters, love triangles, and characters overcoming adversity, among other elements. His key elements to these, too, are they are set in fantasy locations, often divorced from reality—everything from a generic high school to a ski resort or beach community. Doyle argues that the second model of Canadian TV is more "Canadian" and the "hosers, whores, boozers, and losers" category. Doyle puts another famous Canadian export, *Trailer Park Boys*, in this category. In that show, Doyle points to elements such as growing marijuana as a "legitimate occupation" and cigarette smoking, fistfights, and gunplay. *Trailer Park Boys* was a forerunner, but as Doyle expands on it, there is a whole stream of Canadian drama.

These, then, were previous examples of comedy and comedy-drama from the CBC. The most successful/well-known precursors were probably *Corner Gas* and *Little Mosque on the Prairie*. Interestingly, both take elements that made *Schitt's Creek* what it was—small town life, fish-out-of-water stories, and a heartfelt element at the center of the comedy. Following *Schitt's Creek*, the CBC program *Kim's Convenience* was also flying the flag for diversity centering on immigrant and first-generation Canadian experience. We see similar overlaps if we mash up this with the *Corner Gas* model, another highly successful precursor to *Schitt's Creek*. It's the small town storytelling, a small cast (eight in this case); relatively speaking, nothing ever happens. It's *Seinfeld*, the show where famously nothing happened, but with a twist. It's mundane, has no real hero and villain element, and has sweet humor but isn't saccharine.

Add the style of *Little Mosque on the Prairie*, where a fish-out-of-water narrative is again given a particular Canadian twist, and we start to see the mix of shows that led to *Schitt's Creek*. *Degrassi*, that rite of passage for Canadian teens and actors alike, also stepped away from the American model of TV. Like *Schitt's Creek*, it was ahead of its time and more conservative American teen dramas for the way it talked of everything from teen pregnancy to drugs to sexuality. Crucially too, in *Trailer Park Boys*, a couple of characters were gay, and nobody ever minded or remarked on it much. That idea of small town Canada, of a small-scale Canadian drama doing something a little differently from the American model, was sown in this TV genre. It has roots in the gentle culture clash of *Little Mosque* and the low-level social justice model inherent there. Even the more "mainstream" Canadian staple teen soap *Degrassi* was often ahead of its peers in terms of representation. Dan Levy, who is not only the age to have been "raised" on *Degrassi* but also fulfilled the Canadian actor rite of passage and appeared in it, was therefore embedded in a TV culture that was looking to the more inclusive even if it still wasn't the norm.

The point is that *Schitt's Creek* didn't spring from nowhere; as with all cultural production, it is a product of its surroundings. While some specific comedic roots stem from Eugene Levy and Catherine O'Hara, as well as a deep rooting in queer cultural legacy, a certain amount of Canadian cultural heritage is embedded there too.

There are a lot of "what-ifs" around what would have happened if an American network had picked up the show. In one brutally honest world, there's the prospect it would have been canceled after one season for underperforming, never allowing it to grow into the show we know today. Or there's the equally brutal version where the chokehold of network control at best doesn't get the quirky humor written in or wants to recast Catherine O'Hara for not "getting" her Moira. Or, at worst, decides to "count the kisses" as Dan Levy alludes to for gay characters on network TV (Artiva, January 10, 2019). David and Patrick probably wouldn't have been the David and Patrick we love. More importantly, in that scenario, we would have gotten a completely different team, not just different actors. Writers drafted in from the United States along with sets of creative teams who probably couldn't have built the same local team that ended up making the show what it became.

But what was important was the hands-off approach the Levys describe, which may have started as the CBC needing help figuring out what to do with their new endeavor into comedy-drama. Because of the smaller-scale nature of the show, it took a level of trust to maintain the show. Team Levy proved after a few seasons they were delivering a quality product and had done so with minimal intervention. So the CBC was able to stay hands-off. That won't (and probably has yet to) work for every show, but the particular alchemy of this one made it happen. The right home is vital for the show, and the CBC allowed the show to flourish and become what it was. As Levy said in the same interview, the show was a "slow burn" in storytelling as much as a success (Artiva, January 10, 2019). It needed two seasons to grow into itself, and the CBC afforded it that.

There are questions too of *Schitt's Creek* about publicity and promotion. While the promotion in later seasons became more centered on activist elements, it also came easier with the profile of Netflix to boost the show. In the early years, much of the promotion was limited to Canadian media. As Czach asks: how Canadian-centered is Canadian entertainment media? And how did that serve the show? Czach asks how much these programs/media outlets focus on Canadian content or if they focus as much of the wider world on US-based news and content (quoted in Bredin, Henderson, and Matheson, 2012, p. 64). In the context of *Schitt's Creek*, this was important because, like every show, they relied on publicity to create attention. What did work in their favor was the backing of the CBC, who, in their commitment to supporting new original programming, was less ruthless than their US counterparts in their programming decisions. And, of course, the quirky elements of the collaboration worked in their favor too.

Canada has been known as "Hollywood North" since the 1970s, referencing the film production industries in the cheaper Canadian locations, primarily Toronto and Vancouver. For many reasons, this meant that when *Schitt's Creek* took a few seasons to take hold in ratings, it was far "safer" than it would have been elsewhere. Dan Levy often cited this as an element of its success: that the CBC supported it and let it grow. The slow burn of seasons 1 to 3 might have had something other than the might of the US network behind them or even a Canadian system that favored promoting its own. However, it did have a network happy to let it find its own feet and niche.

Canadian Comedy?

When considering *Schitt's Creek*, we might ask, "What is Canadian comedy?" Certainly, it has its unique brand of comedy. But what are the comedy shoulders it stands on in terms of influence? Dan Levy, like any millennial, was raised on a good deal of US comedy, as would the team of similar-aged writers. Equally, almost all Canadian writers were influenced by the context of their country's humor, which is similar yet distinct from their southern neighbors. While Eugene Levy stepped away from the writers' room after the first season, his overarching influence in shaping the show and his position as one of the legacies of Canadian comedy bears consideration.

Canadian comedians have largely been influenced by American and British culture and humor, as well as a smattering of French for the Quebecois-raised. They blend the comic traditions of these cultures with Canadian humor while maintaining an outsider perspective, the latter providing a separation or ironic distance, which has allowed for keen observational humor and parody. That said, their humor also lacks cohesiveness to outsiders. Dark and fatalistic are also used extensively by Canadian comedians. Again, this is something that resonates through *Schitt's Creek* and is generally attributed to the common reference point of the Canadian climate, the dangers of which are well-known to comedians who tour the vast and often sparsely populated country. Changing one's fate in the face of overwhelming forces may be impossible. Still, the comedian allows the audience to use laughter as a coping mechanism.

This unique, slightly weird blend might be why the show is known as one that grows into itself. On an audience, a combination of particularly Canadian humor and a fusing of comedy influences did it. The rest of the world is not quite used to this particular alchemy of influences. This is linked to the previous reflection on the Canadian film and TV pipeline, the element of Canadian actors finding stardom elsewhere. The idea that Canada makes and exports stars has long been a problem for the screen industry. We can use an analogy for that other most Canadian phenomenon, hockey: it's like when the best Canadian players are exported to other teams in the NHL. This happened, of course, with the mum and dad of *Schitt's Creek*, Eugene Levy and Catherine O'Hara. Their Hollywood careers being like Maple Leafs players being traded to the New York Rangers. It, too, is likely to happen for Dan Levy, Annie Murphy, Emily Hampshire, and Noah Reid post *Schitt's Creek* if the early trajectories of their careers continue.The hope being, of course, to keep the metaphor, that these actors eventually want to play for the Maple Leafs again or, at least, fly the flag for team Canada wherever they go.

A Family Show

It is, too, of course, a family show. Much has been written about the Levys creating the show together. This was and is particularly important when considering a father supporting his gay son in creating his queer show. It's a form of activism, a part of the show's politics. The father/son partnership also reflects and expands on the dynamic of David and Johnny within the show and helps create parallels with Johnny Rose as a TV father figure. But how did the show come about as such?

Dan Levy has discussed never bringing an idea to his dad, knowing the comedy, writing, and all-around weight of expectation that would bring both personally and professionally. So he waited for the right idea. Likewise, Eugene Levy, whose career has been built on steady consistency rather than seizing the big money or big exposure roles, was unlikely to have agreed to, even from his son, a mediocre idea. Indeed, Eugene Levy said to *Variety* that he worried at first: "What if he doesn't have the talent to do this as a writer? Do I tell him that he doesn't have the talent, or do we go [ahead] knowing nothing's going to happen with it? And you think Sophie had a choice! That was my dilemma, and there was nothing to worry about right away" (Turchiano, January 14, 2020).

Similarly, Dan feared getting it wrong and incurring the world's judgment. He'd largely avoided being linked to his dad professionally, save for one very funny sketch for MTV Canada where they spoofed "My Super Sweet Sixteen" together fittingly, an improv sketch Dan hadn't needed or wanted to be linked to his dad professionally. Dan also has spoken about needing the right idea and fit to collaborate with his dad. As he said to *Out Magazine*: "I always told myself that if I were ever to work with my dad or approach him about help, I'd want to be completely confident and very sure that the idea I would bring to him—considering I respect him so much—as one of quality. It came down to just being confident in what I could bring to the table" (Picardi, September 17, 2019).

Those comparisons are inevitable, if somewhat unfair. Making the comparison between Eugene Levy's more than five decades of experience in the industry to his son's debut show/performance is an unfair and unbalanced comparison. But they did lean toward the external, and it must be said internal fears around accusations of nepotism in the real world mirrored the privilege of the Rose children in the show. After all, was Moria confessing to buying David's patrons in his art gallery days ("General Store," season 4) all that far from Eugene Levy's son getting his own TV show? In one charming interview, the idea that Eugene was in any way a pushy showbiz parent is refuted in such a charmingly Eugene-Dan-Levy way that it must be true. Dan reflects on that fear and how his dad is far

The Rose Family, Schitt's Creek *promo image.*
Pictorial Press/Alamy Stock Photo

from the driving force in his career: "I think I was very fearful of that headline," he explains. "That I'd somehow weaseled my way into this through my dad, who, god love him, is not a mover and a shaker. He likes to stay home and eat sandwiches" (Dresden, February 12, 2018).

While nobody at CBC was "bought" by a well-meaning parent, and the show's commissioning was, as discussed, hard-won, it would be remiss not to acknowledge the privilege of that situation. Nobody is suggesting that Eugene Levy has the power to snap fingers and get a show made—far

Schitt's Creek *final season promotional poster.*
Album/Alamy Stock Photo

from it if the show's trajectory to its airing on CBC is considered. Still, there is an advantage to having a successful actor father, writer mother, and producer uncle. It is not so much in the ability to open doors; even if Eugene's name did open doors at networks, more was needed to seal the deal or *Schitt's Creek* would have been on whichever network they emailed first. Nor is it suggested that Eugene was bankrolling either at the show's start or his son in pursuing it; we know Dan created his career separate from his parents and on his terms. Like her brother's long path to success, Sarah Levy spent several years forging her acting career through the traditional route. That Dan and Eugene cast her in the most appropriate role of Twyla rather than the bigger and more marketable role of Alexis also says volumes about their focus on the show's quality over nepotism. Therefore, Eugene getting his son cast as his son in a TV show was about quality—this wasn't, after all, Hannah Montana, and nobody here is Billy Ray—but there are other more subtle advantages the Levys were playing with.

Dan Levy knew the advantages and curses he'd endure if he teamed up with his dad on any venture. If a person goes on to create something authentically and with hard work, can that advantage be held against them? Dan Levy went on to prove his worth. While the family name undoubtedly helped a door open for a conversation, a commission, and a further five seasons of the show didn't happen on family name alone. However, the family name or, more, the family influence did make the show what it was. It is also something they've never shied away from acknowledging. First, Dan was conscious of distancing himself from his dad's name. Because while we must acknowledge the privilege that working with Eugene Levy as his partner brought Dan Levy, perhaps more important is the comedic collaboration it also brought. That would come to be the heart of the comedy in *Schitt's Creek*, a mix of kindness amid a sense of realness, drama, and darkness at times that ultimately resolved itself in hope. It was a show borne out of a particularly Canadian network and the Canadian comedy family (both in blood terms and the show family they curated around it). So Canada served the show and became engrained in how it was made. But what beyond that influenced its comedic infrastructure?

2

Comedy (Family) Legacy

In looking at the show's place in Canadian TV history, we cannot ignore the legacy and, indeed, Canadian comedy royalty that is Eugene Levy and Catherine O'Hara. Pulling together the two strands of this chapter is the reuniting of Catherine O'Hara and Eugene Levy once again. Eugene Levy and Catherine O'Hara represent a particular tradition of comedy, and a specific Canadian branch of it. Both character actors are steeped in an improv tradition that is very American and has their Canadian spin on it. Not to highlight a cultural stereotype, but the Canadian *Second City Television* (*SCTV*) branches were always a little less cutting in their humor than their American counterparts, showing how to be funny—and often silly—without malice or meanness. This filtered through into *Schitt's Creek*.

SCTV, where O'Hara and Levy first met, along with their legacy of films, has undoubtedly shaped their approaches to comedy—notably when reunited—and filtered through into the show. *SCTV* was a comedy show that aired between 1976 and 1984. In fitting with the broader discussion here, it is an example of a highly successful Canadian export to the United States, where it also ran on two different networks. The show has its roots in the Second City stage show, which was resident in Toronto for many years as an offshoot of the Chicago institution. Improv in Canada, and as a training ground for Canadian actors, has an equally long tradition. The stage show, even before the TV show, was a space many successful Canadian performers passed through. In 1976 Andrew Alexander, then producer of the stage show, developed it for TV.

The original *SCTV* cast included Catherine O'Hara and Eugene Levy, John Candy, Joe Flaherty, Andrea Martin, Harold Ramis, and Dave Thomas. Mention should be made here of the gender balance of that series. The cast rotated, but Eugene Levy stayed throughout. It's also worth noting that many of the cast initially met in a Toronto production of *Godspell*, including later season additions of Martin Short, Victor Garber, Andrea Martin, Gilda Radner, and Dave Thomas. It's also noteworthy that Eugene Levy got fired from being Jesus in that production for being "too Jewish looking" (Victor Garber, who replaced him, had no such issue).

The show's premise is the broadcast day of a fictitious TV station (later network) in Melonville, a small town of indistinct location, another parallel with *Schitt's Creek*. These small town stories, through both other Canadian programming and the resultant humor they produce, are a through line to O'Hara and Levy's comedy roots. It's a slightly different style of small town humor from American comedies.

In performance, much of O'Hara and Eugene Levy's improv and sketch comedy roots can be seen; indeed, this is something that provides a performance bedrock for many an actor and a reason many a comedy/character actor comes from those roots particularly. What do the *SCTV* roots of O'Hara and Eugene Levy do for the origins of *Schitt's Creek*? A variety of things. First, the comedy partnership between the two gives the show much of what Johnny and Moira are. By the time *Schitt's Creek* came about, O'Hara and Levy had known and worked together for over four decades. The long marriage of the Roses is, in fact, their long professional relationship. There is an embedded working relationship there that couldn't be manufactured. With the vital trust and collaboration, there is also an understanding of how each other's comedy works and how to work with each other more importantly.

Both are character actors capable of being "big" characters, of the kind seen on *SCTV* more than elsewhere. Of the two, O'Hara is more well known for the kooky and outlandish characters, while Levy has ended up more as the "straight man" in comedy. Both traits come through in Moira and Johnny Rose and in performance elements from years of collaboration and trust in the other's instincts. Levy and O'Hara are also incredibly skilled at physical performance elements for comedy. O'Hara demonstrates that in Moira with her slightly over-the-top day-to-day. But it's also a powerful dramatic tool because we see "Moira Rose" and "Moira" as two sides of her personality. If O'Hara can be more "physical" in the role with her comedy, Levy also understates that aspect. While O'Hara can fall out of wardrobes using physical comedy, Levy can, pardon the cliché, do the same with an eyebrow raise. Referring to his most famous asset aside, Levy is a master of facial expression and gesture. Even while playing the "straight man" in Johnny, he incorporates much of that comedy legacy. Johnny is never mean to his wife, who he adores, but Levy expertly and hilariously communicates his frequent bafflement or exasperation with the slightest shift in facial expression.

A lesser-known comedic legacy is also incorporated into the show in the form of Chris Elliott. Much like the younger Levys, he was also born into a comedy family legacy. In his case, his father was American comedy legend Bob Elliott. Like the younger Levys, Elliott, too, ultimately worked with his dad in the "family business" on several projects across his career until Bob Elliott died in 2016. He wrote comedy books with his father, and like *Schitt's Creek*, his father played his dad on *Get a Life* (Fox, 1990–1992). Chris Elliott followed in his father's variety/sketch footsteps to a degree, appearing on *Saturday Night Live* for a season.

Bob Elliott was part of the American variety TV comedy that drew on vaudeville traditions. This tradition was related but different from the later, more subversive *SCTV* model of improvised comedy. The kind of work Bob Elliott did still feeds into American comedy today. As well as being "raised" in that comedy and working closely with his dad on several projects, Elliott has, out of all the *Schitt's Creek* cast, the most experience across American sitcoms.

Elliott, too, has established a long line in American comedy history in his own right. He was part of the *Saturday Night Live* team and appeared in many of America's leading sitcoms of the 1990s and 2000s. He had a starring role in *Get a Life* (Fox) for two years (1990–1992), again appearing with his father. But he also guest-starred or had recurring roles in many more, making him the genre's most experienced *Schitt's Creek* cast. He has made guest appearances on shows from *The King of Queens* and *The Nanny* and recurring roles on *Everybody Loves Raymond*. His most recent and probably most memorable to the thirty-something demographic was Mickey on *How I Met Your Mother*, where, for trivia nerds or simply those who like to make connections in such things, he played Mickey Aldrin, the father to *American Pie* alum Alyson Hannigan's character Lily. And if someone revealed that Mickey Aldrin and Roland Schitt were long-lost cousins, it wouldn't be a surprise. He was an early choice for Eugene Levy, who said of the casting in 2015: "I never worked with Chris, but we had him in mind from the beginning. It's hard to describe what it is about Chris, the insanity in his humor I took to when I first saw him on the Letterman show back in 1982. He does have a kind of a smarminess to his on-camera persona that just seemed like, 'It's there, that's what it is, that's what we want'" (Lloyd, February 11, 2015).

Using the well-established TV model of incorporating one well-known actor with the rest of the unknowns allows audiences to "adopt" the characters into their lives. This also meant including Chris Elliott (Roland Schitt) as the "And" credit in the show, the slot reserved for a "name" actor. So we have the number one and two—O'Hara and Levy—the leads and legacy of Canadian-American comedy, coupled with a pretty heavyweight "And" credit in Elliott. All are bringing a legacy of humor with them.

The *SCTV* roots are certainly felt in *Schitt's Creek* not only from the leads but actually for any writer/actor who comes up through the Canadian system; it's a reference point and influence. The sketch show may not be the most trendy in popularity, but it is still influential. There too was something quite fitting in that post *Schitt's Creek*, Daniel Levy was invited to host *Saturday Night Live* with, of course, a cameo from Eugene, which made some of this feel full circle (Eugene himself never got to host: his episode was pulled in 1985 due to a writer's strike).

Influences on the Show

Because there is something of a multilevel comedy going on in *Schitt's Creek*, it's at once what made it unique, perhaps for some difficult to get into, and ultimately different from other offerings of the time. The final piece of the puzzle comes from Dan Levy and a younger team of writers' influences in comedy, which does differ from their parent's generation.

A particular brand of short-form comedy developed in the 1990s and 2000s. The sitcom model is what we've become most used to. The joint 1990s juggernauts of *Seinfeld* and *Friends* led a distinct form of comedy. It rests on witty one-liners and a particular kind of urban friendship group. While *Seinfeld* and *Friends* have different types of humor in some ways, their success with that style of comedy program truly shaped the following decades.

However, *Schitt's Creek* isn't a sitcom; it's a single-camera comedy-drama, putting it in a slightly different television category. This is not a difference the casual viewer might pay attention to, but it matters stylistically and content-wise. In terms of comedy legacy, it also puts it in categories with other shows that no doubt influenced it. So, for one, the name-checked-by-David-Rose *Sex and the City* (1998–2001), while thematically worlds away from *Schitt's Creek*, showed a proper balance between comedy and drama in the original run. The storylines between the women and their lives were as important as the big laughs, and that influence can be traced. While *Schitt's Creek* isn't out to "shock" in the same way with sexual humor, *Sex and the City* paved the way for a more permissive TV conversation. *Sex and the City* and the more traditional sitcom *Will & Grace* also did much for their time for queer representation in comedy. It is important that these comedies, along with other recent shows like *Modern Family* and *Brooklyn Nine-Nine*, all took strides in making jokes *with* queer characters, not just about them. This style of humor also is woven into what helped create *Schitt's Creek*.

Of course, it also stands on the long tradition of small town and dysfunctional family comedies. So while dysfunctional families were seen on the peripheries of *Seinfeld* and *Friends*, and even in later traditional sitcoms like *How I Met Your Mother*, they weren't the focus in these. In many other shows of the 1990s and 2000s, the focus was the young twenty- and thirty-somethings in the city, working out life, not their family life at home. Other previous comedies exploring that dynamic were *Married with Children* or *King of Queens*, many of which in a similar ilk focused on working-class families around the cities the other glossier sitcoms concentrate on. The most hybrid of these was *Frasier* which, while focused on adult children in high-flying jobs, also had a family dynamic at its core. More recent shows that center on family dynamics include *It's Always Sunny in Philadelphia*, which also has a similar element of not always likable characters you still root for, *Arrested Development*, *Curb Your Enthusiasm*, and of course, *Modern Family*, which before *Schitt's Creek* was also foregrounding queer characters in mainstream comedy in a way that felt like progress (with some caveats around the amount of physical affection they showed).

Schitt's Creek also has its roots in oddball comedies. Much like the previous references to *Corner Gas* and *Little Mosque on the Prairie* in its native Canada, we can also see similarities with collective-oddball comedies like *30 Rock*, *Brooklyn Nine-Nine*, and *Parks and Recreation*, to name a few recent examples. They all center their heart and care about characters as much as they do the sometimes outlandish comedy in them.

Storytelling

As a comedy show in the twenty-one-minute format, however, *Schitt's Creek* offers a departure from the "big hitters" of the genre. The "classics" of the 1990s and early 2000s focused predominantly on the idea of "Big City Life" and what that brings—from *Seinfeld* and *Frasier* to *Friends* to *How I Met Your Mother*, the big city life was the focus. The latter two of the sitcoms, in particular *Friends*, imprinted on most millennials' lives;

the emphasis on "growing up" and the story stopping when you hit the milestone of marriage and kids was the focus. Similarly, the clue in the title of *How I Met Your Mother* strongly emphasizes the wild time of your twenties and then life not being interesting enough in your thirties to catalog. Meanwhile, *Frasier* and *Seinfeld* were more about dysfunctional "grown-ups" who had somehow "failed" the marriage and kids test of their later twenties and therefore slipped into something else. The alternative to these "coming of age" or "oddball" sitcoms is the family-based sitcom.

There's much to find in the Roses' dynamic across many TV families, particularly those that center on small-town life. They're not exactly the sentimental idealized family of *The Brady Bunch* or other classic US comedies. They would be more *The Simpsons* if Homer were somehow a millionaire: a family that is dysfunctional on the outside but ultimately love and care for one another. Thought it is not a comedy per se, the Roses, aesthetically and emotionally, are more like *The Addams Family*: strange from the outside, but under it, a caring, loving family, just in their peculiar way.

Similar is Micky Aldrin, mentioned earlier from *How I Met Your Mother.* Mickey and Roland offer parallels: they're both incompetent at many things. Still, they also would go to the ends of the earth for anyone they care about. It feels like *Schitt's Creek* and its plethora of interests are pulling together the best and often weirdest of comedy-drama and creating its version of that model.

The family drama has much in common with more recent works like *Modern Family* and *One Day at a Time*; all come back to the value of family—however you frame it—which is part of the through line *Schitt's Creek* offers. However, an essential element is the idea of chosen family. An important aspect of queer people's lives—surrounding themselves with people who support them, even if that means being apart from their "real" family—is explored subtly in *Schitt's Creek.*

But with all this, we must recognize the more traditional comedy roots of the 1990s/2000s sitcoms that *did* have a hold on our comedy landscape. The writers of *Schitt's Creek*, in particular, are all of similar age to Dan Levy. So while Eugene shaped the premise of the show—and he and Catherine can shape (and also Chris Elliott) the perhaps "older generation" of comedy influence there—*Schitt's Creek* comedically becomes that melting pot of influences, so it doesn't feel like it's an awkward mix of all these influences because what's happening is a true fusion of them. Across the 2000s, in particular, most comedies were chasing that 1990s goal of *Seinfeld* and *Friends*, so huge was their collective cultural influences. Since then, comedy has proliferated, splintered even. To the extreme oddball of *The Good Place*, for example, back to the more traditional set-up, with a modern twist like *Modern Family* or *One Day at a Time*. Somewhere in between are things like *Brooklyn Nine-Nine*, which is character driven with an element of screwball or visual comedy, or *Parks and Recreation*, which in a similar way to *Schitt's Creek* was a slow burn/acquired taste that eventually created a devoted and large fanbase who just "clicked" with it.

Comedic Roots and Impact

We see a fusing of comedy worlds and influences that made the show what it is. The combination of Dan Levy's approach to world-building and the show's devotion to creating the characters and the world before concentrating on the jokes is important too. We also see a desire from Levy to build something from the ground up and be part of controlling, yes, but also curating what that looked like from a storytelling point of view.

For the collaboration, too, Dan was mindful of the steering, particularly at inception, the show might need. For that, his father's influence and comedy legacy were an immediate thought. He realized it "had the potential to be broad in the wrong hands." He had long admired his father's work, "particularly in co-creating the Christopher Guest anthology—[, and] felt like it needed that kind of comedy: it needed sophistication, it needed care, and it needed a heart" (Turchiano, January 14, 2020).

But really, what facilitates this melding of intergenerational comedy is the drama and story at its heart. The idea itself was also an out-there and quirky one. The format could be more "cookie cutter" for comedy or drama. It falls into the "sitcom" format in terms of run time and uses many conventions and influences of the genre. However, it can't be strictly termed one in TV: it's a single-camera show (multi-camera filming style being a hallmark of sitcom style). While not all sitcoms utilize the live studio audience, *Schitt's Creek* also eschews this being part studio filmed and part shot on location. Technical television definitions aside, the dramatic style also defies some traditional conventions. It is a character-driven comedy-drama that, despite an outlandish concept on the surface, has its characters' emotional journey at its heart.

Of course, it becomes suitably "Levy" in multiple ways: Dan Levy is a product of not just his dad and his contemporaries (O'Hara, of course, but also the late John Candy, who was good friends with Eugene, as well as Martin Short, Victor Garber, and other members of the *SCTV* Canadian comedy era), but also from his mother, Deborah Divine, who Dan often cites as the "funniest of them all." But from that mix of family influence and growing up influenced by his tastes and experience in comedy, Levy has managed to curate something that balances all of those things. In addition, he keeps it kind.

The difference in comedy approaches was something Dan Levy was mindful of going into. Still, he recognized it as a successful formula too. As he says: "They are two different sensibilities, but that made the show so special. It's become this kind of amalgamation of young and old—not that my dad is old per se—but two different philosophies and sensibilities and two different senses of humor rooted in the same idea" (Reddish, May 23, 2020).

The show that *Schitt's Creek* was to become was a legacy show. Not in a nepotism way, but in that amalgamation of influences and approaches to telling comedic-dramatic stories. Eugene, too, was an integral part of shaping the stories. He spent a long time with Dan before they properly wrote a pilot creating the world and the characters and mapping out the stories. Eugene's guidance here is hugely important in piecing together the show. This was crucial to making the show as it would become. It was inspired by the kind of character work that was the bedrock of Eugene's work both in *SCTV* and the Christopher Guest films, making him and Catherine O'Hara even more of a comedy staple of the 1980s and 1990s.

As a veteran of TV and film, his knowledge of screen storytelling from the ground up is something many first-time writers wouldn't have. His input in creating the characters with Dan drew on his years of experience as both an actor and a writer (credit here too to the quieter influence of Deborah Divine, who, while not officially a creator, certainly would have brought her experience and instinct to the conversations at home about the show). Eugene also was part of the writers' room in season 1. While he stepped back once he was confident the show was up and running, his influence as the executive producer continued, and that experience came from a space of an instinct for the comedic and dramatic storytelling that shaped the show. Eugene Levy's influence and impact in creating the show are acknowledged, not just out of courtesy for him as a co-creator but in understanding its comedic and dramatic roots.

There is rare alchemy of ingredients that created the success of *Schitt's Creek*. Still, a key one was the comedic legacy it stood on the shoulders of, used, fused with the new, and made a little bit queer. It was, in fact, a queering of comedy—that taking the existing formula and making it new in terms of subversive elements within the show itself, the off-the-wall quirky humor, and the ability to marry drama and humor like many a comedy had forgotten how to do. *Schitt's Creek* queered expectations comedically.

One of the show's greatest strengths is the intergenerational through line in how you think about comedy and make quality drama. Indeed, that balance between the real world and the show's world keeps audiences and fans returning to the show. But it is all a clever alchemy of the show's impact both in the moment and beyond the show. This drama and the social conscience and activism of the show bring to mind *Schitt's Creek* as standing on the shoulders of the previous near-perfect example of those things: *M*A*S*H.* The two shows are similar in comedic sensibilities in that they veered between set-piece or visual gags in broad strokes and acerbic wit.

Levy talks of the importance of that drama focus to *Variety*, and in a form that brings him full circle to his dad's influence on the show they created: "Ultimately, my dad and I have always considered it to be a drama—that's always been the through line—it is a drama that happens to involve hilarious circumstances and characters that are not equipped to handle those circumstances. I've taken away from working with my dad by basing something in a kind of foundation of truth and honesty" (Arthur, April 4, 2020).

Romcoms and Queering the Conventional

Dan Levy has made no secret of his love of the romcom: it is "the best genre of the film" (*Entertainment Weekly*, 2020). His love of the romcom infuses the storytelling in *Schitt's Creek*. The genre's influence permeates the show, but is also updated, taken apart, and, yes, "queered."

"Queering" here is in the broader sense. It is more than just reworking the main love story into a gay one, though that is important. It is "queering" in reevaluating and shifting to a new set of values not governed by heteronormative values or the rules of the TV stories that accompany those, while honoring the spirit and influence of romcom-sitcoms and fusing that with elements of queer drama of the past.

In *Schitt's Creek*, there's a balance of that "unrealistic romcom" level and an often humorous but down-to-earth element. And when we talk about "queering," we also talk about updates. And the whole show sort of feels like the writers taking all that they loved about the genre—and the comedy/drama genres from TV—and giving it an updated twist.

3

Queer TV Legacy

The hoped-for progressive and hands-off attitude of the network the Levys wanted for their show was important for the LGBTQ+ content they wanted to include. From the start this inclusion was central to Dan Levy's vision. He hoped to build on—and correct—in comedy history, was part of. As he told *Variety* in 2020: "It was really important to represent my life, my friends, my family. . . . My life is not a lesson to be learned. My life is my life, and we're going to depict it as effortlessly as we can. That's the philosophy" (Turchiano, January 14, 2020).

That, of course, has been the heart of, and the making of, the show. Yes, it fuses multiple influences of comedy and drama, and the network supported it in a right-place-right-time manner. Still, Levy's central philosophy made it what it was. That sense of heart is at the center of comedy and kindness but also telling stories with honesty.

The show's "queering" is not just limited to gay storylines (as referenced in later chapters). This is "queering" in the broader sense where queering is the verb form of the word queer and comes from the shortened version of the phrase "queer reading." This technique emerged from queer theory in the late 1980s through the 1990s. It challenges heteronormativity by analyzing places in a text that utilize heterosexuality or identity binaries. Queering is a method that can be applied to literature and film to look for places where things such as gender, sexuality, masculinity, and femininity can be challenged and questioned. Initially, the method of queering dealt more strictly with gender and sexuality. Still, it quickly expanded to become an umbrella term for addressing identity and a range of systems of oppression and identity politics. The queer theory involves fighting against normalization even in the field itself.

Queer History

Cultural history for queer stories is to be part of a series of "hidden histories," the narratives that were kept tucked away or hidden in plain sight from the writers and artists who couldn't be themselves or tell their stories, but who still belong to that story. Or those who began to take those tentative steps but could not fully be themselves or tell their stories. Queer cultural history is complex: examples include the "hidden histories" of literature from E. M. Forster or Tennessee Williams, men who didn't write about their "real life" in fiction dared not reveal it to the world, or Gore Vidal, whose work was blacklisted by the *New York Times* for its gay themes. There were, of course, those who broke through; Christopher Isherwood was open about his sexuality for all of his career and included queer characters in his work, most notably *Goodbye to Berlin* (1939), the stories that would later become *Cabaret* which was, of course, part of *Schitt's Creek*. One writer who was open about his sexuality while writing about his community too was Amistad Maupin with *Tales of the City*, serialized in 1978 and published. Later adapted for TV after that, it managed to depict an out, proud, and largely happy queer community. These are probably some of the most famous examples, and there were a scattering of many other authors who paved the way: Edmund White, Andrew Holleran, and Manuel Puig all told stories of gay men in literature in the years when it was still a risk, if not outright dangerous, professionally and personally. These writers were forerunners in carving out a culture of queer people at a time when TV and film certainly weren't giving LGBTQ+ characters a look in aside from when coded as villains or figures of fun.

In the spirit of this "queering" approach, how the show took all these elements, from romcoms to musicals, and queered them in the broader sense of the word was exciting. The idea that there is a through line in queer stories, from Wilde, through to Christopher Isherwood, to Evelyn Waugh (who, like David Rose, used a wine metaphor in his novel *Brideshead Revisited*), to the contemporary stories that *Schitt's Creek* sits in. Meanwhile, it was taking the historically very "straight" genres of TV comedy and romcom and making them queer, which was exciting. It also takes Dan's (and David's) beloved romcom and throws it into the mix—this means along with references to *Notting Hill*, we also see fragments of queer history and stories. From visual references to fashion divas and drag queens to those queer stories, we get a true queering of the genre. Across the series, a number of both are directly referenced in dialogue but more obliquely in visual references, plot arcs, and other nods. Some of them are obvious and deliberate, and some of them perhaps coincide. Still, there is a self-awareness within the show of the legacy in which it sits. And the fact that it then plays with these as an essentially queer narrative.

TV history doesn't exist in isolation, either. It exists in the social, political, and, yes, current history—queer and otherwise—in which it sits. So while we must acknowledge *Schitt's Creek* didn't independently reinvent or move forward queer/LGBTQ+ representation on TV, it has a huge role to play in the ongoing through line of that cultural history.

When we think of the significance of the types of stories *Schitt's Creek* was telling, it's against the context of this backdrop—when Eugene Levy was starting his career, all these stories remained hidden. Even in Dan Levy's lifetime, there was little to choose from culturally as he grew up in the 1980s and 1990s. The TV legacy of queer representation Dan Levy was keen to create—and has contributed to in *Schitt's Creek*—doesn't exist in isolation; it exists in the broader web of queer culture (including music, fashion, and art, which also gave queer artists a voice in popular culture). And so, before TV could, theatre told gay stories. The way was paved in theatre by writers like Mart Crowley and *The Boys in the Band* (1968), the first "mainstream" Broadway play about openly gay men. *Cabaret*, well known to *Schitt's Creek* viewers and discussed in chapter 10, was a diverse set of progress and sideways steps in depicting queer characters. A little later, *La Cage Aux Folles* (1984), was the musical and was an early contender for gay "happy endings" and positive depictions of gay relationships.

These TV legacies of queer representation don't exist in isolation; they exist in the broader web of queer culture (including music, fashion, and art, which also gave queer artists a voice in popular culture). And so, before TV could, theatre told gay stories. There's a whole host of queer stories taking place in theatre that eventually fueled the quiet and not-so-quiet revolutions in TV stories. Of course, in all formats, the 1980s and the impact of AIDS drastically altered the trajectory of representation and inclusion of gay stories, shifting toward activist works about the AIDS epidemic. But out of this, seminal, game-changing works like Tony Kushner's *Angels in America* (1994) shifted conversations by showing that works about gay people could also be masterpieces of drama. As ever a step ahead of TV and film, theatre paved the way for telling new gay stories with relative freedom. This has also resulted in, particularly in recent years, more and more "happy" gay stories on stage, particularly in musical theatre—from *The Prom* (2018) to the adaptation of Alison Bechtel's seminal coming-of-age story *Fun Home* (2014) or even *& Juliet* (2019) written by *Schitt's Creek* writer David West Read.

David and Patrick in "Happy Ending" (Season 6, Episode 13)
Comedy Central/The Hollywood Archive/Alamy Stock Photo

Because queer people are a minority telling stories, they are not the dominant cultural narrative. So, they become interlinked, consciously or otherwise. Therefore, even if in the subject matter they seem worlds apart, the existence of work like *Angels in America* has allowed work like *Schitt's Creek* to exist. In the same way, as we have any rights as queer people, we needed people before us to kick down that door to ask for more. Most often, the theatre did a lot of that door-kicking for queer representation so TV and film could follow.

TV Representation

While representation might have increased on TV—perhaps more so than even in theatre and certainly in films—shows such as *Black Mirror* or *Grey's Anatomy* continue to bring queer characters into a more "mainstream non-queer" show.

We have begun to tell better stories over the last twenty years on our screens. But it has been a very up and down journey. There was great promise in British TV in the late 1990s when *Queer as Folk* burst onto screens. Funny, camp, and indulgent, Vince and his best friend Stuart were both a cultural moment of late 1990s TV: the risqué boundary-pushing epitome of late-night Channel 4 drama, and a cultural moment of their own. We can take this, along with *Will & Grace* in 1998, as two shows which burst through the closet door on mainstream TV. Indeed twenty years later, the *queerness* of *Queer as Folk* and the mainstream appeal of *Will & Grace* might just have helped create the hybrid child of *Schitt's Creek*. But what else happened around these watershed shows to get us to David and Patrick's "happy ending"?

By the time *Schitt's Creek* aired, Levy and his team were working with a broader church of inclusion across drama, where shows had begun to include "incidentally queer" characters (that is, characters who happen to be queer) without that being their own/whole storyline. Several long-running US drama shows like *Grey's Anatomy*, famed for diversity, are very good at this. Dick Wolf's plethora of shows, from the *Law and Order* franchise to the *Chicago Fire, Chicago Med,* and *Chicago P.D.* shows, all manage their ensemble casts to include a range of queer characters. Drama has made progress, then, as has comedy. The 1990s and early 2000s were sitcoms where gay characters were very much the punchline, and anyone outside white and middle-class gay/lesbian characters didn't exist.

What else hasn't existed on TV for queer people? Sex.

It's a double-edged sword of over-sexualization and fetishization (something that also comes into play with fan engagement, as we will see in chapters 15 and 16), but also, how many queer couples have had a fade-to-black even before they kiss?

Most of the time, the show focuses on the romance, especially with heterosexual counterparts. Sometimes, there's a smattering of smut too. The trouble with sex between queer characters is that, all too often, it ceases to be sexy and becomes a scandal, either within the drama itself or off-screen.

Another strong example is Shonda Rhimes' Netflix hit *Bridgerton*. Rhimes, known for her inclusivity in other dramas like *Grey's Anatomy*, gave people high hopes for the costume drama. However, while the drama became infamous for its sex scenes (one episode had a nearly ten-minute explicit scene set to a Taylor Swift soundtrack), the one solitary gay character was depicted entirely sexlessly. Similar patterns occur in other big "costume dramas" like *Downton Abbey*, where the "gay butler" was allowed only the most chaste of dalliances, usually with negative consequences. The impact isn't limited to the shows themselves but also the reaction. Case in point: when *Bridgeton* aired, so did *It's a Sin*, a drama about gay men and AIDS, which was condemned by tabloids as "scandalous" for its sex scenes, which were no more explicit than those in *Bridgeton*. For many millennial viewers who grew up in the shadow of AIDS, this condemnation felt all too familiar: gay sex was not to be discussed.

Meanwhile, much "queer drama" has gone the opposite: over-sexualizing. The same idea that if "mainstream" drama won't allow queer sex or even affection, then drama made for specifically queer audiences leaned into the sexual elements. So, from the original *Queer as Folk* to *The L Word* to *Looking*, sex—and often explicit sex—has been a huge part of the narrative. Now sometimes, that's necessary. Sex is a part of human relationships and dramas, after all. For queer stories, particularly gay men in a post-AIDS world discussion around sex, even the act of sex has both personal and even political implications. Sex is part of queer life and should be celebrated, analyzed, and seen in queer drama. But are there lines between over-sexualization for the sake of over-sexualization? Are there even ideas of fetishization from audiences and TV makers alike? Quite possibly. When we consider fan culture later in this book, even in a very "PG-13" show like *Schitt's Creek*, sexualizing and fetishizing queer characters, particularly gay men by straight women, is something to be kept in mind. But still, queer people deserve sex in their stories like straight people, and Levy created a sex-positive show, as explored in later chapters.

What about queer-centered stories? Aside from the iconic and groundbreaking *Tales of the City* and *Queer as Folk* in 2015, when *Schitt's Creek* was being created, few shows still centered on a queer main character. Things had begun to shift in that period. But when a queer character was centered, a considerable part of their story was often a coming-out story. So, from teen shows like the Canadian classic teen drama *Degrassi* which had many coming out stories over the years. Now, most teen dramas feature a queer-identifying teen across often a broad spectrum of identities. We get to see their coming-out stories, which is excellent, enormous progress. But are there more than just high school stories to be told here? Yes. Because queer people spend their whole lives "coming out"; it's not a one-time deal. So, stories like Rosa in *Brooklyn Nine-Nine* declaring her sexuality at work are more relatable for older audiences who do that every time they move jobs. But also, the people who didn't come out until later need stories like Patrick in *Schitt's Creek* coming out to his parents later in life. They need complicated coming-out stories like Callie Torres in *Grey's Anatomy*, who takes ownership of her bisexuality, or Schmitt in the same series, realizing he's gay as an adult too. These are some of the less prolific but perhaps even more critical coming-out stories TV offers for older generations.

While historically TV hasn't done brilliantly, by the time *Schitt's Creek* hit screens, it was part of a quiet queer revolution that would later become a small explosion. Is this because someone who lost out on TV as a kid channeled some of that pain into humor? Maybe. But in doing it, perhaps also they asked what kinder humor where minorities and particularly queer people aren't the punchlines look like.

The sitcom/comedy drama has possibly provided some of the best queer representation in recent years. If we consider the sitcom model, the first "gay character for gay audiences" was Will Truman in *Will & Grace*, a heterosexual actor played. On the one hand, gay audiences finally had a sitcom character who looked like them, but for all Eric McCormack's good intentions, he wasn't the complete package. So, Levy offered both a character in David Rose who expressed queer experience eloquently, in all its flawed, complicated glory, and an actor (and writer) in himself who also could empathize that was powerful for audiences. It was a case of on-screen representation and the sense that representation came from an authentic place. For those audiences who were teens with *Will & Grace* and *Queer as Folk* and thirty-something adults with AIDS drama *It's a Sin* and *Schitt's Creek*, there was a feeling of finally having a set of shows and actors who spoke to their experience.

In addition to *Schitt's Creek* and its seminal portrayal, in *Brooklyn Nine-Nine*, *One Day at a Time*, *Modern Family*, and *Crazy Ex-Girlfriend*, an array of queer characters across gender/sexuality representation happened in American comedy programs post-2010 in particular. Shows like *Modern Family*, *One Day at a Time*, and particularly *Schitt's Creek* meant so much. They gave people the chance to feel represented in "normal" TV rather than "queer" TV. It wasn't the TV to keep hidden in the bedroom, but TV your parents could watch and laugh at too, and ultimately shed a tear over and understand their queer kids more. These shows reach beyond just a niche queer audience. This both normalizes the existence of queer characters on-screen and has the potential to open questions: if viewers can be comfortable with fictional characters in a show, they love being queer, what then of the people in their real lives. Humor, too, has a disarming quality; if characters can laugh at themselves, then audiences have permission to laugh with them, just not at the queer characters. It's the shift, crucially from not just telling queer jokes but queer stories.

Why Does That Through Line Matter?

Several obvious queer-connecting dots with *Schitt's Creek* fall into various chapters of this book: Moira's drag-esque clothing, the use of music, David's wine metaphor, and the entire *Cabaret* arc. But there are lots of smaller connections, intentional or otherwise, that a queer viewer might make. Why? Because, again, as a minority audience used to scrambling for the scraps that broader culture throws, it's a natural thing to do. But also because queer creators, like Levy, have likely consumed every bit of that media that they can and are participating knowingly or otherwise in that through line.

But also, in a critical reading of anything, it's a legitimate exercise to find those links. So when we expand on Patrick's ties to the *Carbaret* characters Emcee and Cliff, we do so as critical reading and reinterpret both texts. In the same way, we might make parallels with David or Patrick with queer characters from the queer canon; we make these links because of those through lines in culture. But also, in contextualizing David and Patrick with the queer characters before and around them, we understand their significance. We might also reinterpret them beyond what is on the screen or page, asking more profound questions about their identities and sexualities because that's what we have always had to do as critical readers and consumers of queer culture. It isn't saying, "This is what was intended by Dan Levy." It's saying, "this is what we as a queer community might take from it." It's also saying, "why is it essential in TV terms?" and "why is what Levy did important?"

Most people in their thirties and older remember the first "gay [insert activity or persons here]" on TV. For millennials, shows like the seminal *Queer as Folk*, in its original British incarnation and the American remake, and *The L Word* offered one slice of "gay life" on TV. This was also the days before streaming services and prolific broadband, and all of these were viewed on TV late at night or smuggled in on VHS and DVDs away from roommates or parents. Because on mainstream TV, there were very few queer people. And even in these "gay" series, things as seemingly simple as a happy ending for the characters are lacking.

So lacking in fact, it's become a well-known TV trope. The "bury your gays" trope refers to the fact that often when a gay character appears on a TV series, they'll meet with a tragic ending: from Willow's girlfriend Tara on *Buffy the Vampire Slayer* to Matt Fielding in *Melrose Place* to Loras in *Game of Thrones* (which might get a pass as his death is fairly indiscriminate in Westeros). Back to British TV, our "first lesbian kiss" in a soap character also died, but "so what people die all the time in soaps, usually in ridiculous ways" (as Moira Rose could attest). And so, what does become political is giving these gay characters a happy ending. More specifically, it feels like it shouldn't be too much to ask, but they often don't die. Dan Levy recalls being asked not to make "anything terrible" happen to Patrick when he joined the show (Artiva, January 10, 2019), which might seem like an overprotective fan reaction. But considering how often a gay character has met an unfortunate end on TV, it seems like a logical fear. And while, yes, characters die on TV all the time, the ratio of gay characters on TV to dead gay characters on TV is alarmingly high. It's become a trend of gay publications to compile "actual happy ending" gay films/TV series (which is an added pun for the final episode title). Giving a happy ending to your gay storyline is still a rarity.

Ellen came out in the 1990s, and that was a seismic TV moment. And yes, *Will & Grace* also happened, which redressed the balance of shows like *Friends* and *Seinfeld*, which, as much as 1990s kids like me still fondly remember them, did not have the greatest track record on queer representation. More accurately, most comedy from the 1990s and early 2000s still used queer people as the punchline all too often. It's hard to criticize the shows that taught many of us to love comedy or influenced us on TV. The writers' room of *Schitt's Creek* was made up of writers who likely grew up on *Seinfeld* and *Friends* and *How I Met Your Mother*—none of those shows was trying to hurt queer people. Often, they probably believed they were doing good work. *Friends* did have recurring gay characters. *Seinfeld* won a GLAAD award, the same award *Schitt's Creek* would later win for inclusivity. But times change, and queer audiences deserve better.

The bigger question is about how these works serve the bigger picture of queer visibility and community. In that, *Schitt's Creek* joined an ever-growing amount of positive queer visibility on mainstream TV. Shows like *Brooklyn Nine-Nine* integrated queer representations into their characters without ever explicitly framing themselves as a "queer" show. Another example is *The Good Place*, which embraced sexual fluidity and queer acceptance as just part of the makeup of its world. Shows like *One Day at a Time* and *Modern Family* are further examples, where the show's queer characters are an integral part of the narrative and aren't glossed over or ignored regarding identity and the importance of the issues they face.

In TV drama, the integration of queer characters has steadily become more mainstream, led by writers like Shonda Rhimes, whose shows *Grey's Anatomy*, *Station 19*, *How to Get Away with Murder*, and others have all integrated queer characters with diverse storylines across the series. Indeed, long-running ensemble TV series in North America have often been forerunners of inclusivity, including Canadian stalwart teen drama *Degrassi* which integrated many queer storylines aimed at a younger audience (the show also featured Dan Levy in one episode in a rite of passage for any Canadian actor). There's also a whole host of "gay drama" that has sat in its own, sadly separate box, for which *Schitt's Creek* owes its legacy too.

Again, trailblazing is often overlooked or put in its category. Programs like *Queer as Folk*, first in the United Kingdom, broke the mold for showing gay life on TV in 1999 (and subsequently in the American reboot in 2000). And the gay TV drama owes a lot to trailblazer shows in "mainstream drama." While *Sex and the City* might have focused on the "camp gay best friend," it still gave its gay characters real stories and personalities. Elsewhere, *Six Feet Under* gave one of the drama's most fully rounded characters, David Fisher, in a show that gave him a healthy, normalized relationship storyline and a believable dynamic in coming out to the family. Again, these elements were incorporated into *Schitt's Creek*. TV has caught up in recent decades.

What *Schitt's Creek* did expertly broke down a few barriers between "queer TV" and "mainstream TV with queer characters," which is still a rarity. In the last twenty years, there has been an increase in "gay TV" in which queer experience is foregrounded. Russell T. Davies' *Queer as Folk* burst onto Channel 4 at the start of the new millennium. The (mis)adventures of Stuart and Vince, and Stuart's sometimes hooking up with Nathan, looked set to change how gay stories were told on TV. It was the first post-AIDS gay drama that deliberately never mentioned the pandemic. It was hedonistic, irreverent, and very British in its sense of humor. *Queer as Folk* didn't hold back in showing the sexual side of gay life and what the gay community looked like.

What it feels like *Schitt's Creek* is doing, then, is a combination of righting some wrongs and offering something missing. It seems still surprising to millennials of Dan Levy's age that there can be a sweet, gay narrative, where being gay isn't the punchline, and nobody dies. While it is (thankfully) no longer the only show with a positive representation of queer characters, it is not the kind of show Levy's generation grew up with.

There are many Easter egg–type references fans of the romcom will find across the series. Some of them are intentional and some of them are not, but the influence of romcom as a genre is evident across the series. A few of these in the romcom side include visual cues like the aesthetic of Rose Apothecary bearing a striking resemblance to the store Sandra Bullock runs in *Practical Magic*. Also similar is the scene where she chastises her sister for the lack of help and focuses on sampling the products, much like David does to Alexis when setting up the store. Other references might be more subtle or in the eye of the romcom beholder. Patrick's "You make me feel right" speech might be a neat reversal of Darcy's "I like you just as you are" sentiment from *Bridget Jones' Diary* in the right mindset. But in that same scene, David's reference to the "Downton Abbey Christmas

Special" is followed by him declaring himself "damaged goods," the exact words Lady Mary uses to describe herself in the *Downton Abbey* Christmas special.

More important than any specific nods, deliberate or otherwise, are the romcom sensibilities that permeate Levy's influence. And he namechecks several across the series. Usually about David torturing the long-suffering Patrick with his choice of films. The comparisons between Levy and David blend into one there, with Patrick lamenting, "You have to stop watching *Notting Hill* David, it's bad for our relationship" ("The Hike," season 5, episode 13), as his attempts to give David a romantic picnic fall short of his romcom aspirations. David is perhaps a neat metaphor for everyone raised on romcoms with slightly unrealistic expectations. Mr. Darcy doesn't always appear out of the lake and perhaps that's given unrealistic expectations of romance. But in *Schitt's Creek*, there's a balance of that "romantic romcom" level and an often humorous but down-to-earth element.

The show takes those big moments from the big romantic gestures, like the proposal Patrick is planning when he complains about David's ridiculous standards, and makes them an offbeat version of the romcom ideal. Patrick's proposal is a perfect example of that—we expect an organized, sure-of-himself Patrick to do something well-executed and pitch-perfect. Instead, he misreads his boyfriend's willingness to try new things and gets a stick stuck in his foot. It's ultimately charming and romantic and a lovely play on the big *Notting Hill*–like gestures of a perfect romance.

There's a nice through line in the not-quite-romcom ending too. In Alexis' storyline, we get the bittersweet romcom ending instead. It's *The Way We Were* or *The Bodyguard* or, of course, *Casablanca*. The girl doesn't get the boy. But they both get what they need, or where they should be instead. But instead of "we'll always have Paris," it's "we'll always have Schitt's Creek." And that's the kind of contemporary love story for young women we need. It's a nice twist, too, that Alexis, with all her leading lady looks and the quirky tales of love (and lust) gone wrong that bring her to this point, should be running off into the sunset by romcom standards. So, it's a strike for a twist on the genre that instead, we leave her better than we found her, having known the first true love of her life, but also happy to be on her own. The idea of telling women they are allowed to be their own happy ever after is the romcom update everyone needs.

The romcom genre also loves a small town tale, perfect for influencing *Schitt's Creek*. *Practical Magic*, for example, features picture-perfect small town life; the same goes for Sandra Bullock being name-checked in the show *The Lake House*. For the slightly more dysfunctional, *Footloose* also fits the show's ideas about community and family and the changes the community can make. *Groundhog Day* rests on the change the external circumstances—the small town of Punxsutawney—have on Phil Connors, and this is similar to the Roses' story. That the film also features Chris Elliott (Roland) and Robin Duke (Wendy from Blouse Barn in *Schitt's Creek*, *Second City Television* alumni) is a lovely bonus. Similar could be said of *Waiting for Guffman* and its charming portrait of small town life. It's not technically a romcom, but it's worthy of mention for, of course, Eugene Levy's involvement as writer and star. It's the kind portrayal of small town life, in contrast to many a film's approach, which would later be seen in *Schitt's Creek*'s approach too. And, of course, it's the use of a musical performance as part of the narrative, another element that ends up included in the show.

Queering Small Town Stories

4

Queering the Narrative

The town's "could be anywhere" status helps the idea of it as a queer space/utopia. Many queer narratives rely on going to a specific place to be queer. So think *Tales of the City* making San Francisco that space you can be free to be queer or the original *Queer as Folk* making Manchester's gay village the United Kingdom the height of queer cool. Instead, Schitt's Creek is never given a geographical identity. Most fans unofficially decide it's somewhere in rural Ontario in line with where it was filmed. Still, the show deliberately never names where it was.

Small Town Stories

Small town TV was also prominent in the 1990s and 2000s when Levy and most *Schitt's Creek* writers grew up. Some examples include the similarly named, but otherwise wildly different, *Dawson's Creek* uses the backdrop of small town America for teenage angst and drama and *Gilmore Girls*, which offers a similar coming-of-age in small town America drama. These shows offered an idyllic cut-off from the wider world, always picturesque backdrops. An escape perhaps from the fraught real world. Or, in TV terms, when aimed at younger audiences, it may be an element of guarding them against the "real world." For grown-ups, too, though, small town drama often provides an escape. In the 1990s, the small town counterpart to the big-city glamour of *Sex and the City* was *Desperate Housewives*. There were and are grittier small town takes. Some comedies mentioned using working-class rural backdrops and also using dramas like *Friday Night*

Lights, which follows the ups and downs of small town life through the lens of high school football.

Similarly, in the late 2010s, *Riverdale* and *Stranger Things* would lean into the weirder side of small town life. But Levy is also careful not to make the town a negative joke. The joke is how the Roses initially interact with—or don't—the town; the drama is how they grow into it. So while the townsfolk have elements of the weird and ridiculousness, they are treated with love and affection and ultimately become the people the Roses learn from. It contrasts a lot of comedy tradition that uses both working-class and small town dynamics as something funny. Instead, *Schitt's Creek* finds the quirks in the people that make them amusing. It's not that Roland is the mayor of a nowheresville town that's funny; it's all the ways he manages to mess things up. It's not that Twyla works in a tiny diner; it's that she is fabulously weird and quirky. It's another way of queering the expected narrative.

It's also that the town becomes that protective bubble that allows all the Roses to grow (gardening puns throughout intended). That small town life becomes the antithesis—the queering—of the traditional narrative of leaving a small town to become who you truly are. The Roses become themselves, their best version, in this town. This was an extension of the idea that the show—and the town—are both a kind of safe space and a very queer space. As Dan Levy says: "I wanted this town to be hyper-accepting. It's the most incredibly open-minded place, and I think it's because I had the reigns of what I'm creating, and I'm going to put out into the universe this utopic world where I feel it's just as it should be" (Dresden, February 12, 2018).

The town's location and if or how this might impact the "without prejudice" element is a subject of discussion if not debate. The show carefully never names the location in the broader context of the town. Instead, it resides within a cluster of larger towns that include Elmdale and Elm Glen but without mention of any real nearby locations. It's rural, but without any real geographic markers. Even the "creek" of the town's name doesn't feature until season 6. About the characters, it's close enough to wherever the Roses lived before for people from their old lives to visit (such as Moira's sister, old friends on their way from dropping a son at college, Moira's old Sunrise Bay acquaintances) but not close by. Again, it's a kind of nowhere and everywhere. This works narratively for the kind of town you could drive through on the "scenic route," as Johnny and Moira's old friends do, or just rural enough that someone looking to run away from their old life, like Patrick, could end up in. This also works as a narrative as it's not tied to a particular location and preconception about that region—a rural Deep South US setting, for example, has wildly different connotations to rural New England, even for global viewers. There's a certain shorthand there. This does two things. First, it's reductive to the work the show is doing and the conscious decision to show a place without hate. Second, it does a disservice to the need for ongoing conversations about discrimination and prejudice within Canada, which the show has become a part of. Most importantly, the "nowhere and anywhere" is important for how the "town without prejudice" idea works for the idea of "leading by example" and how the world could look.

The Town without Prejudice

It's well documented that the show came from an idea of "what if the Kardashians weren't the Kardashians"? What would they be without the wealth and everything that came with it? But an additional part of the story is the idea of owning a town—something that was inspired by Kim Basinger, who allegedly bought a town hoping to make money from it. This idea, and the show's name, are credited to Eugene Levy's wife, Deborah, who had an idea for a show about boomers moving in with their kids (Wong, January 12, 2015). From there, the idea of the Roses buying the town as a joke and having to live there became integrated into Daniel Levy's existing idea.

This idea then became the framework for the show. The Rose family loses all their money through a business manager's fraud, and the one asset they're allowed to retain is the town Johnny bought David as a joke present years earlier. Moving there and living at the town motel the first couple of seasons rest on a classic fish out of water narrative, with the Roses learning to adapt to life without a staff of fourteen and the idea of having to work for a living, with varying degrees of success.

The first two seasons rest more on the quirky humor and misadventures of the Rose family. And while there are moments of real dramatic heart—Johnny needing to swallow his pride and go to the unemployment office, David's "coming out" to Stevie and their sexual misadventures—it is the end of season 2 that shifts *Schitt's Creek*'s dramatic arc to the story and the attachment to characters fans took to heart. In part, the slow-burn narrative makes it take a much longer time for the characters to ingratiate themselves in the viewer's heart. And that is a real strength of storytelling. Fans of the show often tell friends they're trying to "convert" to it to stick it out through the second season. A moment of "falling into place" happens in the final episodes, specifically the season 2 finale. When Johnny and Moira defend their new home and new friends to the old friends, who are determined to mock it, something has shifted. Instead of laughing at the Roses, the audience is now fully on their side. When Johnny declares, "It's called Schitt's Creek," it's a kind of shout-at-the-screen moment of "hell yes" as a viewer. Then in the final scene, where the Roses dance together at a party, it feels like the moment to truly fall in love with the family and their journey.

Season 2 cements the characters and the narrative that the remaining four seasons can build on, which makes the final resolution and emotional payoff all the more impactful. The show as a slow burn refers to it in rating terms and how audiences engaged with the characters and their story. In both respects, this cemented the show's power—in rating terms, a loyal baseline became a word-of-mouth hit that eventually exploded in popularity. In terms of engagement with the characters, the slow-burn effect of the show allowed the audience to truly fall in love with the characters; it began to feel like they'd already shared the journey with them this far, and by the time it finished, the Roses had become a kind of extended TV family for fans.

The power of all of this also rests on the premise of a "town without prejudice," a space where these stories can be told without interference, but also the promise of what a world can look like without homophobia specifically but more broadly an absence of other prejudices. And this, with the arrival of Patrick and the start of his and David's relationship in season 3, was a fundamental shift for *Schitt's Creek* into the landmark piece of television it would become.

Much of this rests on the character investment and development Levy put into the early seasons, but it also rests on the world-building that went into those first two seasons. An integral part of that, and the show's broader message and impact, is the concept of Schitt's Creek as a "town without prejudice."

Queering Small Town Stories

The town itself is just very queer in many ways. We discuss sex positivity elsewhere and its importance to queerness and the show, but the town is, just in small ways, very queer in its outlook. First, unmarried women abound, and nobody comments on it. From Stevie and Twyla to Ronnie and a handful of other women whose marital status isn't commented on, there's never a single comment from a woman or man about another woman needing marriage. The town has very few "traditional"-looking families, at least in the heart of the show/its stories. We'd expect a show about small towns to be composed of very "traditional mom and pop" stories with children at the center of the narrative, but children rarely feature. This reinforces, once again, that family is what you say it is.

The town, too, is full of people going their way in life. Stevie, Twyla, and Jake are young people forging a life away from chasing a career and doing what you "should" in life. All are unmarried, educated, intelligent people who have chosen a life in the town, doing what they love. Stevie doesn't know she loves owning a motel until later, but she's also stayed long enough to hint that she loves the town, the job, or both. Jake is so talented at his woodworking and the other romantic and sexual benefits of big city life that we'd expect him to be off chasing big-city-high-success dreams. Still, he's happily making coffee tables in a small town. Twyla, of course, who, as we find out, has the means to do anything she wants, chooses what makes her happy. All of them have. Even Patrick, who actively chooses to move to the town, could be off doing all manner of "bigger things" and chooses a life with a store and a husband. Yes, it's all part of the broader lesson of the show—that less is more—but also, it's a brilliantly queer notion: choosing the thing that brings joy.

The people, too, embrace queerness in their peculiarities. We focus on Moira and David's unique approaches to life, but, in the town, they are accepted because everyone is, well, a bit odd. Crucially, though, nobody is mocked for it.

On a low level, there's Bob, a sweet naive man who doesn't seem to see what his wife is up to but who also is just charmingly eccentric. He would be the town's oddball if everyone weren't equally allowed to do their own thing. From Stevie, being unapologetically herself running the motel, to Twyla and her unique outlook on life, to Jocelyn who reminds us all of that one teacher who was cool and strange all at once. And yes, to Roland, the man who (allegedly) runs the town uniquely. In any other story/show/town, any one of these would be the "town kook"; indeed, Chris Elliott has previously been that character (it's a pretty solid bet that Roland is the cousin of Mickey Aldrin in *How I Met Your Mother*). Still, here, everyone is . . . a little different.

The contrast between the small-minded and the small town is most clearly seen in the season 2 finale. When Moira and Johnny run into old friends at dinner, these "friends," who the Roses haven't heard from since losing their fortune, spend most of the dinner mocking the town they drove through and complaining about the restaurant. Their taunts are snobbish and juvenile at once—mocking the town name, pointing to the low-quality food and drink, and exhibiting a thinly veiled disdain for Jocelyn and Roland. They are a stark reminder of what the world outside the town is like: judgmental, cruel, and ultimately selfish.

Meanwhile, Johnny remembers—and tells his old friends—how welcoming, kind, and generous their new friends have been. Johnny points out how they shared "what little they have" with his family. It's a cruel reminder that in the "real world," Johnny and his family have been abandoned by everyone they knew, as well as a reminder of what is possible with a shift to kindness. The critical difference between their old and new friends is that the Schitts would never judge the Roses based on what they did or didn't have, and the Roses are as welcome in their town as anyone. The town's influence is already evident in Johnny when he declares triumphantly, "It's Schitt's Creek." And instead of dinner with their old "friends," the Roses return to the town, dancing joyously in a barn with their family and new friends.

The town without prejudice benefits everyone, allowing them to thrive as themselves and grow. For David, much of his character arc centers on his ability to find a functional relationship—and ultimately the love of his life—after the damage of his past. The narrative around David's past relationships is that they generally were not good people and that he made repeated bad choices. When Moira talks to David about Patrick's impact, she speaks of "drawing a line" under the previous life in which he'd had terrible relationships ("The Barbeque," season 4). Much like his parents and Alexis, this also comes after an encounter with their previous life ("Sebastian Raine," season 3), all needing one final reminder from the outside world before they shift and change, embracing what the town can offer. This is partly made possible due to removing him from the impact of the wider world of homophobia (and, in David's case, biphobia for added measure). The town's safety plays a big part in David, self-described as "damaged goods," to heal and find true happiness. At the end of the show, David's decision on where his future lies speaks to that positive influence; who wouldn't, given a chance, ultimately choose safety where they feel most themselves? There is an essential connection between his choice of Schitt's Creek over New York and his telling Patrick in their wedding vows that he feels safe with him. Whether he knows it or not, the town, as much as Patrick, created that feeling—having one without the other wasn't possible.

What removing homophobia does is free the writers to tell other stories. In another setup, David moving to town would have resulted in numerous encounters of homophobia to deal with. Patrick, first in realizing his attraction to men, then in developing a relationship with David, and later coming out, would have been diverted, dominated even, by him dealing with outside judgment and obstacles. Even Jake, "everybody's ex and nobody's ex," would have probably spent more time fending off homophobic comments rather than deciding who his next throuple might be.

Here, we see queer love stories and hookups unfold without fear or consequences of prejudice; they are seen as people. To watch David and Patrick develop a relationship and stumble through various roadblocks on their way to marriage, the usual ups and downs of any relationship, shouldn't feel quite such a television storyline revelation, yet it does.

On the surface, Patrick seems the most together when he arrives in the town, but you have to speculate that life didn't quite go to plan for him to end up in Schitt's Creek working for Ray. Despite that, Patrick "clicks" before everyone else with the power of the town. Even Stevie takes until the Roses leave to realize the town lets her be who she needs to be. For Patrick, it is moving to the town that, in every sense, allows him to be who he is. Whether you read it as his relocation, his meeting David as a revelation about his sexuality, or his coming to terms with it, the town and its safety play a huge part. It asks if Patrick had lived somewhere like that his whole life, would he have spent so long in a doomed relationship with Rachel? Would he have had to wait so long to, as he puts it, "understand what right felt like"? Would he have found David had they met elsewhere? Patrick explains his reluctance to come out to his parents by how comfortable he'd gotten with David and his family in the town. That the town has created this almost-perfect oasis where someone like Patrick can quietly learn about, accept, and act on his true sexuality is powerful.

For those reasons, wanting to stay in the town is important to Patrick. It is where he's become himself, where he feels safe and able to thrive. While the Roses are the focus of the towns' power to let people be who they are, Patrick's story and the reasons he fights so hard to stay are also important. Having already scoped out a house as the final puzzle piece for his life, Patrick already knows it. It's why, too, Patrick is so upset about leaving (something Noah Reid manages to heart-wrenchingly portray virtually without saying a word at the end of "The Pitch," season 6, episode 12). Patrick knows the town has allowed him and David to find each other, their purpose in life, and where they will be happy. When he says then, "It's gonna be a tough goodbye, this is where we started our life together" ("Start Spreading the News," season 6, episode 13), it's about their relationship but much more. It's about finding a life that works in a place that lets you live unjudged and free to be yourself.

The heart of what made *Schitt's Creek* a hit is its story of love and acceptance, whether that is accepting who you are, who your family is, where you end up in life, or all of these. The themes of unconditional love, healing, and family are all at the show's heart, but the show also challenges conventional views of what that looks like, or at least how we interpret it. The Rose family is the show's heart, and their journey to love, acceptance, and healing is its core. The idea of a family depends on a "chosen family" at the heart of queer relationships: the idea that queer people often rejected from their "real" families form bonds with other people that are stronger than the "real" family bonds ever were.

Similarly, at the heart of the Roses' journey is the idea of reconnecting with their family by expanding it. When they were just the Roses, they were disconnected and lost their sense of love for one another. But by becoming part of the town and bringing other people into their wider, "chosen family"—Stevie, Patrick, and even Roland and Jocelyn, specifically, but also becoming part of the town "family"—they find their connections again and grow as people individually. The town is at the heart of everything, and the idea of a "town without prejudice" is at the heart of what lets the show tell the stories it does. It also connects with fans and casual viewers and becomes a queer political statement.

A Queer Safe Space

The town as a "safe space," much like queer safe spaces, works as an allegory because queer spaces mean different things to different people. For some, it's a place they need when growing up to help them figure out who they are and what they need, like Alexis. For others, like David, it's about realizing trying to "fit in" with other places and people didn't work for a reason, and finding your place in the world matters.

Is it a really easy life lesson? If you make spaces where everyone—including queer people—can be their authentic selves, this filters through and lets everyone be their best selves.

For queer viewers, it's a chance to see their stories told as everyday stories, which—we already know—they are, but so often have to be filtered through the impact of others' prejudices. More importantly, they get to see a happy, relatively carefree version of a gay love story, something rarely seen in cultural portrayals. Usually, any gay love story is filtered through the lens of overcoming external prejudice. The town as a physical space is important too. Because it's a space where queerness is never questioned, it is an extended version of the "gay villages" in New York, San Francisco, London, and Manchester—those spaces within cities where queer people are themselves.

Radically Queer Stories

"Queering" here in the broader sense than just reworking the central love story into a gay one, though that is important, but a "queering" in a re-evaluating and shifting to a new set of values not governed by heteronormative values or the rules of the TV stories, all while honoring the spirit and influence of romcom-sitcoms and fusing that with elements of queer drama of the past. In *Schitt's Creek*, there's a balance of that "unrealistic romcom" level and an often humorous but down-to-earth element.

There are a few things at play. First, it's a lack of queer romcoms. The handful is expected to serve every identity, personality, and desire from a film. That's why *Schitt's Creek* was important, and that's why it fits so well into the "know your history" model of reading queer cultural history. Like all aspects of queer life, TV is far from perfect today. But things have changed. TV, too, speaks to multiple generations.

The story of love and acceptance made Schitt's Creek a hit. Whether that is accepting who you are, who your family is, where you end up in life, or all of these. The themes of unconditional love, healing, and family are all at the show's heart, but the show also challenges conventional views of what that looks like: the idea of family in the show is very dependent on the concept of a "chosen family," something at the heart of queer relationships: the idea being that queer people often rejected their "real" families and form family bonds with other people that are stronger than the bonds with the "real" family ever were. The town is at the heart of everything, and the idea of a "town without prejudice" is at the heart of what lets the show tell the stories it does, but also connect with fans and casual viewers and become an accidentally political statement in the process, what Dan Levy has called a "lead by example" approach.

Because queerness often aligns with a specific anti-capitalist, anarchist state, in terms of TV stories, the small town chasing big city life feels like an incredibly queer notion when it's for young people. It's not crucially framed as "the young people had their wild life then settled down in a small town to raise a family like you're supposed to." It's "these young people chose this life" that's what queerness teaches us: choosing the life that serves you.

This aspect highlights the idea that spaces where people can be their authentic selves benefit everyone. As queer people, we see it all the time: in the places we can be our authentic selves, everything from romantic relationships to work thrives. The show itself is a marker of that, with a culture of inclusivity fostered from the top down, meaning everyone involved in making it does their best work. And in the world of the show, then, we see what happens when you take away the fear of prejudice and replace it with support: everyone elevates one another to be their best selves, and it also snowballs. One person feeling supported and able to be their best self will support other people to do the same. It's truly a "town without prejudice."

Queerness and the show as a queer show come in many forms, as we'll explore, but this is the lynchpin. It's not *just* that David and Patrick can have a big gay wedding in the town hall, though that is vital. But it's that Moira can walk down the street being Moira. Alexis can be supported as a high school student. Johnny, the fallen-from-grace businessman, can be picked up again and supported. All of these are queer ideas that the town and the show enable.

5

Everybody Fits in the Town: Differences and Acceptance

"A Delightful Half and Half Situation": On Jewishness and the Roses

When discussing *Schitt's Creek* and its attitudes toward prejudice, we focus on the queer love story at its heart. But the overall message of tolerance and acceptance goes beyond that. The Roses' Jewish identity is of particular importance, subtly woven across the series. While the show isn't about Jewishness, it is a show that incorporates and comments on its Jewish identity. The Roses mirror the Levy family as a blended family of Jewish and Christian heritage. Eugene Levy's wife (and Daniel's mother), Deborah Divine, talks of their "combined world." Eugene and Dan Levy reference their Jewish heritage in interviews. In the show, the Roses equally reference their shared heritage. Unlike other comedies where Jewishness is the joke (often in an outright or unintentionally anti-Semitic way). And while the Roses don't reference their faith and heritage in any necessary character-defining way, the series is peppered with enough references to their estate to make it clear they aren't avoiding defining themselves as such. And while the jokes aren't *about* being Jewish, there's humor in their Jewishness too.

So we get, on the one hand, David referring to himself as "a deeply embittered mildly Hebraic looking Elf," or Moria calling Johnny a "Sephardic Mr. Clean," or Johnny referencing his Hebrew school baseball team (the brilliantly named Flying Latkes). Alexis and David mention their Bat/Bar Mitzvahs, mainly concerning Johnny's terrible gift buying (he got David a basketball court, then a nose job after David tried to play basketball . . . and the nose job was what he wanted all along). There's a lovely, warm set of almost-in-jokes and references that might bypass non-Jewish viewers, and that's, in its way, a joy. It feels like Dan and Eugene Levy are integrating the kind of family and Jewish humor they know, and the world can get it or not.

One episode that brings Jewishness to the fore and makes a statement about the Roses, Jewishness, and overall acceptance is the Christmas episode. We certainly see Johnny lean into the season. The episode ends with a beautiful rendition of "Silent Night" (led by Sarah Levy as Twyla) with the Christmas tree and menorah on display in the motel room. Having "Silent Night" sung to him after David jokes about Christmas being a holiday that his dad "technically has no authority over" being the Jewish parent in David's "delightful half-and-half situation" is a subtle nod perhaps to inclusivity. Drawing on the Levy family, the Roses are a mix of Christian and Jewish parentage. Never heavy-handed in its messages on inclusivity, the combination of self-deprecating jokes earlier in the episode and incorporating a sweet Christmas moment for the whole family is an excellent moment.

The message of inclusivity is within the metaphor of the town here. The town welcomes them; they celebrate together regardless of differences in faith (we don't get many hints the town is particularly religious anyway). But the duality is accepted, and Johnny's menorah proudly on show. But the menorah, too, is a powerful symbol; the Roses must have brought it with them. Since being there, they haven't celebrated the holidays, so they haven't bought one. Therefore, Johnny's faith was important enough to include the family menorah in what they could carry from their home. They lost a lot, including other meaningful possessions, and while the giant family portrait has been done away with, the family menorah remains. Of course, in typical fashion, Moira hopes it also burns down the motel.

It's a commentary on the "half and half" Roses and how they are welcomed and protected even in the town. With Johnny and Moira's being arguably the strongest love story in the show—a marriage that flourishes for forty years—this feels like a subtle but incredibly powerful counterpoint to *Cabaret*'s Schulz and Schneider's doomed love. Placing the Roses next to this musical makes a powerful point for anyone who makes the links, knowing not everyone can live in a place like *Schitt's Creek*. It is characteristic of the approach of Dan Levy's writing to guide the audience to this rather than laboring the point. Again, to parallel *Cabaret*, which does not lecture an audience and merely shows them the chilling consequences of inaction, *Schitt's Creek* offers the opposite: what happens when you remove prejudice?

We see this too in the one time the show does address anti-Semitism and indeed uses it as a bit of a wider metaphor for how this town treats outsiders. In one of the most brilliant scenes of the show's six seasons, local businessman Bob comes to Johnny for help opening a bagel store, which Johnny initially takes as a compliment. However, it quickly becomes clear that Bob isn't asking because of Johnny's business sense; he's asking because Johnny is Jewish. After Johnny explains to Bob that he would need to make "good bagels the real way," Bob assumes Johnny must know how to make them based solely on the stereotype that Jewish people love bagels. What's even funnier is that Bob can't say "Jewish" out loud because he thinks it's an anti-Semitic slur. "I didn't know if I could say it, but boy, do you all love your bagels," he says nervously. "I mean, I do too, and I'm not even—." When he's too scared to finish his sentence, Johnny reassures him that the word is not offensive. "I don't know why it feels like a swear," Bob continues. "What's the one you can't say?" ("Bob's Bagels," season 2, episode 5).

The show powerfully offers an alternative to comedy and even drama interpretations of Jewish men. Instead of portraying Jews as one-dimensional characters like Hollywood so often does, Eugene and Dan have managed to create an authentically funny show that addresses Jewish stereotypes about looks, athleticism, and even bagels. But what it does also offers an alternative to the traditional Jewish male stereotypes in comedy.

First and foremost, even in his former business mogul persona, Johnny Rose avoids the cliches of Jewish money-grabbing characters. Instead, he's portrayed as a compassionate, ambitious, but not money-driven business owner. Even in the glimpses we get of their previous life, it always seemed that Johnny's ambitions lay in being seen as successful over the monetary reward. Either way, riches aren't seen as his focus, and even when it's the lesson, the Roses have to learn about money, not buying happiness. The show skirts the right line away from Jewish stereotypes. Johnny and David's business models are collaborative and integrated into the community, and they define their success away from just the monetary caricature we're all used to.

Traditionally, male Jewish characters are presented in conflict with the women in their lives as weaker: Rick Moranis as Seymour in *Little Shop of Horrors*, Jason Alexander as George Costanza in *Seinfeld*, or Dustin Hoffman as Benjamin Braddock in *The Graduate*. Previously the nebbish character, an impotent, neurotic male as a foil to the Jewish American princess and Jewish mother stereotypes, emerged from Jewish insecurities and a warped performance of patriarchy. With the Roses, there's a balance between this and any hypersexualizing of the Rose men.

Instead, we get David, who rejects traditional norms in his pansexual, gender disregard, all-around progressive, and sex-positive stance. He manages in his portrayal of a man developing healthy approaches out of (some) trauma as a healthy portrayal of LGBTQ+ sexuality and a healthy portrayal of Jewish masculinity. He also had a strong example in Johnny Rose, who once demonstrated a healthy marriage and a healthy attitude to masculinity. No, he might not be out chopping firewood (they did, after all, pay people to do that). Still, Johnny was attempting to (and eventually mastering) a barbecue and doing household (motel) tasks like fixing things successfully, which contrasts the weak-willed Jewish stereotypes of old. We also get two Jewish men, seen as unquestionably handsome and desirable by their significant others, which is a huge shift in those portrayals. Johnny Rose and David Rose show that future generations of Jewish men on TV don't have to be hypermasculine to subvert expectations of Jewish masculinity. Patrick does think of David as the "Jewish Channing Tatum" after all ("The Premiere," season 6, episode 5).

Johnny and David are not above using their Jewish heritage to get out of situations either, and it also shows in the way they demonstrate the strong father-son connection. When he's trying to find excuses to expose Bob's "cheating" in a poker game ("Sebastian Raine," season 4, episode 10), Johnny plays into the need for Kosher snacks. Johnny Rose is not above using Jewishness to escape awkward social situations. Something David manages (of course) to level up when he declares a need for "Kosher wine" to get out of the sex party organized by Jake. This is possibly the first time Kosher wine has been used to get out of a sex party on network TV. Either way, Johnny Rose raised his son to use his identity to his advantage sometimes.

There's also, obviously, comedy in the Jewish references in the show. There are a couple of self-deprecating jokes on David's part about his appearance: again, a nod that it's okay for minority groups to have a sense of humor about themselves and that funny doesn't need to be cruel. The idea that Johnny was on a Jewish boy's baseball team called the Flying Latkes is funny on multiple levels: the name and the fact that Johnny's Hebrew school buddies were as athletic as him. It was like watching a team of Davids play, coupled with Johnny's self-assured faith in his abilities. Finally, there is the running joke about Johnny's (and David's) love of pork chops and bacon. Nobody ever mentions it, but because the show is unashamedly Jewish in other ways, it is a subtle joke (based on the Levys' love of food) that is typical of the charming yet witty approach to Jewish humor in the show.

"Day Three of a Panic Attack": Mental Health and *Schitt's Creek*

Like much in the world of *Schitt's Creek*, elements of neurodiversity are largely unspoken but also positively represented. Even without actual naming of anyone's conditions/illnesses, coding characters with mental health struggles or neurological diversity is as important as the queer-coding and queer stories in the show. For both queer viewers, who are statistically more likely to suffer from mental illness, and for a wider audience, it shows a world where characters have these struggles but aren't judged for it.

Across the series, we get hints that Moira's mental health has long been unstable. From the obvious elements in her behavior, she often responds dramatically and exhibits more signs of depression than the rest of the family when they move to the town. She clings to the past (her outfits, wigs, etc.) to regulate these feelings and hints at her medication, past and present. Like David, we never get named conditions—could Moira have bipolar disorder? Certainly, she seems to suffer depressive episodes and slightly manic episodes too. But in some ways, it doesn't matter; Moira has mental health conditions, and her family cares for her with them. They all seem to have various methods for managing her when she's unwell. Johnny, most of all, is practiced in looking after his wife.

As we peel back the layers of her character, we get a revelation about where this all comes from. On the one hand, we have the foundations in season 1 that she is a small town girl who escaped. With the help of being a pageant girl/actress and then her marriage to Johnny, we see she escaped small town life, which perhaps played a part in her mental challenges/outlook on life. Mixed in with that, we know all the Roses have been victims of their success, and none of them are mentally healthy as a result, even Johnny, the most balanced of them, is affected by the trappings of success. But we see in season 6 behind all that, too, is the impact of Moira's treatment on *Sunrise Bay*. The gaslighting and poor treatment of her in that role had a subsequent impact on her mental health, culminating before they ended up in the town; it was at first exacerbated by their fall from grace, then healed by it.

After she locks herself in the wardrobe following the news about the *Crows* film, Johnny calmly disperses the party, as it seems he's done many times before. In sweet small details too, when the opener to season 6 ("Smoke Signals") returns to that scene, the area by the closet is cluttered with books and other items, indicating that Johnny or someone else has been sitting there with Moira during her exile to the closet. This is a sweet indicator that the family has an array of coping mechanisms they use to support her. The idea that these are tried and tested gives Moira a little more rounded approach than a cliche "rich woman" or actress with a pill/alcohol problem.

The Roses protect Moira, and there are hints of a long history of doing so. They also never mock her for it, but they do mock her ridiculous elements. Johnny isn't immune to saying his wife's name in exasperation, but her issues, while never talked about explicitly, are also never mocked. There's a low-key acceptance of family and friends with mental health struggles that we don't see on television. Usually, mental health issues become just that, an "issue" for a character, which is used as a negative character trait and becomes a huge storyline. While mental health storylines are important, so is the acknowledgment *Schitt's Creek* provides: people deal with mental health struggles daily. It's part of their lives and character and doesn't always warrant commenting. The show also demonstrates partners loving people with mental health struggles not even "despite" them, just including them. Having Johnny and Moira, who have a textbook-loving marriage in many ways, with Moira's mental health as part of the picture is important. That Patrick follows suit and sees David's various struggles as part of him, too, is a beautiful positive spin on including the characters' mental health struggles in the bigger picture.

Across the series, David's mental health is a subtle undercurrent to his character. The first was David's panic attack in the first season. We see him struggling to breathe and having chest pains. With the absence of a "real" doctor, Alexis takes him to Ted, who diagnoses a panic attack. The incident is handled with comedy for the situation—taking David to the vet—but not comedy at the situation. The joke isn't that David has a panic attack but that the town—unlike his old life—is ill-equipped to deal with his troubles. His sister and Ted both care about David and want to help. Later, when David goes to yoga class, he's also met with compassion, and his final line, "I think I'm lonely here," is incredibly moving. We see here the balance of how the show handles mental health and neurodiversity with humor but compassion.

We also see the shift in that when he gains real friendship with Stevie, he strengthens his relationship with his sister and, of course, begins his relationship with Patrick. Alexis delivers one of the most mind-blowing revelations to anyone with anxiety (like David) when she tells him, "Nobody is thinking about you like you're thinking about you" ("Driving Test," season 3, episode 4). This is at once a reassuring and revelatory mantra for David (and viewers who share his anxiety). We see various manifestations of his anxiety across the series: when he's planning the store and tells Stevie, "Some guy at Ray's told me my business was a failure" ("Motel Review," season 4, episode 8), it's a manifestation of his anxiety, which Stevie sees and supports him through (admittedly with the help of some weed she finds). Patrick, too, sees anxious David from the start, and instead of making fun of him, it endears him to David, and he wants to help (he does make fun of him, but not for that).

Patrick shows time and time again he's happy to "manage" David's mental health and support him through it. Indeed, in talking with Johnny about their upcoming wedding, Patrick promises to "protect" David from "all the things that can set him off," noting that there are many things that can set him off. While done with trademark humor, Patrick here acknowledges he knows David has several issues and struggles, and he doesn't mind, accepts them, and takes them as part of his husband-to-be.

The reason all these relationships are important is that they accept this part of David and support him. But Patrick, in particular, takes on the job as nobody has before. We see elements of it early in their friendship when Patrick treats David's anxiety with fond teasing and actions that alleviate it. So while he gets on David's case for not fixing the lights, he also recognizes David's anxiety over the store opening and helps out. The deeper into their relationship they get, the more Patrick steps in to support David's anxiety—whether he knows or appreciates it or not—so even when Patrick is offering his olive branches to David following their argument over Rachel, he's also behaving in a way that will reassure David's anxious nature. This, too, is why Patrick is different from anyone in David's old life: he takes action to support David's mental health, not work against it.

Patrick's care for his husband mirrors Johnny's care for Moira, who struggles. Johnny steadfastly and consistently supports Moira; however extreme, strange, or unreasonable she seems to outsiders, Johnny is unflappable. One of the most significant moments of this comes in "Life Is a Cabaret" when she has a meltdown and locks herself in the wardrobe. Johnny calmly ends the party, sending everyone home so he can attend to his wife as he has done before. It's both beautiful and sad all at once: a glimpse into the real struggles of Moira, and indeed Johnny, despite the money and often funny, ridiculous behavior. In the next episode, "Smoke Signals," Moira is still in the wardrobe, but touchingly there's a stack of books next to it, where presumably Johnny has been keeping her company. Either way, he (and possibly David) have been watching her. Because despite the family's distance, there's a sense they've been looking out for their mom for some time.

Patrick knows the level of teasing that's healthy for David to push him out of his comfort zone, but he never takes it too far. A lovely example is when he tells David he loves him, something he knows will spark anxiety, so he manages it, speaks to him in an offset way, and gives David the out he needs. These are simple, subtle elements in the storytelling. In another show, Patrick might have told David he loves him, which sends David into an anxiety spiral and causes tension between them. Instead, Patrick is aware of David's mental health. He responds and manages how he approaches big things in line with that and supports David through it. His simple but sincere "you don't have to say it back" to David allows him to process it without pressure and realize he is ready. The fact that someone takes care of his mental health needs makes David love Patrick all the more. Perhaps, too, because of the example set by his parents.

In the bigger moments, too, Patrick behaves in this way. He preempts David's reaction to his "I love you" with reassuring words and body language, allowing David to process it in his own time and respond. Patrick isn't perfect—he makes several mistakes that set off David's anxiety, from his secrets about Rachel and his parents, to his choice of proposal approaches. But the way he fixes them shows Patrick understands David's mental health needs—seen most tellingly when David wets the bed. Patrick makes no fuss other than some friendly jokes, which are standard in their relationship. He plays down the incident, so even while David is dialing it up to thirteen (with some help from his mother), Patrick keeps them grounded. He also doesn't try and dismiss David's reaction outright—he gets it's a big deal to him—but he lets it play out supportively without using it against him. In other relationships, David wouldn't have had that, and in other shows, the joke would have been what happened to David, with his partner joining in. Instead, the joke becomes about Moira's misguided publicity and some charming, even romantic-comedy (in the literal sense) between the couple.

The fact that it's not talked about is important. It's not a show plot point that Moira or David has a mental health episode. Even when Alexis is depressed after her breakup, it's accepted, and she's supported, but it's not made an issue. Equally, when Stevie drags David (in this case, literally) out of bed when he's depressed about Patrick, it's done in the spirit of Stevie knowing what's good for her friend. Similarly practical is David seeing his mom is close to a meltdown over her performance at Asbestos Fest. Instead of making an issue of it, he steps in with practical help and averts, at that moment, her spiraling. Little things like this show the low-key management of the mental health of those around you while being conscious of their bigger issues. Like Johnny knows how to manage Moira daily to keep her level and support her, David does for his mom, and ultimately Stevie and Patrick do for him.

Neurodiversity

The panic attack aside, David and Moira's mental health struggles are never named. Still, for both of them, we could speculate on the show showing a subtle depiction of neurodivergent conditions accepted along with mental health struggles. Across the Rose family and, indeed, across the town, there are examples of potentially neurodiverse characters who are part of the town's fabric. The show might not do well on disability representation overall, but perhaps something in its take on neurodiverse characters not played for laughs in the way, say, *The Big Bang Theory* has been heavily criticized for, is a positive piece of representation. It also plays into the idea that the town doesn't express prejudice, that the show doesn't particularly like to label people, and that this might be part of the characters but it remains uncommented upon.

Do David and Moira, in particular, display neurodiverse traits? Possibly. Regarding the show, it can be positive that nobody is labeled—much like things like sexuality—as it allows audiences to project their meanings onto the characters. Certain elements of David's personality lean toward some autistic traits. He needs things to be a certain way, not in what we first assume is his spoiled brat manner, because David adapts to the world of no money in some ways better than the other Roses. But the way he orders the store and the way he has his bedding point to a need for physical spaces to be a certain way. His clothing mirroring his mom's look is also crafted for particular comfort. All his clothing has a softness to it, a certain breathability. While stylish, it also eschews a particular type of fashion look and is tailored to what David wants and needs. Even his need to eat when he needs to eat and his particular patterns of eating pizza, bacon, etc., fit a certain way of approaching food many neurodiverse people have: a list of "safe" foods they revisit repeatedly. Even his fastidious skincare routine reflects a need for order and routine, a trait for autistic people and people with ADHD. David, too, avoids tasks like phone calls (called out by Patrick on a couple of occasions) which, while used as a joke about David's attitude to work, are also neurodiverse traits. The way David is with other people, too, such as the way David centers narratives about himself like his mother, are ways of creating empathy and are autism-coded traits. In addition, David is an introvert; he doesn't do well with people. He likes attention to a point but on his terms and is ready to retreat to the safety of his room (or, tellingly, Patrick's place). For Moira, too, there is a clear alignment with maybe more neurodiverse traits and specific mental health struggles we see explored. Similar to her son, there are several explanations—from autism to ADHD or, in Moira's case, possibly bipolar disorder. Like David, her lack of a filtered way of talking or Moira's invented language could all be autistic traits.

While we can't diagnose a character from the show, it is again that these traits are not a punchline as such that makes for refreshing reading. Patrick doesn't struggle to love David because of these. Instead, he pledges very clearly to Mr. Rose to make David's life as easy as possible. The loving support of family—from Mr. Rose worrying to Patrick as his partner—is a refreshing take on potential neurodiversity and mental health. Maybe too, the Roses needed to be where they were accepted for their neurodiversity, and nowhere but Schitt's Creek could be more perfect than that. It also simply and effectively extends Dan Levy's metaphor of a town where everyone fits in, because none of this is explicitly commented upon. Like sexuality, it is an element that exists as part of the characters rather than a defining characteristic. Similarly, because it goes largely uncommented upon—whether these are diagnosable conditions or simply exaggerated eccentricities—it allows for that extended idea that everyone is welcome and valid, and nothing is "wrong." In that way, the town is very "queer" and becomes the ultimate queering moment; the innate queerness means all are accepted and welcome.

Class, Contrast, and Life Lessons

"Money doesn't buy happiness" is the show's and the town's clear moral message. Still, the Roses and their relationship to the town, money, and even issues of class and identity are important in what the town allows them to be.

Is Johnny Rose originally working class? Maybe. After all, we hear him talk about his work in the button factory. This reading also fits Eugene's family background: his father worked in an automobile plant as a foreman and his mother was emigrated from Scotland in the 1940s. There is certainly a "working your way up" element to Levy's own story that would make sense to align with Johnny. It also somewhat offsets the narrative that the show is unsympathetic as the characters are rich. Both Moira and Johnny allude to working-class beginnings. When we add to Johnny's Jewishness, we can see an element of their struggle—admittedly slightly forgotten—that influences their reactions in the town.

Moira, of course, embodies the opposite. She is the idea of working-class aspiration given what it wants and more. Once Moira had it, she struggled to let go. But also, even when she lived in a small town, she longed for more. That's where her idea of "dress up" comes from, the idea of creating a version of herself. Of course, Dolly Parton's adage of "it costs a lot to look this cheap" also comes to mind in some of Moira's more choice outfits, and we may also see her roots there. Moira wasn't born into the idea of glamour like David and Alexis. Instead, it was Moira's early years, imagining, presumably scraping by and scraping together a look in her pageant days, and then transposing that to the "real thing" when she could afford it. Combine this with the look of a soap opera actress in North America, and you end up with a Dolly Parton style poor-upbringing glamour meets drag queen look that Moira embodies.

Johnny and Moira's approach to class and money reflect two sides of people who have moved up the class ranks. Johnny is proud of where he came from, embracing his roots as part of the story, a kind of his persona. Moira does anything to hide it kindly. She only mentions her background once to Jocelyn when drunk. She also avoids mentioning her sister or contacting any other family she might have. Is this out of pride? Maybe in part, but also out of shame and distancing herself from them. We don't hear anything about Johnny's family, and we can assume both parents are no longer around, but Moira has at least a sister alive, yet she has cut herself off from all family ties. It would almost be peak at Schitt's Creek if the sister and extended family were from one of the "greater Elms" towns in the surrounding area. But regardless, Moira left that life behind her and refused in any way, shape, or form to return.

The twist in the show's story is that David decides to stay, perhaps because, for David, the town gives him what he needs: a place to be himself. Be that with anxiety and mental health struggles or neurodiversity. David finds peace, unlike Moira, who is still away from that kind of life. He gets that in the town and gets everything he needs. David perhaps never knew what he needed, but there was no reason to leave when he got it. The others need things outside the town: Alexis needs to be independent, truly, for the first time, so she has to leave the town for that. Moira needs to finally prove she is not a joke and step into the career that is finally what she deserves. Johnny might be the exception in that he *could* have run the business from the town, but what Johnny needs is his wife, so he goes where she is. David and his dad are more similar than the series to this point allude in this way; career is important to them both, success and all it brings are important to them both, but not as important as the one they love. The neat parallel at the end, where Johnny leaves, even though he might have been equally happy to stay, for his wife while David stays for his husband despite always thinking he wanted to leave, is poignant and beautiful.

It's almost as if David was never the problem: it was his world. It is a very queer notion, even if not directly connected to David's queerness. Like queer people often have to change their environment to be their authentic queer selves, David, too, had to change his environment to be his authentic self. And while not directly connected to his queerness, if we take queerness as the whole person, how they are, how they carry themselves, how they see the world and themselves in it, then yes, this "town without prejudice" was what David needed to be fully himself.

6

One Must Champion Oneself: Women and *Schitt's Creek*

The women of *Schitt's Creek* also manage life and careers in a way that puts other comedy dramas to shame, partly possibly because the small town setting gives them "real" jobs, unlike some other comedy dramas set in big cities with vague "jobs in public relations" roles for women.

First, there's Ronnie. Everyone's favorite local "woman of business." Ronnie is one of the great and underrated characters on the show, and she's a great feminist icon. Quietly going about her business, running a business, and being part of the town council, Ronnie is a rare thing in TV drama: a quietly competent woman. That Ronnie is also a gay Black woman in this town is an integral part of the show's depiction of the "town without prejudice." And that her sexuality is both barely addressed but quietly present also makes her an important character. She's an incidentally gay character who isn't defined by her sexuality. She's butch presenting, but it's never a defining characteristic. She has a "butch" job, but again it's never an issue or facet of her character (other than her competence). In the episode "The Wingman," (season 6, episode 6) when she goes into the town bar and picks up a woman, it's a lovely point of both illustrating the acceptance in the time and inclusion. The fact she picked up a woman isn't a plot point, and the punchline isn't the gender of her hook-up but that she, not Bob, is the one to be going home with someone. And that perhaps, sexuality aside, it's because Ronnie is just a bit cooler than many people in the town.

It would be remiss to talk about women's roles in the show and the town and not talk about Twyla, who comes to embody the show's message as much as, if not more than, any other woman. Twyla spent all six seasons being quietly supportive and kind to everyone, being a friend to Alexis even when she didn't ask for one and being uncompromisingly kind. She embodies what women should be to each other: supportive and championing of each other. The feminist twist on Twyla isn't that she does that through naivety or misguided trust; she does it because it's the right way to treat people. Previously, other women have treated Alexis as someone to be used for connections, as a love rival, or as some other kind of competition. Twyla treats her as her friend. In the final twist, when Twyla has been sitting on a huge lottery win all this time and could do anything she wants to, it turns out she is doing what she wants. And that's a brilliant message for anyone, but particularly women. Those pressured to be and do so much are up against even more obstacles. Choosing the things that make you happy, rather than any sense of what you "should" do, is just as powerful a message for women as Alexis choosing her career over a relationship.

Jocelyn also does quietly brilliant work representing women in the show. At first, she seems to be the "nice but not that bright" wife of the equally "nice but not that bright" town mayor, Roland. Very quickly, though, it's clear that she is both intelligent and capable. Jocelyn is an excellent example of women unquestioningly supporting and uplifting other women, something she constantly does with Moira across the series. In a situation where Moira is used to being the "leading lady" in every sense, Jocelyn is happy to fill the part of a supporting role in her life. But hers and Moira's story is about a strong female friendship, one told without rivalry or conflict. Too often, women are painted as rivals to each other, for work or men; Moira and Jocelyn are a refreshing counterpoint to that.

"I Do What I Want": Stevie Budd

Stevie refuses to change for anyone else, and it's not that she doesn't change or evolve. It's that she does it on her terms. We see Stevie struggle with feeling stuck in a life she didn't choose and fell into. And she reflects on where many thirty-somethings have found themselves: unsure exactly how they ended up stuck but equally unsure of where they're trying to go. And Stevie is also a refreshing antidote to TV twenty- and thirty-something women with glamorous big-city jobs in trendy industries, and a reminder for most people that isn't reality, and that's okay.

Stevie is also unapologetically romantic and sexual. Stevie is another example of sex positivity on the show. She engages in casual sex across the series, is open about it, and is not shamed. The idea of a town without prejudice extends to not slut shaming. So Stevie engages in sex with Jake, which ends up being one of the longest continuous relationships on the show, spanning several series and presumably beyond. As a woman in a TV narrative, she's allowed to be both sexually free and show emotion around relationships, but ultimately isn't defined by them. When David and Patrick find her at Jake's sex party in season 6, Stevie declares, "I do what I want." And while they leave, Stevie is staying. In another show, this, and other elements of Stevie's sex life, would be a vehicle for slut shaming. But she's allowed to carry on without shame. It's also a great moment of counterbalance: David and Patrick aren't a couple comfortable in that kind of situation, but Stevie is. Queerness in sexuality takes many forms. Queerness in the form of deviation from heteronormative, or in this case monogamous, norms is something Stevie embraces. In this instance (though as discussed later, not entirely ruling it out), David and Patrick seem to adhere more to those "norms" while Stevie is sexually adventurous, progressive, and "queer" in her approach to breaking norms. Even if she's not canonically "queer" in same-sex attraction, perhaps there's more queerness in Stevie than meets the eye.

Is it strange that Stevie is "queer-coded" in the show? And that perhaps there was a missed opportunity for another bi/pan protagonist? Slightly. There's an argument for characters not living up to stereotypes or being judged by their appearance. Stevie's outfits, and we know outfits and fashion are carefully curated on the show, are very clearly coded for queer women. The plaid shirts, straight denim, and Converse all shout "queer woman" to an audience. But Stevie, as she says very clearly, drinks only "red wine" (is straight).

It perhaps feels more of a missed opportunity because Emily Hampshire credits the show with a revelation about her sexuality: on hearing "the wine not the label" speech, she later considered her sexuality and recalled its impact on her. Hampshire, who previously identified as straight, now identifies as pansexual. While not always appropriate to align actors with their characters, an arc about Stevie having similar revelations would not have been out of place in the show. Especially perhaps being around David, and in particular, Patrick, seeing his journey to being who he is, might have made for a nice alternative arc for Stevie.

In a traditional story, the uncoupled Stevie would have a moment in the final episode where she decides to "look for love" inspired by her best friend getting married. This is because, usually, we can't conceptualize a woman not having her only priority being love. However, Stevie's arc is written so that her "win" is that she gets to run the motels as she wants to, with Mr. Rose and Roland. It's not written as a sacrificing love for a career. Instead, Stevie's wants/desires as a character are focused elsewhere.

She ends the show professionally fulfilled—with exciting opportunities ahead of her—surrounded by friends and an adopted family. Stevie wins without romance, which feels like a win for women viewers. That, too, feels refreshingly queer.

Ultimately, Stevie's strongest relationships are her friendships, and she is a woman whose life isn't defined by some endgame romance. Instead, what she gets from that ill-advised affair with David is her best friend and a stronger relationship than when they started. She also has a friendship with Patrick that is entirely separate from that with David—again showing women having friendships with men, former lovers, and their partners and being fully functional and adult about it, able to separate that part of their lives and move forward. David and Stevie give us a friendship as valuable as the endgame romance. David is who he is in the end, yes, because he finds love with Patrick but also because he finds love of a different kind with Stevie. What the show gives us are both male/female friendships that are real and of value but equally weighted as romantic ones.

Stevie's importance is shown most of all by Patrick, who asks her for her blessing before asking David to marry him. Again, the story puts the importance of friendships in parallel with family. While, yes, none of the Roses can keep a secret, Patrick knows better than to tell them in advance; his asking for Stevie's blessing is a much more important one: he's checking that he is "good enough" for David and that he is "good" for David. If Stevie, his best friend and the chosen family who made David in part, thinks Patrick can be the man David loves, it's okay. Patrick, too, acknowledges the importance of Stevie in David's life and their lives going forward. In asking for permission, he's also recognizing and welcoming her as part of their family. They don't know then that the Roses will leave them behind in town, but it paves the way for their micro-family of Patrick, David, and Stevie.

I Love That Journey for Alexis: Women Not Defined by Their Relationships

In *Schitt's Creek*, women aren't defined by their relationship status. This is a "queering" approach to the narrative and something we don't realize we sometimes lack, because romantic relationships are always the endgame. Stevie and Alexis seem so refreshing because, both in their ways and for their reasons, they don't end up with romance as their win. Stevie finds her purpose and contentment in her career, and Alexis goes to chase after her dreams, neither of which are dependent on men.

Alexis' story is also about how love enables success, just not in the usual way. In an excellent B-side to David and Patrick's story, Alexis and Ted are still a success of a love story and just as powerful a story. When she first meets Ted, Alexis says, "there must be some other girl [in town]." Flirting and getting the guy is her currency, and she sees getting together with Ted as the "win" for both of them. When they say goodbye, she tells him, "I'm sure there'll be some other woman somewhere." She knows "winning" the guy isn't all there is and isn't the best thing for either of them. It's sad, yes, but also so hopeful. Because Alexis' growth is also Ted's here, and he gets to put himself first, too, in a good way.

For Alexis, too, having her heart broken is the making of her. She doesn't need a man to be who she's supposed to be, which is a refreshing lesson. But getting her heart broken is an important lesson on that road. As Annie Murphy says: "Her first heartbreak is so significant; she has it at 30, just after graduating high school. [*Laughs.*] I'm so proud of how she deals with it because we all know how nasty it can be" (Ivie, April 11, 2018).

Alexis has led a charmed life in more ways than one: she leaves a trail of broken hearts in her wake, never investing in or caring for others. Having someone care for her for once shows her what that can mean, and having it taken away is a step toward becoming who she can be. As Murphy says: "She's come into this situation having broken a lot of hearts and not caring about it. She never truly cared for another person before, or being in the position of not having what she wants" (Ivie, April 11, 2018).

It becomes a neat twist on what we expect from a female protagonist: the love story is her endgame but not how we expect it. It's what makes her who she is, and it's what lets her go out in the world and be the best version of herself. It doesn't disregard the impact love can have on someone's life. Indeed, it puts it as what Alexis needed in hers. The impact of stepping away from love can be just as powerful an impetus, and that's what Alexis gets to learn. She becomes a powerful role model for female viewers, turning what they're told from most other shows—love and only love is the happy ending—and telling them to put themselves and their careers/whatever else fulfills them first. It also cleverly twists the "selfish" Alexis from the first season into a person being selfish in a good way, prioritizing themselves and what they need. The most moving is when she says she can't go to the Galapagos Islands; Ted thinks he wouldn't have let her, not in a controlling boyfriend way, but in the form of knowing what's best for her way. Alexis has never had a boyfriend who acted in her best interests before, but also Alexis has never acted only in her best interests either.

Instead of a romantic endgame, we get a story of a woman growing into her potential. If that's not a "queering" narrative, what is? Every romcom and every TV show most people Alexis' age were raised with had "get a husband" as the end goal, with countless problematic examples of women who put their careers first being "wrong" or "sacrificing happiness" for it. Instead, we see Alexis stepping up and taking ownership of her success. She gets flowers as a thank-you for work, and it's the first time she's received flowers that were not from a man. But we see her work for it; we see her misstep—she accidentally does public relations for a cult and gets her mom a terrible voiceover job—and it's not plain sailing for Alexis. Still, she puts in the work, and it pays off. But also, a huge catalyst for all this is Moira showing how she believes in Alexis. Going from the awkward lunch date when they first moved to the town, when Moira took notes for conversation with her daughter, to fully supporting her in getting success shows both Moira Rose being a good mom and Moira Rose as a champion of women.

The Other Woman Isn't Evil

Another refreshing counterpoint is how women-as-love rivals are painted across the series. Alexis was, again, doing away with the idea that women are only to be used as competition. Or to be angry girlfriends (or ex-girlfriends). So even when another woman gets "in the way" of a love story, it's never the woman painted as the antagonist. Seen several times in Alexis' dating life, in the case of both Mutt and his new girlfriends—be they Twyla or Tennessee—it's never the woman Alexis blames. Similarly, when we meet the woman Ted is now dating, what's played is Alexis' hurt and regret, not painting the new woman as in the wrong. And it shows the power of this from a storytelling point of view; it makes for more heartbreaking watching that his girlfriend is so nice, that she's kind to Alexis, and that Alexis doesn't treat her as a rival, instead admitting her hurt to her brother.

When Patrick's ex-finance turns up, the episode takes time to set her up as a real person, which is important for depicting women in TV and telling queer narratives. Rachel is neither a "crazy ex-girlfriend" nor a throwaway woman that Patrick "experimented" with before "discovering" he was gay. Whichever way you read it, following her ex-fiancé to his new life in a new town displays some boundary issues, but we don't hate her for it; we assume, like Alexis, who bonds with her, she has her reasons because she's drawn as a person first, not just a plot point of the "other woman."

Ultimately, Patrick doesn't come off well in this scenario: telling your ex that you're in a new relationship and to stop texting might have helped. While we're at it, tell said boyfriend you were previously engaged also. But even in that, in the complication Rachel causes for David and Patrick, it's equally important she isn't painted as a throwaway woman he encountered on the path to finding out he was gay. So often in narratives about discovering sexuality, women end up a spare part, used and forgotten about. Or worse, they are painted as some terrible experience that allows a man to discover his true self. Rachel isn't that; she's a genuine relationship from Patrick's past that meant something, that he tried hard to make it work. And while yes, some of his communication skills could use some finesse, the subtle reframing is important: instead of a terrible previous relationship that "pushes" him to be gay, it's the joy in the new relationship and "feeling right" that finally allows him to close the door on the relationship with Rachel. And in doing so, too, she remains a real if flawed human, just like the other women on the show in their attitude to relationships.

This is important in how the show reframes the "queer people stealing girlfriends/boyfriends/husbands/wives" TV trope. Historically the trope of gay people only being "allowed" if they either died (the bury your gays trope) or went back to a (heterosexual) relationship at the end was a hallmark of queer narratives. Even if that didn't happen, there was a moral judgment often ingrained in the story, the "bad gay" who "broke hearts" by leaving a partner for a person of the same sex. There was a danger the Rachel storyline could veer toward this, and this is what the story, in a way, wants us to think will happen.

Moira as a Feminist Icon

Moira, of course, is a feminist icon in the show. Her general take-no-nonsense attitude is inspiring, but so is that she is never anything but who she is. Nothing Moira does is to appease anyone—least of all men—and she is so uncompromisingly herself, often outside the bounds of what society says anyone should do. Fashion has long been a feminist issue, and Moira takes ownership of fashion and does it her way. Showing creativity in clothes but purely unapologetically dressing for yourself is key to fashion. But camp women are also strong women; they're often the women dealt blows in the entertainment industry who come back fighting. Camp might be about excess and how you present yourself to the world, still, camp and queerness go hand in hand because camp comes from a place of outsider status.

"Different Orchard": Moira and Her Kids

In TV, Moira's character is important as it takes us away from the cliched "TV mom" who is a stay-at-home parent whose whole life is focused on her kids, etc., that has been the hallmark of so many TV shows, particularly comedy shows. That the only time we see Moira cooking is a complete disaster is a brilliant antithesis to this.

The "fold in the cheese" scene, while a moment of high comedy and a very early scene, indicates where Moira's character will go and where she stands in opposition to other TV moms. It's a brilliantly comedic scene with a lot of heart. We see David taking care of his mom—again in his particular way—by helping her and googling a recipe. We see Moira opening up to her son by talking about her past. We also get an insight into the fact that Moira Rose hasn't always had it as easy in life as we might have assumed. That there's no magical resolution to the fold in the cheese incident is also a lovely touch. The meal is a disaster; they'll return to eating at the cafe. But Moira didn't need to become a domestic goddess to be a "good mom." Again, a more "traditional" narrative would have the Roses settling down in the town, becoming "normal," and having Moira turn into a "real" mom, cooking and all. But for several reasons, this doesn't happen. First, the narrative is that you don't have to change *everything* about yourself to be a better version of yourself. The Roses, Moira included, are still very much themselves at the end of their time in the town; they've just brought out better versions of themselves. It wouldn't serve the moral of the story for Moira to become a "normal" mom because Moira Rose is the best version of herself she can be.

She's not fluffy and caring in the usual way, but she helps her kids when it counts. Her relationship with Alexis grows over her time in the town. They go from Moira having to bring notecards to lunch with Alexis to Alexis expressing how much she loves her mom and hugging her when they prepare to leave. We go from Moira having no involvement in her daughter's life to supporting and encouraging her career. It's also a nice touch that Moira (not Johnny) helps her get on the career ladder, once again emphasizing Moira is her own woman and, in her success, takes her daughter along with her.

There's also a brilliant irony—and proof that Moira is a better mom than even she realizes—that she leaves the town with two more "children" than she started with in the form of Stevie and Patrick. Although different from Johnny's relationship with the two, there's no denying that Stevie and Patrick have become a part of the Rose family. In other ways, Moira has somehow become an unconventional mother figure to them, too, possibly whether she wanted to or not.

There is no doubt of the mother-son similarities between Moira and David. There's a sense of David's unavoidably of being like her and an element of a son who worships his mom. At times, perhaps David sees more in Moira than she sees in herself. When Moira officiates the wedding, we see her version of the caring mom. She steals the limelight slightly, and David would expect nothing less anyway. But she does it with heart and love for her boy. We see her carefully planning her speech, partly because Moira Rose always prepares a performance. Still, she prepares careful (and ultimately touching) words for her son's wedding. Again, she might go full "Moira Rose" in her outfit, but Moira is also there to care for her son. That she is also convinced she must take charge, that her husband would be too "emotional" about it too, is lovely.

Working Women—and Taking Back Power

Perhaps the show's most significant feminist moment is Moira's win for her career in the final season. Over the seasons, the show takes her career, initially framed as a joke by her role as the ridiculous soap opera actress and her outlandish life, and instead peels back the layers to reveal a woman who seems to have worked incredibly hard against many odds to get where she is. Moira could have been a very one-dimensional character. It would have been enough to have the fish-out-of-water rich wife character. And indeed, that was what was first written. But Catherine O'Hara, bringing the kind of comedy experience explored in chapter 1, wanted her to be more. She remembers the initial character being very different: "It's generalizing, but it seemed more like their idea of Moira was like the soap opera character she played, like a snooty kind of rich lady thing. That's probably not how they saw it, but that's how I saw it when I read it. And I thought, 'No, I don't want to do that. I don't want to do snooty rich lady. I'd rather do someone who thinks that she's of this world and hip and avant-garde and has been everywhere and is cultured'" (Lloyd, February 18, 2015).

Back in 2015, O'Hara also thought there was more to Moira: "I like to think of her as more vulnerable than just snobby or superior. I think it's way more insecure. It's more fun to play, I think" (Lloyd, February 18, 2015). This played out in the final seasons, where we find there was always more to Moira. Indeed, she was a greater feminist icon than the initial woman with wigs would suggest. She's a woman we discover—particularly in the last season—who got truly screwed over by the men in power—a familiar tale.

We assume that Moira is just another washed-up soap actress, either a relic of another time, or we believe she just wasn't very good at her job . . . maybe Johnny helped her into it, or perhaps she got by on looks, a set of familiar judgments. However, in the final season, we get a twist showing we all underestimated Moira. Not only does she step up and make *The Crows Have Eyes 3* a success, but we find out her soap career was far from the joke it has been until now. The joke is on us, the audience, for believing that. But it is also on everyone around Moira.

What had initially looked like a failed soap opera career had been a woman asking for what she was worth—and being rejected because of the men around her. After years of thinking she got dropped from *Sunrise Bay*, her career taking a downturn that, she'd thought she negotiated herself out, that is, she'd asked for too much. What had happened was her male co-star had her written out and gaslit Moira over what happened. It's an incredibly moving revelation about Moira and partly why and how she is, and a sad indictment of the state of the way women are treated in many industries, not least entertainment. That Moira then puts the men in their place when they beg her to return (and yes, throws a drink in their faces) is a great win for her. And it tells the audience what we all know: Moira is a powerful woman and a force to be reckoned with.

Beyond the show, it's a nice nod to Catherine O'Hara too: that older women actors should not be underestimated but also that they can get what they deserve later in life. In her Emmy acceptance speech, she thanked Eugene and Daniel for letting her play a woman her age. That's such an important thing. There is little work for actresses over some seemingly increasingly low age threshold. And those women who work are often asked to play older characters, quickly becoming a "little old lady in a corner," or they're asked to hide their age as long as possible. For a show to embrace a woman her age and let her play that—without it ever being a focus—was a revelation. And Moira is also a powerful feminist statement: she's a woman in her sixties fighting for her career, a career she knows she's good at, a career she knows she deserves a seat at the table in.

Along with Moira, O'Hara has that seat at the table, and the recognition she deserves is tied up in that too. Like Moira, it's too easy for O'Hara's comedic character actress career to be dismissed as silliness. Having a career of such longevity in this industry takes real strength of character. Moira and O'Hara both proved that true.

The show treats her "win" in getting her career back as important; Johnny's need to regain his career is significant. The most powerful statement comes when Johnny changes his plans to fit with hers. The simple decision that he can and will change his plans so Moira can have her dreams puts her career on equal footing with Rose Video, where it has always been if we pay attention to the clues. Johnny used Moira in the promotional videos and calendars in accompanying him to events not because she was his "token wife," the soap opera star on the powerful businessman's arm, but because they always were, and always will be, a power couple. And while, thanks to how the industry treats women, it went wrong for a while, it's never in doubt that she deserves her time to shine. And she takes it thanks to what the town gave her.

7

I'm Not Done with This Place: *Schitt's Creek* and Chosen Family

Traditionally, queer people have ended up with "chosen family." This relates to the idea of finding your community and the sad reality that many queer folks are rejected by their biological family. The whole of *Schitt's Creek* can be read as a metaphor for chosen family and aligned with queer lives and a queer reading in this way. Finding a place where you fit in is related to your chosen family and is obviously at the heart of *Schitt's Creek* and the Roses' journey. In the show, the Roses have to leave where they were to be who they can be. They go from being worse versions of themselves, or more accurately, not the person they're capable of being, to being their true—and good—selves in the town. This is where "queering," rather than just LGBTQ+, themes come into play. If we approach things in a "queered" view and take a different approach, we see the world differently.

Friends as Chosen Family

Roland and Jocelyn also have a sense of community and solidarity that they immediately extend to the newcomers, the Roses. There's an element of "queer elder" about Roland, the one who knows how to navigate the world the Roses find themselves in and is willing to pass on the wisdom. Much like queer elders, he has nothing to gain from it; he sees it as a moral and social obligation—this is a very queer notion from Roland, perhaps the most unlikely of mullet-wearing queer icons.

Many viewers dislike Roland because they don't know what to do with a working-class person who isn't necessarily the butt of the jokes. Roland is funny and meant to be the butt of jokes, but unusually the joke isn't

"Look how poor they are." The show never really goes there despite that being the joke of the show. It's flipped that the joke is on the Roses. Perhaps then, it's how audiences view it: is Roland the "gross" and "incompetent" town mayor, or is he the good guy who helps out everyone in the town as best he can while doing the best for his family?

In some ways, Roland is a lot like Johnny. He's proud of his name, heritage, and status in the town. It might not be Rose Video, but to Roland, how the town is part of his legacy is important. Like Johnny, he has expectations around his son, about whom he is somewhat disappointed, and he has to learn to accept what his son will be (and won't be). Roland also struggles for money, and like Johnny, he hustles. Just because he does it by offering to clear gutters and fix things around the motel doesn't make them much different—Johnny might wear a suit to do it, but he does the same thing. Equally, Roland has a sense of pride like Johnny's. Ultimately, they're two guys wanting to provide for their families and preserve their family pride and legacy. But Roland and Jocelyn also have a sense of community and solidarity that they immediately extend to the Roses.

The way that Roland and Jocelyn rally around Johnny and Moira but also care for their children is a particularly "chosen family" notion. As referenced in chapter 6, it is also a trait of working-class communities (and small towns, the two of which go hand in hand). But in a broader sense, how Roland and Jocelyn care for Johnny and Moira does buy into the idea of a "chosen family."

Jocelyn and Roland give everything financially and personally to help the Roses succeed. In terms of the motel business, they are tied together, if not for life, then for many years. They're also personally invested and caring. From Jocelyn making sure Moira knows she is excited for her about the *Crows* trailer (even writing a mini-essay) to Roland encouraging Johnny to talk to Patrick about his marriage to David. Ultimately, Roland is rooting for Johnny to win; in his moving speech during "The Pitch," (season 6, episode 12) he shows he values Johnny as a businessman, but also as something more than a friend. They become more than friends: in Johnny and Roland's case they're co-workers and eventually business partners. But much like Johnny and Stevie's relationship is more significant than just co-workers, Johnny and Roland are also the kind of close friends that feel like family. As much as Johnny would never have anticipated it, Roland is perhaps the younger brother in this scenario of chosen family within the town. Similarly, Moira would never have envisioned a friendship with Jocelyn, but in her case is a direct contrast to Moira's sister, who we meet early in the series. Jocelyn is always there whatever Moira needs, from when she was at her lowest. For the Roses and the Schitts, their bond becomes one of chosen family, in the most unlikely of circumstances. Chosen family isn't limited to queer people, but chosen family does find a way to help people who need it the most; that's what the Roses get with the Schitts.

Patrick and His Chosen Family

Patrick's is the kind of "chosen family" we're more used to seeing: a newly out queer person finds support and solace in a family that isn't his own. Usually, we would see this narrative with Patrick moving to a town with a queer population, finding other queer people, and discovering his identity. That is a valid and important story, and the absence of other queer people is one thing this very queer show sometimes misses. But we can take something else from this: as long as the community is supportive, that is the most important thing in helping queer people flourish. In Patrick's case, it is partly because he separated himself from that world when he started dating David—the world where he was being who he was supposed to be. So while the chosen family is a queering narrative in the wider sense, there is a literal depiction of a chosen family helping support queerness to flourish. This supports the wider thesis of Levy's show and idea. If you support people—in this example, by surrounding them with the community—they flourish. Patrick is a throwback to how that largely functions for queer people.

Patrick symbolizes finding a chosen family as a queer person, with Johnny as a figurehead. As loving and supportive as his parents, Marcy and Clint, are, Patrick needs to be separate from them and the version of him they see to carve his own identity. This is important for so many queer people who grow up in a heteronormative society with parents who assume—often, through no fault of their own—that their children will be "like them." When Patrick is removed from the familiar environment, he can consider who he is without the gaze of those who have always known him and instead consider who he might be. When he comes out and expresses the fear that his parents will see him differently, he is, in part, right: they will see him differently because the version of their son they always had is changed.

Patrick has slowly become part of the Rose family in the final two seasons. In "Meet the Parents," (season 5, episode 11) he talks of how comfortable he got with David's parents. Later, he tells Johnny how thrilled he is to join the Rose family. For Patrick, much like David, the chosen family is the whole town; both of them, on moving there, found who they are and who they're supposed to be through the town. For Patrick, the Roses are the first real example of a family that accepts him for who he is. And so he feels close to Johnny and puts him as an important figure. It's not so much that his dad won't accept him; it's that Johnny is the first "father" to accept who he is. And for queer viewers, whether their parents have yet to accept or reject them, that is what Johnny represents as well: what a parent to a queer child can be, what love and acceptance can look like. And watching him care for Patrick, who is not his child, feels like being accepted. The idea that Johnny—or the Johnnys of this world—could accept the queer kids who don't yet, or might never, have their own parent's acceptance is an important message for queer viewers.

For Patrick, the town gave him more than just his relationship. It gave him a family. While he has loving parents, he is an only child, and in adulthood, he seems not to be that close with his extended family. Either way, he has moved away from where they are and, like many, finds himself alone as an adult, until he finds not just David but the Roses. It's why Patrick is so upset about leaving (something Noah Reid manages to vividly portray without saying a word at the end of "The Pitch," season 6, episode 12). It's because Patrick knows the town has allowed him and David not just to find each other but to find their purpose in life and the place they will be happy. When he says, "It's gonna be a tough goodbye; this is where we started our life together" ("Start Spreading the News," season 6, episode 13), it's about their relationship but also a lot more. It's about finding a life that works in a place that lets you live unjudged and free to be yourself.

Queering Family

The Roses are a "queered" version of family, in that while on the surface they are "traditional"—mom, dad, married, two kids—they are nontraditional in many ways and queer the model of what family looks like. As the reflection on Moria as a character indicates, they are not traditionally weighted in power dynamics, eschewing traditional male and female roles. Even in the town, when their lives shift—Moira is the first breadwinner: Johnny's job at the motel initially involves domestic labor more than anything else, while Moira is on town council. Meanwhile, their previous lives have been blurred in the "traditional family" sense, in addition to David's role as a "parent" to Alexis in their younger years. Arguably, David somewhat parents Moira at times; there's more than one indication he looks after her in professional settings. When her mental health challenges get the better of her, David appears as a caregiver.

Wrapped up in this is the entirely conventional while wholly unconventional marriage of Johnny and Moira. The Roses' marriage is the emotional touchstone at the heart of the family and the show. They are, refreshingly, an unusual thing: a long-term heterosexual couple who remain in love and fond of each other. There's no doubt that Moira is challenging to live with. Nobody pretends otherwise, least of all Johnny, who rolls his eyes and exclaims "Moira!" or sometimes a bewildered "Sweetheart" at regular intervals. Johnny doesn't understand everything about Moira; even over forty years after beginning their relationship, he doesn't have to because he loves her. Equally, Moira is not above telling Johnny exactly when she thinks he's being an idiot. But it's real and heartwarming all at once. They're not above being irritated by and pointing out one another's flaws, but they'd be lost without one another. In a world of comedies where the joke is how useless or awful a husband/wife is or dramas that center on the breakdown of marriages, theirs is refreshing. For many, it might seem like the show's ultimate "fantasy" element—parents still happy after forty years together—but it's also the most reassuring and hopeful.

By the end of the series, we realize their parents' marriage is what Alexis and David have, in a way, been looking for. Alexis doesn't have it yet, because she needs to become someone who can have that relationship first. And David takes a while to realize that once he has it, he doesn't need all the other things he thinks he does. And for audiences, it is powerful to have a mom and dad on TV to look up to and be a surrogate for what is missing in their lives.

Plans Change: On Babies and What Family Looks Like

Many queer shows are only "allowed" to be queer if they emulate heteronormative society. And while *Schitt's Creek* does this to a degree—David and Patrick's courtship and wedding are fairly heteronormative—Levy digs his queer heels in on not giving them the baby route to "complete" that. Not only does he not give it, he actively comments on it through both straight and queer characters.

Other sitcoms had women like Alexis married off with children as a central plot point by her age (*Friends*) or would incorporate the having/not having children as a point of trauma/reason a relationship broke down (*How I Met Your Mother*). Instead, the whole set of issues around her and Ted's relationship, being them getting to pursue their passions rather than having children still in 2020, felt wonderfully refreshing. Nowhere in their relationship was a conversation about babies, nor was it a reason they broke up. They broke up to pursue careers and be who they could be. And Alexis never once has someone mention a "biological clock" or pressure her to settle down and have babies. This is where *Schitt's Creek* gets it right. David and Patrick had their white wedding (black and white for David), the traditional "happy ending," but we don't get them being "incomplete" until they have children. And we don't get a narrative of something being "missing" in their relationship or flawed in the one who doesn't want it.

The notion of what family looks like is also queered and challenged in another way by David and Patrick. Their decision not to have children, and happily so, is both a wildly revolutionary one in TV terms for an endgame couple but also quietly queer in the notion of what makes a family. So, while David and Patrick follow the heteronormative model of a traditional wedding, one important factor in offering alternative life plans is that they not only do not have children but actively talk about not wanting them, and that being okay.

We know by this point David is not exactly inclined toward babies. He said, "This is why I hate babies" ("Baby Sprinkle," season 4, episode 10) and showed his lack of babysitting skills with Roland Junior ("The Hospies," season 5, episode 8). So it seems a given that David doesn't want children. Patrick has never raised the issue until, on the way to having his wisdom teeth out, he casually mentions he thought he'd be married with a kid by now. Later, high on painkillers, he starts talking about babies to David. He says, "I wish you were my dad." Much of this can be blamed on the medication's effects, but David is understandably taken aback (or indeed horrified) at the sudden turn of events. But Patrick quickly shifts the conversation, telling David, "plans change" and acknowledging that he knows David doesn't want children.

It's a narrative seen repeatedly in TV and films and placed where it is in the arc of the series—midway in the final season—we would expect this to be a dramatic fork in the road for David and Patrick. That Patrick wants children and David doesn't could be a means to keep them apart in the run-up to their wedding, the dramatic thing that might break them. But Levy skews it in favor of David. This feels huge for anyone who, like David, doesn't want children and has been repeatedly told they're selfish or wrong. Usually, that narrative would be framed as David "denying" Patrick what he wants—though it is usually framed as a need—and blame being assigned, even going so far as to suggest the idea that something is "wrong" with him. But the show illustrates another way: Patrick happily compromises his expectations in life and agrees that "plans change."

On the one hand, it shows a couple capable of discussion, compromise, and a healthy attitude to accommodating what each of them wants and needs. In a wider sense, it's a comment on not conforming to heteronormative expectations. There's a lot of pressure on queer people to emulate straight society to be accepted. There is, too, since marriage equality, the idea that queer people should want exactly what the "normal" path is for straight couples: marriage and babies. Moreover, it's the dominant heteronormative concept of "family." The idea is that a couple is "incomplete" as a family without children. Levy says a firm "no" to that and shows us David and Patrick are a family without children.

TV shows have long replicated this idea, too. *Modern Family* opens with the gay couple adopting a baby, and shows like *The L Word* have in-depth storylines about queer couples conceiving a child. These stories are important too, and we should show TV viewers what different kinds of families look like. But different families include those without children, and Levy chose to show that.

It also goes back to queer chosen families because David and Patrick don't have biological children or "adopt" them in a traditional sense, which doesn't mean they won't have children in their lives or create families another way. Patrick, who seems to like children, could have children in his life in other ways: coaching sports teams or similar seems likely. But family isn't just children and parents in the traditional sense. David, like his dad, may become a "father figure" to grown-ups later in life. David shows he is filled with nurturing and caring abilities time and again, another important facet the show illustrates is that this isn't confined to childrearing.

Father Figures

We know Moira isn't exactly a traditional mom, but when Moira does parent, she does it with a queered approach to what we expect from TV families. She encourages Alexis to go and pursue her career. Having a mother figure who isn't obsessed with babies and grandkids is another characterization that shouldn't feel revolutionary, but it is in the moment. It's also part of the show's broader "queer" outlook. Traditionally, mothers in TV drama and comedy are there to encourage their offspring to marry the nice [insert applicable gender here] and give them grandkids. It's a very strange preoccupation when you think that the parents of adults are the drivers in their reproductive habits, but it's a social norm reinforced by the media. The "give us grandkids" mentality is nowhere to be seen with Johnny or Moira. This shouldn't be a point that needs commenting on: why on earth would Alexis's breakup or David's marriage be cause for comment from their parents on the lack of grandchildren? Why indeed! But it has long been an established trope of TV drama the link between adult children, marriage, and parents wanting grandkids. And it all loops back around to queering the family model.

One of the show's most important "chosen family" themes has to be Johnny Rose as everyone's dad. Looping us back to queer people finding family outside of their own, Johnny is the steadfast one in the Rose family, often bumbling and embarrassing to the kids, but he's also always there. It makes sense that he "adopts" the people closest to his kids. We get the feeling that Eugene Levy would do similar, and indeed that's an important part of the wider narrative of the show: Eugene and Johnny and what they both mean to queer viewers.

Showing Johnny as a father figure to Patrick but as someone outside his family is also an important signal to queer viewers, telling them that it is possible and okay to find father figures outside of their family. Sometimes they might need them. They might offer something missing in even the most accepting of families, reinforcing the idea that "family" extends beyond who you are born related to. And Johnny's relationship with Stevie also encapsulates that. We don't learn much about Stevie's family; she rarely mentions them or her dad. And we can assume there isn't a close relationship. And so, in the show's narrative, which for Stevie's arc rests on finding herself and her direction in life, Mr. Rose becomes integral to that. They have ups and downs—he infuriates her with his computer skills, embarrasses her, and she teases him—in short, he is a dad. He also lifts her, supports her, and is that friend in a way that only a surrogate dad can be. But it also becomes a two-way street; Stevie shows Mr. Rose she believes in him and the business, which gives him the confidence to get going again. She also comforts him when he's sad about not having the money for David's wedding. Johnny's kids might have a stronger relationship with him now, but Stevie also fills the gap of a child who needs and is there for him daily.

Stevie is the one that seems to "need" a father figure more. We don't see her family; other than the aunt who left her the motel, we assume they're largely absent. So when Johnny comes into her life, she seems to need him as a father figure. One particularly moving moment is when they think Johnny has a heart attack. Stevie's upset at the moment is apparent, and there's a lovely moment of tenderness on his part, too, at her concern ("The Hike," season 5, episode 13). Similarly, Johnny shows across season

6 how much he's in Stevie's corner where her life and career are concerned; we see him support her decision to leave the motel, offer her support in business, and welcome her back. Stevie becomes what Johnny's kids never did: a business partner who is also family. It dives into the broader chosen family narrative, much as Roland does, that family takes many forms. Of course, as future father-in-law, Johnny automatically becomes a father figure for Patrick and much more (as discussed in Patrick's coming out story in chapter 9). That aside, it's clear that Patrick respects and admires Johnny as a businessman and person, and well before Johnny gives him a speech about taking him under his wing ("Moira Rosé," season 6, episode 7), it's clear Johnny means a great deal to him.

The more "traditional" Rose parent, Johnny's relationship with Stevie and Patrick extends the way he has become "everyone's dad" to viewers of the show too. For different reasons, viewers feel connected to Johnny (and, by extension, Eugene), and his relationship with all his kids in the show is part of this. Running parallel to the show's themes of the family is the nature of it being a "family show" in the literal sense. For fans, it's both a charming additional element of the show and something they strongly identify with: Dan and Eugene's dynamic—from the cute anecdotes about Eugene not liking getting his hair wet and mouthing the lines with his kids to the deeper loving bond between father and son that is apparent on the screen and the promotion circuit.

That connection is mirrored by a lovely sentiment from several fans reflecting on their experience of the New York event, which Eugene Levy attended. A fan interviewed for this book, who accompanied Mia, loved the opportunity to see them together and witnessed Eugene's clear pride for his son: "Seeing Dan and Eugene together talking about the show and each other was so heartwarming. Their love and respect for each other, especially Eugene's pride in Dan's abilities and creativity, was life-affirming."

Nicole agrees, "I have never seen a father more proud of his son than Eugene that night." Magaly observes, "My favorite moment was when Eugene talked about how incredibly proud he was of Dan. Dan just sat through those moments incredibly humble, and his expression was overwhelmingly sweet."

It's hugely important to queer audiences to have a father figure and an older one, not a young "woke" dad like Randall on *This Is Us*, but someone who is the age of their dads okay with a queer son, and not just okay, but so okay that they make a big queer TV show with them. But also Eugene is quietly so much more activist than Dan in that. To have an older man go on every major talk show to say, "Look at this brilliant queer show, made with my son who is gay and who I love and support." To have him do that time and time again . . . it's hard to quantify what that means. To hear it from a parent figure feels like such a huge step. But it also feels reassuring, like someone who is a parent, who is that age, is there looking out for not just Dan but all the queer kids out there. That's why he's become a TV dad for so many.

As TV parents, Catherine O'Hara and Eugene Levy have been there across milestones. O'Hara as Kevin's mom in the *Home Alone* franchise was there when today's thirty-somethings were in elementary school; the film was usually put on as an end-of-term Christmas treat or put on by parents for a break from whatever Disney film was driving them crazy that year. Kevin's mom and Jim's dad (in *American Pie*, Eugene Levy played the protagonist's father) formed a slightly dysfunctional pair of iconic screen parents even before they teamed up as an admittedly slightly dysfunctional pair of parents on *Schitt's Creek*. O'Hara offered unconventional mothering role models for thirty-something years, and Levy offered well-meaning but occasionally misfiring fatherly advice for fifteen years. It is again why elements of the show hit home harder for certain age groups, specifically those of David/Alexis/Patrick's age, and the power of these on-screen parents in that shouldn't be underestimated. It's also endearing that, as an older actor, Eugene gets "adopted" by an audience for simply being nice. Especially as the show ended in 2020, with many people of that age group also being separated from family for a long time, it seemed the world needed Eugene as much as Johnny.

Because their family feels authentic to us even though we only know the tip of the iceberg, Dan's honesty that coming out was still a struggle even with understanding their parents is an authentic relatable experience. As is Eugene's honesty about that time, as he told *Bustle* magazine: "I would have done things so much. Differently, you know? I would have gotten more involved in discussing what was happening" (Peele, December 18, 2020). That authenticity and that they've both told that story repeatedly is hopeful because a queer child's story is happy and supported. Ultimately, as Dan recalled in his GLAAD award speech in 2019, his mom and dad's support for him as a gay person also was intrinsic in what he has been able to do with the show: "Had I not had the love to give me a sense of security, I don't know if I would have found my way out of the closet, let alone create the opportunity for myself to tell stories on television that have affected some kind of positive change in the world."

It is a kind of full circle that he gives Eugene/Johnny back to the world as a support to other queer people, showing everyone, even those who didn't have a Johnny or Eugene, that it was possible, and that, for the duration of the show, they could "borrow" him as a dad too. Eugene becomes a dual role model through his role as the fictional Johnny Rose, who takes care of David and Patrick as the loving dad of queer sons (and sons-in-law), but also as his real self, Eugene, expressing his support for his gay son publicly and often. Role models of both kinds are important, especially for the queer kids who grew up or have ended up without. The fact that Eugene is celebrating his son's achievements for fans stands out, saying something of the pride and affection fans hold for the Levy family and the broader creative team. Still, it also says that Eugene's character in the series and himself have come to mean a lot to fans. As Mads says of him at the book event: "Honestly, my favorite part—this is going to sound weird—was at the very end when Eugene was asked to say something to us all, and he asked us to get home safely. It was such a dad thing to say, and considering Johnny is like a dad to me, it had the most impact."

And that's just it—the idea of Eugene caring that the younger fans got home safely—cements him as TV dad. The person you look up to is, however, distantly, looking out for you is important. It doesn't matter that Johnny isn't real or Eugene is a celebrity; that role model, that feeling that there is a dad out there for you, matters. The idea of Johnny being a TV dad for so many fans—this writer included, but more on that later—his inclusiveness, pride, and support of making this queer show are important, as is the broader, often extremely powerful, impact the show had on queer fans. Eugene Levy makes it feel like Johnny Rose exists. Both of them let many imagine, even for a while, that the TV dad is the dad they wished they'd had. And for a moment, he can be.

Chosen Family and Choosing Your Family

But *Schitt's Creek* further queers the idea of what queer chosen families look like. Traditionally, the "chosen family" for queer people meant leaving their origins and finding a new family. On the one hand, the Roses (and Patrick) do that. Finding a chosen family usually involved moving to urban centers and finding a new "tribe" of queer people to replace your traditional/genetic family. However, *Schitt's Creek* queers this by asking what if the town was the chosen family? What if this ordinary, small town could be the chosen family, not just for the queer characters but everyone who needed it. That is a very queer notion and is the premise for the whole show, because what Dan Levy calls the "town without prejudice" is, in fact, a town of queer chosen family.

The point of chosen or queer family is finding space and people who accept you for who you are. The Roses never had that, but the town of Schitt's Creek always has—as far as we can tell—been this way. The town is like a queer village or set of queer spaces that we find in many places. From the store to the cafe to the bar, the town is an interconnected set of queer safe spaces.

8

Curating a Story in Fashion: Clothes and the Roses

The clothes the Roses wear are part of the show's storytelling, a visual shorthand, but they also serve each character and are also an integral part of the storytelling on the show. Across the series, the clothes David and Moira wear are particularly important. They are the most expressive in their fashion, and it is the most of who they are, as well as conveying their mood or state of mind at a given moment. But other characters communicate who they are through their clothes. The clothing is an expression of queer aesthetics.

Moira and Camp

If anyone embodies camp aesthetic, it's Moira Rose. Camp is a traditionally queer expression; its roots are in a police investigation into "homosexual acts" which they deemed "campish undertakings." From there, and the original aesthetics of working-class gay men in France, Christopher Isherwood cemented the association and the definition in his novel *The Word of an Evening* (1954). Camp and queerness are intertwined.

We see this too in the drag influences Moira also embodies. Her over-the-top looks mirror those of drag queens (to the extent that in a full circle moment, there are now many queens inspired by Moira Rose). The essence of a drag is an exaggeration, and Moira lives that in everything she does. Drag is also about defying society's expectations of how to dress and act—all very Moira-like qualities. Drag attitude and culture, of course, have deep historical roots in queer culture. With roots in theatrical culture, from vaudeville shows of the 1920s through to the underground queer scene in the 1920s and 1930s, drag has a long tradition. It rests on being both an exaggerated, fantasy version of yourself and fully yourself. Moira's aesthetic would give any queen a run for their money.

The idea of "camp" varies culturally but is also inexorably linked to queer culture. It is an over-the-top, ostentatious, often performative approach to clothing and behavior. In the case of Moira, she's not trying to "perform" camp. She *is* camp. In the tradition of every iconic camp woman, she is strong, has a unique sense of style, and is over the top in personality and attitude.

While it was once about a carefully curated public image for "television's Moira Rose" and "Moira, wife of Jonathan Rose," when she's in the town, she plays a character every day to shield herself from what reality has become. A pivotal moment for this is when it's rumored she has died ("RIP Moira Rose," season 4, episode 5) when she spends hours agonizing over an outfit to present herself to the press. Of course, it is of concern not that the world thinks she's dead but what she looks like when she presents herself as alive. She gets so wrapped up in her outfit choice that she misses the press. However, she still goes to dinner in the outfit so as to not waste it. That Stevie compliments it might be a more significant "win" for Moira and part of her overall journey with the town.

"The Girls!" Moira and More Than Wigs

Moira, of course, has an image that is carefully curated; from wigs to her heels, it is a thought-out look at every opportunity. To an extent, "Moira Rose" and "Moira" are two different people: the public persona and the wife and mother at home. It's an element the show subtly pulls through the series: the Moira at home is a different version of the Moira carefully curated through the image of "Moira Rose" over the years. However, that performative "Moira Rose" takes on a different meaning when she gets to Schitt's Creek, as she defiantly clings to the image she curated in her old world.

Moira's wigs are a huge part of her identity: "anything but the wigs," she screams in the first episode. Moira's hair/wigs are exquisite in their ability to tell stories. When we see Moira without her wigs, too, it's like the Moira Rose/Moira divide illustrated. Wigs have a deep history in queer culture and fashion. Beyond drag, she is dating back to the 1920s queer scene, where men and women alike would appear in wigs and makeup, making gender often indistinguishable. Wigs are about presenting an exaggerated, more fabulous version of yourself to the world. But they are also about giving a version of yourself you wish for and keeping elements hidden. And while Moira isn't a queer person, she is keeping with the show's queer-inspired aesthetic and roots. How Moira displays the wigs adds a particular camp aesthetic to the motel room.

When she puts on a wig, it makes a statement about her mood and about who she wants to be that day. But when she takes one off, it is too. Sometimes, there is something vulnerable and exposing about seeing Moira without her wig, like seeing a drag queen take off their wig, we're getting a peek behind the curtain, perhaps at something else. She doesn't always wear wigs in public, so they aren't a "must have" or something masking day-to-day insecurity; instead, they're a mix of dress-up and glamour and provide a particular "personality." She does tend to wear them when facing the public in any sense, and they are curated to the occasion.

Of course, Moira's curation of her image—or many images—is part of being "Moira Rose" and presenting a particular image to the world. Moira's wigs each have their own personality, which she selects for a specific purpose or mood. She doesn't wear them all the time either; they are used for moments or days when she needs an extra lift or armor to undertake a task or face the world. There is an elaborate set of visual storytelling in every one of Moira's outfits, along with her hair and makeup, which Ana Sorys and Lucky Bromhead expertly craft.

Moira's use of clothes to present a specific image nods to queer culture. Her clothes allowed Moira to "perform" the previous version of herself, which had money and another life. In effect, Moira's clothes allow her to perform as "Moira Rose," doing that against the town's backdrop. It was all part of Moira's demonstrating her vulnerability. She's putting up a wall with her clothes, much like in her acting days where she could hide behind the characters (who were no doubt just as fabulous). And camp is often used as a defense against the world, a way of playing a character to present the version of oneself you wish to be, or as an act of self-preservation. Both things apply to Moira.

O'Hara initially drew on Daphne Guinness in many situations for her monochrome aesthetic and high-concept looks. For O'Hara and Levy, the leveling up of Moira doing that in the ridiculous backdrops became a jumping-off point for the character, but the clothes also tell a story and reveal much about what Moira thinks or feels at any given point. Moira thinks she's "hip" and "cool," and annoyingly, for her grown-up children and husband, she is. After all, despite being uniquely herself in her fashion choices, her choices were still on the fashion pulse (at least in 2015 when they had money). That, of course, becomes part of Moira's story; she has paused. Moira treats each day in the town as if it were still the world she left behind. She sees no reason to adapt her clothing choices; she leans into them further. And we get the "Moira Rose" look we know and love.

Moira's premiere dress is a massive moment for her ("The Dress," season 5, episode 4). She orders the dress—the first new thing she's ordered for herself in years—and is incredibly proud to show it off. It was also the only new piece of designer clothing Dan Levy used in the show, in keeping with the idea that the Roses wouldn't have had anything new (and in keeping within the show's budget). The dress is the most beautiful of anything Moira wears. And, of course, it's imbued with meaning. It's rose-gold in a nod to the family name and covered in feathers in a nod to the movie in question. Letting Moira look different at this moment, and later in "The Premiere" (season 6, episode 5), because she kept the dress is a moment of real celebration for Moira. We also see her look transformed; her hair is natural and her makeup is softer and glowing. Ironically, when she puts on the premiere dress, everything of the Moira Rose facade falls away in public for the first time, and she is entirely herself.

One overlooked Moira "look" is her self-styled Sally Bowles for *Cabaret*. When she thinks Stevie will be a no-show, she arrives ready to go on. It's a perfect nod to Fosse-esque costuming, with a waistcoat, suspenders, and bowler hat. Her makeup is also Fosse-perfect. It's an understated Moira moment that subtly proves her credentials as someone from the performing arts. Before we get the confirmation in season 6 that her career was not the joke or sham we suspect it is, Moira shows up, ready and entirely on brand. It's not so much that she's there to steal the limelight (though she happily would), but she knows exactly what the outfit should be. It's an authentic theatre person look put together with nods to the back catalog of the era, director, and style of the show she's directing. That Moira had this on standby, not just for her but for the show, is a little nod that despite her dramatics, she's an industry hoofer through and through.

Another overlooked, or as understated as Moira gets, look is in "Meet the Parents" (season 5, episode 11). Only Moira Rose could make a silver sequined dress at the cafe a toned-down look, but that is what she achieves. For Patrick's birthday party, Moira is wearing a long-sleeved, silver sequined dress with a (relatively) simple necklace. Her wig that night is a long red-haired one styled in a half-up half-down with bangs. First, she looks beautiful (Moira's red wigs suit her coloring), but she also looks as close to a "normal" mom as Moira is likely to. She's looking, as best she can, like a mom-of-the-boyfriend for David. This point well documents Moira's devotion to her son's happiness with Patrick; it's the one time

Moira Rose wouldn't dream of her outfit pulling focus and causing any upset for her son. So she does toned-down, albeit Moira style.

The wedding was one point when Moira didn't worry about overshadowing her son's moment. Once asked to officiate, Moira leaned in. She leaned in so hard she turned up as the pope. So much has been written about Moira's wedding outfit. It became countless memes and even more Halloween costumes; rightly so, as it's iconic. And really, what else could Moira Rose do at a wedding? Technically she followed David's dress code of black and white, just with added gold. When your everyday is Met Gala–level fashion, where do you turn for your son's wedding when you're also officiating? The outfit says that Moira cares for the family and her son, if only in her peculiar way. In Moira's mind, she undoubtedly gave David the spectacle he deserved, and she wasn't taking away from his day. David, unlike Alexis, somewhat enjoyed the theatrics of his mom's life as a kid. He is as camp as she is and shares her aesthetic; he wants to be her aesthetically and otherwise. But ultimately, her look came from a place of love, of wanting to do the best she could for David's wedding, and in Moira's eyes, there is nothing so important to do your best as serving the best outfit you can.

Moira's story doesn't quite conclude with the wedding outfit; for a woman who has used clothes to cope with the town, her departure outfit is important. She leaves in a checkered suit (monochrome, of course). Moira's hair is longer and softer in the final season, and it's styled here softly, framing her face, which is made up of her trademark bold lip and dark eyes. Her jewelry is reserved for an array of rings—not unlike her son's, just with more bling—and she carries a smart plain handbag. It's a power-suit and matches her husband's uniform of suits in her way. It's saying Moira Rose is back, but also mirroring her husband saying what we've always known: these two are equals in marriage and career. They're leaving the town united, more so than when they went in, and moving forward with their lives and careers together. Most important, Moira is together, stylish, and ready to take on the wider world.

"I'm Reorganizing My Knits": Clothing and Queer Aesthetics

David's style will, like his mom's, always be a suit of armor, and it also settles into a more authentic expression of who he is as David grows into himself across the series. David's sweaters chart his arc in various moods across the series and at significant moments. But overall, too, they showcase his subtly evolving style. We meet David in his quirky mix of sweaters and shorts. In season 1, he focuses on skinny jeans and fitted sweaters, often with embellished styles. They're more structured; geometrical patterns spiked even through season 3, episode 7. Across seasons 1 to 3, David's most iconic look is the Helmut Lang hooded sweater he wears on his Amish adventure ("Happy Anniversary," season 2, episode 1). And his seasons 1 and 2 looks are mainly plain, simple black numbers except for one white-with-grey floral ("Little Sister," season 1, episode 11) and the black-on-white stripes he wore to "fold in the cheese" ("Estate Sale," season 2, episode 4). David incorporates some slogan shirts slowly into his wardrobe, like his "D" sweater ("The Drip," season 1, episode 2) and his "Love Me Tender" sweater ("Finding David," season 2, episode 1). But his slogans get a little more pointed/meaningful later on with "Radical Feminist" and the little more hopeful "I Believe in the Power of Love" in season 5 ("The Hospies," "A Whisper of Desire," and "Meet the Parents," episodes 8, 9, and 11, respectively). David saves the most significant slogan sweaters for the final episode, with "Love" in rainbow colors appearing. Besides evolving slogan sweaters, David's style also evolves as time progresses. His sweaters get softer overall, losing the hard edges of the early seasons, as his style evolves into a more relaxed, more personal one than the try-hard gallerist we meet in season 1. With a couple of, dare we say it, fluffy sweaters (in the literal and figurative sense) and a softening of edges with his cream and black fluffy number in "The Incident" (season 6, episode 2), and an array of cozy-looking sweaters, David is maybe to some degree at least putting comfort over fashion too. The sweaters in the final season are fun, playful, and relaxed, much like David (mostly) is in his happy relationship.

On a more nuanced level, David's sweaters and other clothing also offer signifiers to specific moods and moments across the series. Two of these signal the evolution of his relationship with Patrick. In "Open Mic," he wears a sweater covered in orange flames—the first time we've seen him in anything but monochrome or neutrals—signifying the "heart on fire" moment Patrick's song gives him. Later, in "Start Spreading the News," when showing Patrick the house and finally deciding to stay, his sweater has hands holding flames. That final sweater is an amalgamation of the open mic outfit and the sweater he wore in the episode: a plain open hand. In a lovely bit of visual storytelling, his outfits tell the story of his vital shifts in accepting this relationship is forever. Another final season call-back is in David's last sweater of the season, his black with a rainbow heart and the word "Love" sweater. On one level, it's a lovely subtle "Pride"-themed sweater. On another, its color palette refers to the sweater from "The Olive Branch": geometric (star) patterns in reds, whites, and

David and Patrick in "Open Mic."
Pop TV Network/Photofest © Pop TV Network

blues (season 4, episode 9). If the flames are David accepting and committing to the relationship, then the shapes and colors are him celebrating it.

David's clothes also have a few other critical moments besides wearing them, and they take on another significance level even when he's not wearing them. Beginning with his stress about storing them in season 1, when Stevie offers to store them for him. In this episode ("Bad Parents," season 1, episode 4), Stevie gives David the motel's "honeymoon suite" to store his clothes on the condition she's allowed to wear them. David agrees, and it's the first time anyone in the town has done anything nice for him. That it's also in that room that they'll have their ill-fated hookups is a nice parallel. Clothing also plays a part in the potential downfall of Stevie and David's relationship, in that he's packing them when they "break up" as friends when she declines to live with him ("Town for Sale," season 1, episode 13). The sweaters symbolically become part of a relationship conversation when Patrick looks for his apartment. David rejects the place Patrick has in mind because of a lack of storage space for his clothes (season 5, episode 3). It is a manifestation of his anxieties, which Patrick quells with the idea that the apartment is just for him, and David would spend a lot of time there. However, by the end of season 6, David's sweaters are visible, folded on Patrick's shelves in the background, a sign he has all but moved in, sweaters and all.

A few other fun elements of David's attire are worth reflecting on. One overlooked vital piece of David's wardrobe is his leather jacket. He's wearing it when he arrives in the town (it was one of Dan Levy's personal pieces), but it also comes out at crucial moments in the story. Most significantly, when David is trying to get some romantic action; more accurately, it's his hookup jacket. He wears it when attempting to find some action at the bar with Stevie, again when he visits Sebastian Raine for what can only be described as a revenge fuck, and finally when he and Patrick visit Jake for what can only be described as an orgy. David's sex jacket is a small, repeated detail across the series, but it's a nice throwback to who he used to be. David in formalwear for the family party is a slightly sweeter throwback to who he used to be (season 1, episode 12). When dressed in a formal suit, Moira describes David as "like your father the day I married him," a lovely nod to the Levy father-son duo at the end of the first seasons and a sweet Rose family moment.

A couple of times, David dresses against type (and possibly better instinct) for other people. When his mom suffers nerves around performing at the town's "Asbestos Fest" (season 4, episode 3), David offers to perform "The Number," a musical skit he and his mom would perform at Christmas parties. For it, he wears a very "David Rose Christmas past" outfit and styles his hair in a way best described as 2000s emo chic (straightened fringe and all). For David, the love and support of his mom trump many things, including fashion. He does similar for Patrick, in a demonstration of his softening walls, when he agrees to play baseball. Despite hating all sports and making his hatred for the uniform (the glove is brown and the shoes are black, after all), David puts on the uniform and plays baseball. Again, he's willing to put aside his snobbery about his clothes when it's for someone he loves. One exception to this rule is when David dons camouflage in the episode "Turkey Shoot" (season 1, episode 7). This is the only time he dresses out of his aesthetic for non-altruistic reasons. In this case, it's to prove a stubborn point to Stevie, which while not in terms of clothing on brand, is equally on brand personality. David's other diversion from his usual uniform is suitable "For David" because he borrows Patrick's clothes to pose as a candidate for Larry Air when Stevie has an interview. Despite wondering if David could fit into Patrick's extremely tight (and several inches shorter in the leg) jeans, the look is contrasting and hilarious. It's also perfectly their relationship: when thinking about what a perfect interview candidate looks like, clothing-wise David, in a teasing, slightly mocking manner, thinks of Patrick. The teasing and mockery, through clothes, is part of their "love language," and it's an endearing, if offbeat, sweet moment—again very David and Patrick, very *Schitt's Creek*.

There are so many more little clues to the state of mind, storytelling, and more in David's clothes in particular, and it's a layer of visual storytelling that makes it such a full-rounded work. His use of different patterns, the balance of black and white, and the combinations of when he wears skirts all indicate his mood or state of mind. But more than this, clothes are an essential queer signifier, even within the community. They queer-code David to both the town and viewers. And the lack of comment on his clothes from the town and an affinity we as viewers may feel with him in understanding him as queer-coded from his clothes is important.

David's look certainly does that. While Moira's looks are more performative—mostly hiding many of her true emotions under her "costume"—David's looks are a more sensitive and nuanced insight into his personality. David's clothing evolves with him: a really basic level in restricted outfits—buttoned-up shirts, skinny jeans, and leather jackets—morphs into a softer selection of sweaters, pants, and skirts as David changes.

David isn't trying to be "feminine" particularly; he's just using clothes for expression, some of which are skirts. Sometimes he wears them over trousers (also feeling like a fashion flashback to the early 2000s for many of us). Sometimes they're just a skirt. It's not "drag," but David expressing his femininity through clothing, and David being able to express himself across the gender spectrum or expectations through clothing—and adjacent to that, his personality—is important. This is nowhere more so than in his wedding outfit. It makes sense that Patrick is happy with his "little suit" (as David puts it), simple, classic, and traditional, but David goes for something else. Still in keeping with his usual monochrome style, fitting his general aesthetic-tailored, considered statement skirt and jacket that is masculine and feminine at once because clothes and people can be both. And David embodies that.

The queer aesthetic of his clothing is about embracing all of that: clothing doesn't have to be gendered, but you can use it to express your gender or your queerness if you want to. This is something Dan Levy has extended in his awards show repertoire of outfits—from his Emmy night gray version of David's wedding suit to his yellow Valentino suit for the Golden Globes to the Dior military-inspired ensemble for the Critics' Choice awards; Levy uses fashion as personal expression, as a way of defying expectations. He and David alike use it to embrace queerness. This becomes important for queer viewers, too, seeing a high-profile gay man embrace gender-defiant clothing and fashion and expression through it, which has historically been limited for men but also met with homophobia. Levy taking a version of David's use of clothing as self-expression to the real world felt important for queer viewers too. Aspects of role models come in many forms, and we shouldn't dismiss style and personal expression.

Queer-coded clothing is important to queer expression. And while it's an obvious commentary, it would be remiss not to reflect on David's gender-defiant clothing. His isn't a "drag" performance. It is a gender-defying one. There's a lovely moment at the end of "New Car" when David critiques Moira's outfit, and she says, "It's your outfit," as they are wearing the same clothes. This is funny but also a subtle point on the genderless nature of clothing in David's world.

Queer Coded Fashion and Identity

Clothing and queerness are also closely entwined as a means of self-expression. For people who feel "outside" the norm of society, who are already ostracized for being different, clothing choices can be a way to lean into that difference. Queer clothing is also celebratory of contrast, throwing out societal expectations and norms. There are vast and complex ways in which the queer community uses clothing—from categorizing each other in terms of everything from music taste to sexual preference to a rebellion against heteronormative culture. It is nuanced in every gay "scene" and across gender and ethnicity. But it also boils down to a means of personal expression that throws the expectations of everyday clothing away and goes its way.

Interestingly, if we're reading through a historical lens of queer clothing as self-labeling and self-expression, Patrick's clothing puts him under one of those labels. In part, Patrick's consistent "uniform" is a nod to his similarities with Johnny. But there is also more to his style choice. His "uniform" of straight-legged jeans, blue shirts, and a short, neat haircut feels like a call-back to a gay "clone" look. A hallmark of the 1970s and 1980s queer scene, the clean-cut, masculine-presenting "clone" was often seen in, yes, straight-legged denim, utility boots, or sturdy shoes, with close-cut haircuts and often a mustache. (Thankfully for Patrick and Noah Reid, the latter isn't included.) He's not dressed in *precisely* that form of queer expression, but his way of presenting himself is a nod to it. Patrick "passes" for straight in his fashion sense, but it might be a neat trick on the audience, too, a nod to us assuming Patrick's "straight" look, as David perceives it, is one thing, when it is also a nod to queer history and culture.

He has hidden various Easter eggs of queer moments in clothing, nods to particular trends or subsets of the community within the more "innocent" and "straight-friendly" clothing of David and Patrick. One such nod might be in "Smoke Signals" (season 6, episode 1); Patrick clips his keys to his belt, which is also part of the color codes/flagging system in the queer community (this was a system of seemingly innocent elements of clothing which were invisible to the wider public but sent clear signals about the wearer's sexuality and preferences to those in the know). Although keys on a belt is predominantly a lesbian signal (used also to indicate whether women are a "top" or "bottom"), it's also something used within the leather community. It could mean nothing, but it also could be a deliberate nod, and that's the fun of a show with such detail, down to everything the characters wear (Patrick, by the way, clips his keys to the right).

In the years before being gay was legal, dress and other clothing codes were an integral part of the queer community for identifying each other. One prominent part of this was the hanky code, a means by which gay men identified with each other but also expressed things like sexual preference and where they fit within the community. It can outline everything from which "tribe" you belong to to sexual preference. Patrick's "uniform" of blue shirts, straight-legged denim, and sensible shoes can be read as a slight call-back to this and a comment on it. First, David doesn't identify Patrick as queer because of how he dresses: "He's a business major who wears straight-legged denim. He's not interested in me." David can't label Patrick—who has lived away from queer "tribes" or signifiers—through any of the usual exterior elements he is used to, so he assumes Patrick is straight. Of course, we can also speculate on some of the color coding embedded in Dan Levy's love of clothing as an expression too. It's unlikely their respective color coding is a coded message to viewers on David and Patrick's sex life, but their color-coded clothing is a nice nod to that part of queer culture and could be seen as referencing these historical ways of signaling within the community.

One area in that Patrick truly steps into queerness as an identity is as the Emcee in *Cabaret* (as discussed in chapter 7). Here, clothing and queerness have a symbiotic relationship. The Emcee is also someone who creates their character through their attire. Through costume and makeup, they curate an image that fits what they want the world to see. Compared with David, a peacock of a character, who wears his sexuality and his identity overtly in every situation, Patrick needs a framework for doing the same. Patrick and Reid are "the boy next door," so when dressed up in the Emcee's makeup and costume of suspenders and shorts, it is a striking contrast in character and for viewers. And it is a fun moment to push Patrick—and by association Noah Reid—into that role via the Emcee's eyeliner and suspenders. The taking on the role of the Emcee is a fun moment of seeing both of them in an entirely new light (as does perhaps Patrick keeping his eyeliner for the after-party suggest he quite enjoys it). The Emcee also imbues performers with a certain sexual magnetism, something that seems to be enjoyed by viewers (and if the fanfiction on the subject is to be believed, David as well).

Patrick's "straight-legged mid-range denim" and an array of "youth pastor"–esque button-down shirts also reject the idea that being queer *has* to dictate other areas of your life. As discussed elsewhere, Patrick, as a character who demonstrates sexuality, is not defining all areas of life, and fashion is included in this. In another narrative, a "David" character would "make over" Patrick once they were together. It's often seen with a girl getting a makeover to get a guy or a gay best friend doing the makeover. While all of us—particularly David Rose—enjoy a good makeover in a romcom, it's a problematic element because it supports the idea that someone can only be loved/accepted in a relationship with that makeover. Instead, David and Patrick have a healthy and genuine relationship. David makes fun (lovingly) of Patrick's lack of style—from the infamous straight-legged, mid-range denim to his "Oprah on a Thanksgiving Day hike" shoes, all the way to his "little suit" on their wedding day. None of it is what David would choose for him, but he doesn't try and change Patrick's clothes either. Interestingly, the only time Patrick and queer-coded clothes also align is during his stint as the Emcee. For Patrick, his clothes are queer-coded in less obvious ways, but they do not also speak volumes to the show's queer storytelling.

Fans Dressing Like the Roses

For fans—as well as Dan Levy himself obviously—the aesthetic and fashion of the show have been a real focus. And many fan social media accounts are dedicated to sourcing authentic clothes from the show and replicas. Fans engaging in "everyday cosplay" wearing outfits that pay tribute to the show, either being direct copies of outfits worn, with David's sweaters being a popular choice or a stylistic tribute, has been a big part of engagement for some fans. One fan, Joe Black, has set out to collect all of David's sweaters from the series. When he was interviewed for this book, he had ninety-nine sweaters worn on the show. His collection began with the

Sweater collection from Joe Black.
Courtesy Joe Black

Sweater collection from Joe Black.
Courtesy Joe Black

now often-faked lightening sweater from "The Dress" (season 5, episode 4) and expanded beyond sweaters. As Joe said: "My problem is I'm a completionist collector, which means it isn't enough to have the 'Fold In The Cheese' sweater; I need to have the apron too. And before you ask, yes, I found it" (Joe Black, personal interview, 2022).

Fittingly, Black has ended up like Levy, scouring the internet for clothes. Although, as he says of the impact on his wallet: "I used to be a serious bargain hunter before that, so my normal maximum spend for jeans was $30. Rest assured, the Helmut Lang mohawk hoodie from 'Finding David' was *considerably* more than that. David Rose/Dan Levy RUINED discount shopping for me" (Joe Black, personal interview, 2022).

It's almost like, through fans like Black, David Rose lives on hunting eBay for sweaters and sneakers, which is an interesting riff on the stylistic commentary that Levy was aiming for, that the show became a niche trendsetter. Many fans like Black engaged in levels of "cosplaying" the characters from the show—that is, dressing similarly to them either in the exact outfits like Black or similar style. David Rose became something of a style icon, particularly in the latter years of the show. Similarly, Moira Rose became the fashion icon she deserved to be—at least on Halloween. In 2020 and 2021, the Roses were hugely popular costume choices, with Moira's outlandish Gothic style in particular being a strong Halloween choice. Instagram was flooded with tributes to the show via Halloween costume.

Dan Levy has kept a link to the fashion on the show. He's posted on Instagram images of a box of David's sweaters that he kept, with the caption "reorganizing my knits." During the London Q&A for his book, Dan Levy shared that he kept a key "look" for each of the Roses. He also shared that he didn't keep any of Johnny's suits, to his dad's dismay. Emily Hampshire also fulfilled Stevie's promise to wear David's clothes by doing a cover shoot for *The Advocate* (March 16, 2002) in David's "Radical Feminist" sweater, a neat through line in one of the show's queer actors continuing to carry the (fashion) torch for David Rose.

The clothes were part of the Rose family and how their story was told. Not since *Sex and the City* and Patricia Field's generation-defining costume design has a show been entirely defined by its look. Debra Hanson, the show's costume designer, and Dan Levy's curatorial and character vision created a new, camper, queerer version for perhaps the generation who grew up wishing they were Carrie Bradshaw (just like David Rose).

9

You're My Mariah Carey: Music and Storytelling

Music is a critical part of TV storytelling in any context. It adds an emotional shorthand to a given moment, and we can all remember an iconic song playing over a crucial moment in a well-loved TV show. Of course, like any show, the music used over the top of scenes in *Schitt's Creek* was memorable. For fans, James Blunt's "Precious Love" will forever be the Roses' song after playing during their dance as a family in season 2, as will the heartbreaking reminder of Ted and Alexis breaking up on hearing "Dedicated to the One I Love." Fans will remember—or wish they could forget—the visuals of "Don't Cry Out Loud" when thinking of Roland and Jocelyn's wedding night. They'll likely stick with the "This Will Be Our Year" sentimentality for Moira and Johnny's final drive out of town. So powerful are the music choices connected to *Schitt's Creek* that even songs not directly in the series have meaning: the song "To Build a Home" by The Cinematic Orchestra has been adopted by *Schitt's Creek* fans following its role in the documentary *Best Wishes, Warmest Regards.* A song is a powerful tool in the *Schitt's Creek* universe. That's before even getting into *Cabaret,* as discussed in chapter 6.

Music and Comedy

Beginning with Moira's lead (as she would want), the first musical moment in *Schitt's Creek* is a comedy masterclass and a nice throwback to the more traditional style of the O'Hara/Levy comedy partnership. As discussed in chapter 1, their partnership grew from the *Second City Television* (SCTV) and Christopher Guest performances they gave, many of which did involve a musical—and specifically musical comedy—element. So when

Moira gives an awkwardly over-the-top rendition of "Danny Boy" at Carl's funeral, it gives long-term fans an essence of those days.

It's also a brilliantly comedic bit of big storytelling. Even though it's the kind that only works in the early seasons, before the show grows into itself, it's a highlight nonetheless. It's one of the admittedly over-the-top bits that work—it feels genuine that Moira would take to performing to offset the awkwardness. It's also less awkward hearing her sing than the setup. O'Hara executes it perfectly, with Moira being just over the top enough to sell it but also hilarious. It also gives Eugene Levy the perfect "straight man" moment that he does so well as Johnny, being baffled at his wife's performance while he eats sandwiches at the wake. For fans, too, it's a memorable blooper where they keep rolling through the song and O'Hara, while in character, sings, "Are you going to let me keep singing" while Levy continues enjoying the sandwich he's eating.

A counterbalance in broad comedy musical moments comes in season 5 with the now iconic "A Little Bit Alexis." In the episode "The Hospies" (season 5, episode 8), Alexis is auditioning for the town's production of *Cabaret* and vying for the lead role of Sally (she's very much her mother's daughter at this moment). Instead of a traditional audition song, Alexis elects to perform an original song from her "critically reviewed" reality TV show of the same name. The reality TV show had long been built into her character, but the show hadn't found an excuse to use it. An ill-fated musical theatre audition was, of course, the perfect vehicle.

"A Little Bit Alexis" is a moment of comedy gold, giving us some wonderful character backstory moments and charming Rose family dynamics. We learn that this show was one of Alexis' many adventures. It's also a nice nod to Dan Levy's previous life as host of *The Hills: Live After Show*, which gave him a taste of the reality TV world and the ideas like the Kardashians, which inspired the original setup of the show. Of all of them, Alexis obviously would be the one to lean into that world.

The song and Annie Murphy's performance have become as iconic as Patrick and David's musical performances, albeit for different reasons. Like Noah Reid arranged "The Best" for the show himself, Annie Murphy also created Alexis' memorable song. The appeal of "A Little Bit Alexis" only grows as you discover more about its creation: Murphy wrote those clever lyrics while enlisting two musicians—her husband, Menno Versteeg, and his former bandmate Nick Boyd—as her collaborators. As Murphy told *Elle* magazine: "I was both inspired by and jealous of Noah Reid in the previous season when he did his own beautiful rendition of 'Simply the Best.' So I immediately said to Dan, 'I will try to write this,' not realizing that I am not a musician and Noah very much is a musician! And somehow Dan agreed to let this happen" (Dibden, September 21, 2020). But despite it being a hugely comedic set piece, a lot of work and thought went into the song. Once again, this moment uses music as a means of storytelling. Alexis' big musical number sits up there with David's performance of "The Best," as discussed in the next section: it's about showing how far they've come. For David, he can perform because of who he is, and for Alexis, she's terrible because that isn't who she is anymore. Okay, so from a purely technical point of view, Alexis was always terrible, but the song is no longer who she is. Alexis *is* better off helping her mom with the publicity as a chorus member because that's where she'll shine. It also becomes the last real reminder of where Alexis once was as she manages to lean into who she is in the final season.

"A Little Bit Alexis" also embodied some of the *Schitt's Creek* ethos of giving back. A portion of the proceeds is donated to this great Canadian organization, MusiCounts, which provides instruments and resources in schools that otherwise couldn't afford music programs.

The comedy music moments in *Schitt's Creek* are as crucial as the heartfelt ones for carrying forward the stories of the Rose family while also offering trademark comedy. While Alexis might be in a "different orchard" to her mother, both had moments of musical storytelling that are iconic to the show and essential to the show's arc and the characters.

Choirs, Queerness, and Community

There is a long tradition in queer communities of music, specifically choirs, being a "safe space." Indeed, choirs are a safe space beyond the queer community, being places of support and community. Choirs generally have a long history in European, mainly Celtic traditions. So while the idea of choirs and choral singing dates back to ancient history and religious choirs, community choirs are more recent. Choirs for secular reasons saw a rise with the popularity of opera and the need/desire to sing nonreligious music. Across the seventeenth and eighteenth centuries, choirs increased; by the nineteenth century, they had been established in many communities. Nations like Wales and Ireland are particularly noted for their choir tradition, where even the smallest villages would have a choir. This small town choir was replicated in North America when Europeans moved there and established their traditions. But the small town choir serves many functions beyond just music-making—community and friendship being at the top of that list.

This is something we also see in LGBTQ+ links to choirs. In 1978, the first choir to include "gay" as an identifier was formed in San Francisco (The San Francisco Gay Men's Chorus), though there were likely many more gay-in-spirit-if-not-in-name choirs before them. There is a strong history of forming choir alliances in North America as a stance and haven against broader persecution. The three significant motivations for joining gay and lesbian choruses are community, politics, and artistic quality.

The town choir, the Jazzagals, are part of this camp aesthetic of song integrated into the series, and storytelling through song also runs parallel to this. A tongue-in-cheek element surrounds the choir, which is supposed to represent small-time musical performers, which Moira naturally regards with disdain. But they, like Moira's outfits and demeanor, become part of the larger camp aesthetic surrounding her—a nod to queer culture too. As discussed earlier in the book, the over-the-top drag queen aesthetic is also seen in the camp performance, something Moira embodies in the various musical performances across the show and is a nod to that part of the queer heritage of the show.

When Moira joins the Jazzagals, it's initially a moment of Moira Rose's defiance of her celebrity. But as becomes clear when she asks Johnny not to come back as a Jazzaguy, it's her first taste of community in the town. Are "the gals" the first real friends Moira has made in a long time?

For Moira, then, the Jazzagals become an integral part of her being part of community in town. Is it at first a chance to assert her "star power"? Of course, this is Moira Rose. She never quite grows out of her friendly rivalry with Jocelyn for dominance in the choir, but the choir also becomes something of Moira's own in the town. She begins her journey with the choir in season 2 ("Jazzagals," season 2, episode 3). In typical Moira fashion, she assumed her twelve-time projected Daytime People's Choice award nominee self would be immediately invited into a starring role. When Jocelyn insists she auditions, she is predictably outraged. Still, when she arrives at the audition to find a performer in this small town choir who is better than her (Shakura S'Aida as Lena), she quickly panics and tries to get out of the audition. She eventually gets up and gives a typical "Moira" audition in what will become a long-running joke of Moira's weird and wonderful performances.

The Jazzagals audition is a call-back to several of O'Hara's roles in Christopher Guest films, where several weird-yet-brilliant song numbers have been featured (memorably, of course, "God Loves a Terrier," a duet with Eugene in *Best in Show*). This, along with her performance of "Danny

Boy" at Carl's funeral in season 2, firmly sits within those surreal, funny, and quirky performances we expect from Moira Rose. But this becomes the exception rather than the rule from now on. As the show shifts gears in its third season, becoming less outlandish in its comedy and more focused on the drama, Moira's giving "quirky" performances become less of a feature and more for dramatic effect. Even when she returns to the stage in "The Number" with David in "Asbestos Fest," the weirdness is offset by her vulnerability. The Jazzagals is maybe a part of that too.

Moira then, while she never loses her diva nature within the choir—always campaigning for the solo and picking songs in her range—does become part of the choir and, with it, part of something in the community. We see this particularly when Johnny wants to join the choir in season 4. The moment offers another loving throwback to O'Hara and Levy's various singing moments in the past and is also a chance for Eugene to show off his singing voice. But it's also an important moment in Moira and Johnny's journey with the town. When Johnny joins the choir as an honorary "Jazzaguy," he's embraced by Jocelyn, Ronnie, and the other women, even being invited to after-rehearsal drinks with them. While Johnny rejoices at being part of the choir and spending social time with his wife, Moira is less enamored with the arrangement. She eventually confesses to him that although it was done with "the best of intentions," she doesn't want him as part of the choir as he is encroaching on her hobby, her one piece of life separate to him right now.

Moira is allowed to be herself in the choir. They're a quirky bunch of women seemingly from all walks of life and all levels of talent. But Moira is allowed to be who she is within it. Sure, Jocelyn never quite gives in to all her strange demands and star posturing, but also, week on week, the gals put up with, and even embrace, Moira as, well, Moira. It all feeds back to the idea of choirs, community, and friendship and is a thread that runs through the show with Moria and the gals. They become fixtures in her life and a genuine sad farewell for her at the end. While Moira was never going to stay in the town voluntarily, and while her goodbye to the choir is typical "Moira" in that it's all about her, there is also a sense of genuine friendship and sadness to leave there too. All of the Roses found a place in the town, and the Jazzagals were Moira's.

The Jazzagals also punctuate the time in the town with some genuine, heartfelt performances that parallel the Roses, specifically Moira's journey there. Being in the town allows a gradual erasure of this line, and Moira becomes more fully herself as time goes on—fully herself in only the way Moira Rose can be. Still, there are more moments of the woman behind the wigs in public and private, and the choir is an example. It is the place where Moira is Moira most easily.

Alexis' graduation, at the end of season 3, is pivotal for the Roses. They're finally adjusting to and being part of the town. But they're also turning a corner in their relationship with each other. Alexis thinks her mom isn't coming to her graduation, something she pushed for, no doubt, too, after years of being disappointed by her parents (admittedly, the Roses did go to her first graduation. She just wasn't there, but also her parents didn't notice). But Alexis does want her mom there. Moira uses the planned Jazzagals concert elsewhere as a slight decoy, instead turning up to sing. It's a beautiful moment of growth and family love on many levels. But it also illustrates that the choir is about community and Moira's acceptance while demonstrating her personal growth. The previous Moira would have taken the spotlight of a concert—no matter how small—and the chance to one-up someone else (particularly friendly rival Jocelyn) by taking the spotlight. However, she sacrifices this to make Alexis' night special. Moira presumably went out of her way to organize this, doing something special for her daughter, proving that she is trying to be the mom she never quite was. And okay, yes, there comes with it a certain amount of spotlight—it wouldn't be Moira without it, but it still is a magical moment.

The next significant performance for the Jazzagals is during the show's Christmas episode, where they sing, led by Twyla, "Silent Night." This is probably the most straightforward musical moment in the show; what is a Christmas episode without a Christmas song, after all? But it's nonetheless the perfect tone and the most beautiful of moments. For a show that doesn't linger on sentimentality, it's a surprisingly emotional moment—and the show knows, giving the audience an "out" with Stevie crying and being (lovingly) mocked by David. But as the show rounds out its fourth season and has taken the characters on a fairly emotional arc to that point, the Jazzagals singing "Silent Night" is a beautiful moment of pause for the characters, especially Johnny. To this point, Johnny has been quietly trying to get an elusive "win" for himself and the family. When all he wants is his Christmas celebration, it's a small but touching "win" that his family gives him.

We also get a second instance of Moira using the choir to do something good for her family, but also in their support for her. She'd rallied the choir to attend Johnny's party first but then convinced them to stay and perform because she knew what it meant to Johnny. It's no surprise by this point in the series how devoted Johnny and Moira are to one another, but Moira being Moira, it is still a surprise when she does something sweet and selfless unprovoked. But once she's seen how much Christmas means to her husband, probably for the first time in their marriage, she uses what she has—her choir of gals—to give him something special. The moment is a sweet, classic Christmas moment within the context of the show and, in the context of the story, the perfect level of sweet sentimentality that Johnny Rose seeks at Christmas.

The final key moment of musical storytelling from the Jazzagals is David and Patrick's wedding. By reaching that point, it would seem a grave oversight not to have them part of the day. First, on a practical level, it gives the peripheral characters, Jocelyn, Twyla, Ronnie (who is only there for David obviously), and even Gwen (who has reappeared at this moment), a reason to be part of the wedding. But also it makes the wedding a *town* wedding. It's filled with symbolism, obviously that it ends up being in the town hall, filled with people who were strangers three years before, instead of people he invited from his old life. That this group of women sings for him and Patrick as they get married is hugely symbolic. The choir's women become that community of "aunties" lots of people—especially in small towns—would have, the people looking out and helping out. It's symbolic, too, that they will be there after David's parents leave. He might be a grown-up, but that group of women looking out for him, that community caring, is important.

Of course, the songs are perfectly chosen and romantic, filled with meaning, as we would expect from this final hurrah. As the family walked down the aisle—Johnny and Stevie arm in arm—they sang the song playing at the end of season 2 during Mutt's party. It's significant because Johnny declared, "Tonight we dance as a family," and the Roses said "I love you" to each other at that moment. The wedding represents the culmination of the Roses' time and their personal growth; that throwback was the perfect way to illustrate that. And it is the iconic "The Best" that the Jazzagals leave the show with. It was a song that took on a new significance in the show and beyond, perhaps making it a new queer anthem or queer love song of sorts. In part, it's another bit of excellent musical storytelling, or storytelling through song. And, like any good musical theatre number, it becomes a reprise across the series. The choir follows up with their version of "The Best" in the third installment of that as part of David and Patrick's love story, and it is perfectly pitched as a moment of pure sentiment. But the wider significance of having the women who supported Moira, who represent the town, singing to David and Patrick is as important as the song choice.

Jazzagals go from a way for Moira Rose to assert her star status in the town to a way for Moira to feel like she is welcomed, part of something, and her family is loved. Through several key moments—and key songs—the Jazzagals help tell Moira's story with her. They use the songs for sentimental moments peppered with classic "Moira Rose" moments. Much like Moira herself, its sweet sincerity within the slightly off-key approach to life and performance makes the Jazzagals such an essential part of *Schitt's Creek* stories.

The Best

Every romcom deserves a good soundtrack. David and Patrick's story is no different. And "their" song, Tina Turner's "The Best," has, through the show, taken on a new life as a queer love song. As Dan Levy was right to uncover, it's a truly beautiful song if you listen to the lyrics. Reid's arrangement (he took on arranging the new version himself) highlights the song's beauty: that a person to you is "simply the best" is a lovely romantic sentiment without being overly sentimental. And that's why it works for them and probably now for so many others. It's sweet and sincere but not overly gooey or sentimental. Anything else in that scene might have felt trite and cliché. But this works.

It was the setup as much as the song which made it work too. What starts in the episode as some classic Patrick pushing David's buttons about the open mic night quickly becomes the defining romantic moment of their relationship. The setup is that the store isn't as busy as they'd like, and Patrick, who used to run open mic nights as a high schooler, would like to host one. First, the idea alone is enough to send David into a spin, which naturally delights Patrick. They also get in a cute dig/reference at the comedy legacy on which the show stands, with David declaring, "Worst case scenario, I have to watch improv." But meta-jokes aside, David's "worst case" worsens when his boyfriend (a term he has only declared the episode before) announces his intention to sing. It's another clever bit of meta-trolling from the show: they all know Noah Reid is an accomplished singer, but the audience doesn't yet. It was a brilliant coup de théâtre in that way too.

It works because it shorthands everything they need to say—without saying a word, they've reached a tipping point of their relationship, one that will see them eventually freewheel to the "I love yous" of the season finale. But at this point in the story, they aren't characters in a place to *talk* about that. So they don't. In a borrowed technique from musical theatre, when the feeling is so much, you can't talk about it, Patrick sings it. And it works. It is the perfect musical bridge to show their relationship developing without having to say it. In what might have been a forced, possibly insincere conversation about feelings and "where they are now," having Patrick sing to David and declare his feelings in front of the town becomes a neat shorthand for explaining that to the audience. It takes David and Patrick from "dating" to "this is something" in one scene. It also does it powerfully and emotionally that will also—through song—tie key points of their relationship together.

In the sense of characters, Patrick's "don't talk of love, sing it" approach works. As much as the focus is often on David's reaction, it is also a declaration by and a leap for Patrick. While he is a straight-talking and straightforward guy, he's also not one to be overly emotive or flowery with his declarations. So we see Patrick, perhaps unable to communicate his feelings in conversation, do it in song. This, too, could be a nod to the heterosexual upbringing Patrick has had and how, an episode later ("The Barbecue," season 4, episode 7) where he reveals never feeling "right" in another relationship. This never feeling "right" and being unable to articulate it is also linked to his repressed or misunderstood sexuality and a broader heteronormative consensus where men often fail to discuss their feelings. Showing us Patrick found a way to do that through song is both a nod to that and a showing of the queer relationship he's beginning to untie those knots and letting him open up. For David, too, it unties and opens up so many things.

As soon as Patrick starts singing, Moira is as swept away as David is; she declares to Roland and Jocelyn her "boy" is being serenaded by his "butter-voiced beau." It's a moment of togetherness and support from Moira, something that perhaps, as a mother, doesn't come naturally to the character. But beyond that, for the show, having a parent support a queer child in that way is important. Again, in things that probably seem ridiculous to straight viewers but monumental to some queer viewers, that Moira is excited, moved even, to see her son be serenaded by his boyfriend in front of the whole town is so significant, especially to viewers in David's age bracket, who grew up in the 1980s and 1990s when such things were unthinkable on TV and in real life. It's such a simple thing to have Moira by his side—this serenade doesn't take place in a gay bar somewhere, in a space that's "just for them." It takes full view of the town with his mom by his side. That's huge. It shouldn't be, but it is. And it's a sweet moment of character development for mother and son, too, with Moira finally being there for a big moment in David's life.

The song also becomes a through line in their relationship, bridging a gap in the big emotional moments. Later in the series, through lip sync dance format, the song gives David a way to bridge one of those gaps. For Patrick, singing at the open mic was a way to express his commitment to their relationship, to show they were moving forward from "dating" to something more. David soon after uses it both as an apology—his olive branch ("The Olive Branch," season 4, episode 9)—and as part of their wedding ("Happy Ending," season 6, episode 14). The Jazzagals sing it as David walks down the aisle because nothing else would do. The song now transcends as a new queer love song partly for that reason and also because it isn't a song stuck in a heteronormative framework. It shifts easily and regardless of gender. It's not a song about any of the traditional trappings of love, talking about a boy meeting a girl, babies, or marriage—it's just about love. And it's lovely that this iconic gay love story may have just given the world a new queer love anthem.

As a final piece of the *Schitt's Creek* puzzle, the proceeds from Noah Reid's version go to the LGBTQ+ charity The Trevor Project, a lovely punctuation to this love song made queer, giving back to the queer community.

They have other songs too, which like any good romcom soundtrack now have a deeper meaning for fans, and in this case, have been "queered" too. Notably, Aqualung's "Brighter Than Sunshine" is a well-known song for anyone Levy/David's age possibly, and given new life, as is sitcom/romcom tradition through association with the show. "Brighter Than Sunshine" is perhaps an overlooked chapter in David and Patrick's musical history. It's not a performance, but the song plays while they dance at Patrick's birthday party after he's come out to his parents. It's a beautiful song with lyrics about finding love at last—a perfect choice for chronicling Patrick's journey. It's a song many would have loved in high school or college, and that it has been given to a new favorite queer couple is a powerful reclaiming of and queering that song too. Romcoms have done this for generations with otherwise relatively unknown or unrelated songs, so it feels like a win that Levy has done the same in a queer story.

Of course, at least one song already had some queer associations regarding campness. The diva behind it was "Always Be My Baby" by Mariah Carey, the final piece of David and Patrick's musical story. The song that, instead of vows, Patrick chooses to sing. It's a call-back to their first "I love you" when Patrick accepts David has only ever said I love you twice to his parents, and once at a Mariah Carey concert. Mariah, of course, looms large in David's world and her diva, iconic 1990s pop sensation self is a camp icon in and of herself. Actually, Patrick embracing that is also embracing David's camp diva sensibilities and all that he is. If that's not a perfect romcom song moment, what is?

David and Patrick have a romcom soundtrack to rival even the most iconic romcoms. Their love story rewrote meaning for three songs, giving them to the queer community, which is no small thing. But also, their story shows the power of song and how the right music can tell a story better than words alone. In a world of straight romcoms, with songs long associated with them, it's important that when we write queer love stories, we give the community songs to match. Dan Levy did that with David and Patrick. Will there be gay weddings or proposals to the sounds of "The Best" sung by Noah Reid in years to come?

Noah Reid, Music, and Fans

When Dan Levy set Noah Reid the task of arranging "The Best," it was with the knowledge of his musical prowess. This came as a surprise to most viewers, aside from a few already dedicated fans. That song gained huge attention from its association with the show and David and Patrick. But Reid is an accomplished musician in his own right, and his association with Patrick, "The Best," and *Schitt's Creek* has naturally dovetailed with his music and fans of the show.

A lovely coda to the *Schitt's Creek* musical story is that of Noah Reid's musical career, and the connection with that and fans of the show. Reid released his debut album, *Songs from a Broken Chair*, in 2016, just after joining the show. Encouraged by his mother to make music while his acting career wasn't where he wanted it to be, he self-produced the first album, recording it with friends over two days. He cites the song "Mostly to Yourself" from that album with the feeling of uncertainty about his career direction that led him to that decision. In 2020, he released a second album and toured for the first time. There are several elements to discuss regarding Reid's music—that musicianship was incorporated into his character and therefore led people to his music: those finding the *Schitt's Creek* rendition of "The Best" on Spotify would also find his albums. When that track reached over a million streams post Emmy awards, it undoubtedly boosted listening to Reid's original music. His popularity as a performer also allowed him to tour for the first time. His albums were independently produced, with friends rather than capitalizing on the fame or opportunity from the show. Reid is a talented folk musician whose music stands up in its own right.

Reid returned to the show musically a couple of times after it ended. During the 2019 "*Schitt's Creek* Up Close and Personal" tour, Reid would

*Dan Levy on stage at the "*Schitt's Creek *Up Close and Personal" event.*
Courtesy Leonie Woolf

*Emily Hampshire embraces a fan at the "*Schitt's Creek *Up Close and Personal" event.*
Courtesy Leonie Woolf

Noah Reid with fans after the "Up Close and Personal" event.
Courtesy Leonie Woolf

re-create "The Best" along with "A Little Bit Alexis" on tour, sometimes with the help of Sarah Levy. In 2020, Reid sang on the cast tribute to educators for Barack and Michelle Obama's online series of tributes during COVID-19 graduations. Some of the cast reunited (virtually) to re-create their show characters—Moira, Johnny, Alexis, and David, as well as Twyla, Stevie, Jocelyn, Ronnie, Patrick, and Ray. After a brief skit from the Roses, everybody sang a rendition of Mariah Carey's "Hero" (with a cameo from the singer at the end). Once again, Reid took the lead on singing, along with Sarah Levy. Finally, Reid returned to *Schitt's Creek*–themed music when he covered Joni Mitchell's "A Case of You" in tribute to Catherine O'Hara when she was given the Governor General's Performing Arts Medal in 2021. He filmed the performance in Toronto and perhaps fulfilled a long-held dream of becoming Moira, wearing her wigs (and nail polish). The result was a goofy, charming, but heartfelt tribute to O'Hara with a now trademark Noah Reid sweet personal rendition of a classic. It was a fitting musical bookend for Reid and *Schitt's Creek* too.

In a final crossover of note, it has been adopted by fans naturally for elements of fan engagement such as fan videos (edited clips of the show overlaid with Reid's music) and fanfiction that uses his lyrics for inspiration. But there is also a dedicated set of fans whose focus is supporting his music; with post-tour cancellation in 2020, sharing videos from the concerts that did go ahead is a vital part of their fan engagement. In 2020, Reid's music came to mean a great deal to fans; in particular, his song "Hold On" and the way fans have adopted his music as part of but also an entirely separate element of their fandom is an essential discussion in the face of the show as a whole.

In 2022, Reid released several tracks from his album *Adjustments* leading up to the album's release in June 2022. From online responses, fan enthusiasm hadn't waned for his music, and they were keen for more. The album even included a song ("Minnesota") that reflected on his time in *Schitt's Creek* (specifically the "Up Close and Personal" tour) and perhaps some tangentially that also reflected on that period of his life. While not specific to *Schitt's Creek*, Reid's music and the connection fans feel to it is an enduring legacy of the show. And while they may not all be the original audience he thought he was writing for, the show opened the work up to a broader audience, some who would be unlikely to come across it otherwise but also embraced it and found something in it. That, too, is *Schitt's Creek* very queering the narrative.

10

Perfectly Marvelous: *Cabaret* as a Queer Through Line

Life Is a Cabaret

The musical finale of season 5 acts as all good musicals do: a suitably dramatic finale filled with emotion. And the use of a musical in the form of Kander and Ebb's classic *Cabaret* allows the characters involved in the show—Moira, Stevie, and Patrick—to express themselves through song and theatrics. But for the show itself, using *Cabaret* is a fascinating and essential additional part of the ongoing through line of cultural queer referencing, offering, as the show has been since season five, some cultural and political commentary wrapped up in entertainment. Just, in fact, like *Cabaret* has been doing since 1966. That Jocelyn comments *Cats* was "too political" and they chose to do *Cabaret* instead is, of course, a joke about the hugely political nature of *Cabaret* and perhaps a pointer to viewers that what is about to unfold isn't the usual "musical theatre episode" of a TV show. (That the episode came out after the car crash of a film version of *Cats* only adds a pleasing additional dimension to Jocelyn's comment.)

The use of musical episodes in TV is a well-established one. From episodes within the world of the show, a musical happens, such as *Buffy the Vampire Slayer*'s "One More with Feeling" to characters putting on a show within the show, as in *Riverdale*, which has staged two musicals within the show, *Carrie* and *Heathers*. It is a trope used to explore elements of the characters, further storylines, and create showpiece episodes within the shows. The show-within-a-show approach draws on a long line of theatrical theatre traditions of the same format, such as *Kiss Me Kate* or, for a suitably Canadian example, *The Drowsy Chaperone* or, to be particularly meta, *Cabaret* itself. The musical, in general, is not taken seriously, much like the sitcom, and in the joining of the two, musical episodes of sitcoms have been more tongue in cheek, with shows like *How I Met Your Mother* and *Scrubs* integrating musical episodes or moments across the series usually more as a humorous dig at characters, the genre, or both. It's no surprise that *Schitt's Creek* breaks that tradition, both taking the musical format seriously and using it to make affecting and serious points within the show's context. One fitting parallel within the genre is *M*A*S*H* which, while not specifically musical theatre, used musical moments to reflect on the wider mood and political and cultural commentary the show was famed for.

Similarly, *Schitt's Creek*'s choice of show, execution, and many other factors allows it to give additional political, social, and cultural commentary. *Schitt's Creek* adopting a musical episode storyline is not surprising, given the show's approach to taking influence across sitcoms, romcom, and queer cultural history, all of which have a strong association with the musical genre. It also makes sense, given the setup of the show—the established musical integration to storytelling (as explored in the previous chapter) and the association with showbusiness through Moira and her children—that the show would adopt the "putting on a musical" approach rather than "musical episode." This also allows the plot—and impact—of staging *Cabaret* to resonate beyond a single episode. It feels, in that respect, also an evolution of the musical-in-sitcom trope in its integrated authenticity.

Schitt's Creek leans into this with its musical theatre storyline. Musical episodes are not defined as queer, but the links between queer cultural expression and musical theatre are strong. Sometimes the links in TV are subtextual (for example, in *How I Met Your Mother* when Barney performs a musical number, the audience is reminded of actor Neil Patrick Harris' many queer roles in musical theatre, including the lead in *Hedwig and the Angry Inch* or the Emcee in *Cabaret*) or a more overt queer narrative arc, like the *Cabaret* storyline in *Schitt's Creek*. Musical theatre draws on a long queer history, and when TV uses musical theatre, it also taps into that history. It becomes a joining of the dots that might also have been erased from history for all the reasons discussed in other genres: lack of visibility, lack of documenting history, lack of tying the queer creators to the work that went out in the world.

The use of queer art to tell "straight" stories, where that works—and where it fails—and what that says about the dynamics of appropriating queer culture for entertainment will be explored. In parallels with reality TV and fashion, camp and queerness in musical form often offer a safe, acceptable depiction of queer culture, often within a broader "straight" world, as an expression of queer culture, and indeed queer joy in TV storytelling. Taking a medium that, while "mainstream," has something of an "uncool" and (in the derogatory context of the term) "gay" connotations, placing it front and center in TV shows can be an act of reclaiming and celebrating that culture. *Schitt's Creek* decided to step into the Kit Kat Club. It was a vital gear change for the musical as a queer art form on TV. When TV does that, it reclaims history. Musical theatre is a genre that has long been a refuge of queer creativity that has become especially powerful.

Cabaret is already a musical layered with queer meaning and association. It is one that, for many queer people, is already an important cultural touchstone. This feeds into how, overtly and otherwise, *Schitt's Creek* draws on what went before. The show is the sum of queer narratives that went before it, and *Cabaret*, an iconic queer narrative, is part of that and is hugely important to this cultural conversation. The musical as many know it—the film starring Liza Minelli and Joel Grey—has a long queer heritage and legacy. First, being based on Christopher Isherwood's novella *Sally Bowles* (1937) and later part of his *The Berlin Stories* anthology (1945). The character of Sally Bowles would then be adapted first to the play *I Am Camera* by John Van Druden (1955) and later the musical *Cabaret* by John Kander and Fred Ebb (1966). Isherwood was one of the first openly gay novelists in America, and he incorporated his gay experience into his work (including *The Berlin Stories*). The musical has included an array of queer actors in principal parts, particularly the Emcee and notably Joel Grey in the film version and Alan Cumming in the Sam Mendes–directed Broadway revival. It, of course, also starred queer icon Liza Minelli on film. As a musical then, *Cabaret* has a long and deeply queer history, as well as queer themes embedded in the narrative.

The narrative is extensively queer also. Not least in Sally Bowles being a queer icon—that damaged but strong, yet also fabulous woman adopted often by queer culture. Within the musical also the Kit Kat Club dancers are a queer and diverse group. In the opening number "Wilkommen," the Emcee introduces them with several queer attributes indicating among other things their sexual relations between the dancers and the Emcee and the dancers. Later, in the song "Two Ladies," the Emcee sings about polyamory, and frequently there are hints across the musical about queer relationships of all kinds in the Kit Kat Club. The Emcee themselves is thoroughly queer also, embracing gender fluidity as well as sexual fluidity. The musical also addresses aspects of queerness head-on through the character of Cliff, a struggling bisexual who finds himself torn between Sally and others.

All those previous queer narratives led it into being. In the case of *Cabaret*, it is a mix of narrative themes and external factors which make it an essential queer text, from Isherwood himself to the themes of sexuality are addressed in the musical and the associations of campness and queerness, from the film's star Liza and director Bob Fosse. Finally, the legacy of the Emcee—the sexually fluid central character, most recently associated with Alan Cumming, one of the few openly pansexual actors at the time he played the role, or indeed further back, to Joel Grey. The latter played a role in the film and didn't come out until his eighties. All these can add layers of queer reading and queer meaning to viewers, all of which add meaning to the show's context, deliberate or otherwise.

Given that *Schitt's Creek* represents something of a through line of queer culture integrated with other cultures, it would seem *Cabaret* was the only suitable option for a musical to perform. It is a component piece made up of many elements as a musical—some drawing on a legacy of queer culture, others taking much more heteronormative elements and "queering" them, just as *Schitt's Creek* has done. The 1966 musical, with music by John Kander, lyrics by Fred Ebb, and book by Joe Masteroff, based on John Van Druten's 1951 play *I Am a Camera*, was adapted from the short novel *Goodbye to Berlin* (1939) by Christopher Isherwood. The 1966 original Broadway production became a hit, inspiring numerous subsequent productions in London and New York, as well as the 1972 film of the same name, famously directed by Bob Fosse and starring Liza Minelli and Joel Grey.

It was important, too, as Isherwood was one of the first "wave" of out-queer writers in America. His work indirectly paved the way for queer work today. The stories, and subsequent plays and musicals, offer a social commentary that has been applicable across many incarnations. The stories show various characters, misfits, and "deviants" of various kinds clinging to their previous lives as the impact of Nazism encroaches on them. Through the characters, we see commentary on both inclusivity—through the utopia of the Kit Kat Club, where much of the story is set—through the perils of being blind to politics and the world around you. Set in 1931 in Berlin, as the Nazis are rising to power, it focuses on the nightlife at the seedy Kit Kat Club. It concerns American writer Cliff Bradshaw and his relationship with English cabaret performer Sally Bowles. A subplot involves the doomed romance between German boarding house owner Fräulein Schneider and her elderly suitor Herr Schultz, a Jewish fruit vendor. Overseeing the action is the Master of Ceremonies at the Kit Kat Club. The club is a metaphor for ominous political developments in late

Weimar Germany. It's characters, who are both larger than life and slightly existing both within and outside it, and political metaphor makes it a perfect fit for *Schitt's Creek*.

This combination of a through line to queer cultural history and the indirect political commentary it allows on the characters involved make it an apt choice. Had another show taken on *Cabaret*, it likely would not have gotten the respect it was afforded in *Schitt's Creek* by Levy's writing and direction (he co-directed "Life Is a Cabaret," season 5, episode 14). There is respect for the musical theatre genre and the legacy of queerness within *Cabaret* as a piece. And this legacy of queerness, like other elements across Levy's writing, is worked into the show's fabric and given a new perspective, leading it to be able to fuse, if we'll excuse the expression, "straight" drama and romantic comedy with this legacy. And this is an area the musical-episode sitcoms have lacked.

"Robert Fosse" and "Moira Rose" as Iconic Directors

Moira's story and the contextual compressions with the musical start with her own story around it. In "Whisper of Desire" (season 5, episode 7), where the musical is introduced, Patrick mentions his audition and Moira launches into an anecdote about her history with the show. From David's reaction, it is a well-worn anecdote and a typical Moira Rose story of a young ingénue actress who found herself as Sally. Charting the much-convoluted course of Moira's career is difficult at the best of times; however, we assume this production was just before she met Johnny and before her soap opera career began (something we assume was in motion by the time David was born in 1983), then this was either her breakout role or another in the line of strange but obscure performances that make up her career. It's probably safer to assume the latter. The image, perhaps of a second-rate tour of *Cabaret* around small towns of North America in the early 1980s, seems fitting for Moira's career trajectory. Timing-wise, it would have to have taken place around five years after Liza Minelli's iconic take on the part; it seems fitting Moira would give us a Sally to rival that. A crucial part of Moira's character arc in the show is coming to terms with the relationship between her dependence on her professional identity and her self identity. It is a fitting bookend, too, if her time as Sally was just before her rise to fame, and her time directing comes now after her acting career has peaked, as it does to lots of the greats, and perhaps allows Moira to rewrite her career, taking charge of it herself for once.

It does lead to that kind of career revival in season 6 when we see her stand up to her old *Sunset Beach* co-star and producer; she gets validation and justice for what happened previously. Actually, her role in *Cabaret* as a director is an important one. For women in the entertainment industry—especially those of Moira's age who had to endure far worse sexism than today—standing up to oppressors and doubters is important. And although the accompanying success of the *Crows* movie in season 6 is also part of this, Moira's taking charge of her career starts with *Cabaret*. What she does is prove she is more than capable as a director—something subtle within the episode itself. Cabaret is a success as a performance, a credit to Moira.

It's a great microcosm of Moira's arc as a character and how the audience and people in her life see her. Her directing *Cabaret* starts with another of her outlandish tales of her career—and yes, with one of her children mocking her (albeit lovingly). That she steers her way into the director role is a funny and expected "Moira Rose" trait but also indicative of how differently we still view the confidence of a woman versus a man. In reality, what Moira does with *Cabaret* is no different from what Johnny does with the motel. It is a neat parallel to it; both see something within the town their particular expertise can help with and decide to get involved. Across the series, Johnny's involvement with the motel and his "advice" at times is no better than Moira's particular approach to directing. But also, both of them come good in the end for themselves and the town. And for Moira, like Johnny and the motel, directing *Cabaret* was professionally and personally meaningful.

Moira Rose, the embodiment of campness and queerness, who borrows from elements of queer culture in her dress, demeanor, and character, takes charge of this very queer musical, whose iconic productions have been directed by very straight male figures. We get yet another *Schitt's Creek* reworking and queering of culture, even when the object itself was already queered. We associate *Cabaret* inextricably as a queer-coded work and also with its director in Fosse. He was, however, a contradictory auteur: his work from *Sweet Charity* through *Cabaret* to *Chicago* all have an air of queerness. They star queer icons, including Shirley MacLaine, Gwen Verdon, Chita Rivera, and Liza Minelli. But as a director and a man, Fosse remained a hypermasculine misogynistic, womanizing figure. And so, while Moira might seem more a Liza than Fosse at first glance, perhaps it is the reverse: Moira is more than the camp icon—with the ability to be the auteur, taking over the role Fosse once inhabited is an important one.

Like Bob Fosse, *Cabaret* at the time was her hat in the ring for one last gamble. His previous film *Sweet Charity* (1969) was designed to take him from theatre and choreographer to auteur film director but was a spectacular flop critically and commercially. It worked, however, with *Cabaret*: surprisingly, this dark, slightly strange film that shouldn't have been a commercial hit pulled him from obscurity. For Moira Rose, *Cabaret* represented what might have been a different swan song: her career, relegated to small town amateur theatre, had another odd, dark film that equally altered her life in the form of *The Crows Have Eyes 3* movie. *Cabaret* was Fosse's watershed moment: it rescued his career at the point he very well could have tipped into obscurity. And so, it's easy to see why Moira—still desperately clinging to hope that *The Crows Have Eyes 3* film will perhaps be her *Cabaret* too—also might be seeking her "Fosse" moment with the musical. Moira has a self-styled assurance in her talent that has never been realized. Direct comparison with Fosse is somewhat irrelevant in that broader argument: the simple question of, in another timeline, or as a man, would we see Moira as not deluded and eccentric but talented and a misunderstood genius? Perhaps.

In positioning Moira as the Fosse figure, her drag-queerness persona (as discussed in previous chapters) adds a layer of "queering" to this legacy. Comparing Moira Rose to one of the greatest living theatre directors here may have also fulfilled her career desires. But Moira also sees much of herself in Sally Bowles. Within the show's narrative, Moira can align and later compare herself to the woman she passes Sally's torch to: Stevie.

"Perfectly Marvelous": Stevie and Sally

Stevie and Sally made the most sense in terms of narrative arc and added a great comic moment in Alexis being rejected for the part along the way. Famously, Sally Bowles has often been cast with actors who are weaker singers, Judi Dench in the original London production being a classic example.

Stevie's narrative has played with her attraction to and feelings for David and "queered" our expectations there, and we see that parallel to her Sally storyline. She disappears on the performance day, and we think she's angry and upset over David's engagement. As she sings "Maybe This Time," her microphone is set, and Patrick watches her as the Emcee. It's a standard piece of staging in some respects, especially in mimicking the Mendes staging, with the Emcee as an all-seeing observer to the proceedings. It feels like a flip of the character we've been led to believe: that all this time Stevie has had feelings for David, and we're seeing the traditional "woman in love with unavailable man" or "woman in love with gay man" play out. It feels like it slots in with Sally, who in the musical loves Clint, the historically bisexual/closeted character. Stevie's arc is about to come crashing down as she plays Sally, doomed to do what Sally does and love in misguided ways, defined only by doomed love affairs. However, there's another underlying element of her stepping out and making a declaration within the show's narrative: as Patrick and David's lives are about to change, under Patrick/the Emcee's gaze, Sally/Stevie makes a similar pledge.

So why does it make more sense that it's Stevie who gets the part? Sally, like Stevie, is a little rough around the edges and a little lost in life. She uses performing to mask insecurities (not unlike Moira) but also exists in limbo while not knowing her true worth—all a lot like Stevie. Yes, Alexis has the confidence of her mother to step into those shoes, but Alexis doesn't need Sally like Stevie needs Sally. While Alexis shares Sally's "perform regardless of talent" mentality, Stevie's "making the best of the situation" mentality aligns her with Sally. But Sally is traditionally a tragic figure painted as lost to life (and the men she is with), which is not a very *Schitt's Creek* notion of farming women (see chapter 7). So instead, the song, and Sally, take on new meaning with Stevie.

Moira tells Stevie to "take her by the hand." In so doing, Sally becomes much more "Stevie," proving to her that she was good enough all along. Stevie has felt stuck romantically and professionally since her break up with Amir and watching her best friend David thrive in love and business. We expect her to be jealous of David—specifically because of Patrick—but instead, she's frustrated with herself and longing for more. This is something Sally Bowles never possesses, that self-awareness and agency to change. Sally is a chancer, she stumbles from one exciting-looking thing and one exciting-looking man to another, never really gaining ground. Stevie is more than that, and Moira sees that in her. Convinced to take the role by Moira in the hope it allows her to step into herself more, Stevie's journey with Sally mirrors that of her experience within the world of the show: watching others fall in love and live their lives while waiting for "maybe this time" to happen. However, in casting her as Sally, Stevie (and by extension Emily Hampshire) also gets to step into the iconic queer icon shoes of Liza Minelli and Natasha Richardson while making it her own. And from an audience point of view, a queer woman in Emily Hampshire performing the part adds a layer of "queering" to the text.

Of course, there are similarities, so that Sally might have brought Stevie down a bit. Sally spends her life watching the world from the stage of a nightclub, and Stevie watches from behind a desk. Every night Sally watches people fall in love (and lust) in the Kit Kat Club while she says put, which mirrors Stevie's life too. Moira comes to her when Amir breaks up with her, seeing something in her moment of being "lost" that perhaps Sally can find. Perhaps despite the elaborate tale Moira weaves about her time in the part, Sally Bowles helped her once upon a time too. Moira instructed Stevie to "take our Sally by the hand and go out there and show those people everything she can be. If she were only more like you." It feels like a critical reframing of the character. It's a neat combination of their two arcs, reframing the musical for the audience.

Sally traditionally has been tied up in her romances, to a fault, and she can be painted as naïve or subservient in productions. Again, reframing this through Moira and Stevie's gaze within the show frees Sally from previous misogynistic readings. Sally has sometimes, in previous versions of *Cabaret*, felt misogynistic, clichéd, and deeply unsympathetic; the conflation of femininity and fascism, like that of queerness and fascism, in some versions of the show also leave Sally positioned as a means of showing male intellect versus female materiality, positioning of the "innocent" British/American intellectual against the decadence of Weimar Berlin. Moira, in her role as director, her female gaze directing Sally's journey, sees what Sally is missing that male directors—Fosse and Mendes included—have often missed: Sally has it in her to do better, to be stronger, to open her eyes to the world, to be the star she wants to be, to break free from the men who define her . . . she just isn't given agency to in the story.

There is an undeniable parallel for Stevie, who once fell for David, being left as Sally is by Cliff. The story arc of "Life Is a Cabaret" even leads viewers to the conclusion at first that David and Patrick's engagement is what has upset Stevie. This storyline is a nice way to address any lingering doubt around that and illustrate it is possible for a girl to "move on" from a relationship without falling into the "bitter and upset ex" category. David and Stevie's (and Patrick's) relationship might seem unconventional in TV terms, but their mutual friendship seems a very real, contemporary one resolved during the musical storyline.

Usually, "Maybe This Time" is a melancholy song; as the title suggests, Sally longs for something good to happen. It usually feels like a desperate plea for life to change. However, in the context of Stevie's character, she's taking ownership, making the change herself. So instead of a lament, it becomes a declaration. It's a nod to how musicals are constantly reinvented, and context is key. Seeing the song through the eyes of Stevie, we see the defiance in the number and the power she gives to herself and the character of Sally.

It's partly a Sally through a female gaze that does it, and we see Moira instilling this backstage in her conversation with Stevie beforehand. Moira, her female gaze directing Sally's journey, sees what Sally is missing from those male directors. That we also get a "queer" Sally in Emily Hampshire's performance adds to a pleasing meta-layer to a woman who so many queer icons have played, including, of course, queen of the queer icons Liza Minelli. It is again taking things out of a male gaze, out of ownership of men, into the hands of, as Moira would say, a very cool woman. It's a messy-meta take on a woman whose story has always been defined by men, onstage, and in productions. It feels like Schitt's Creek the town and *Schitt's Creek* the show are rewriting the narrative.

Cabaret is directed by a woman, where the gaze through which we view Sally is not just the male gaze of her composers. Instead, we have her steered through a woman's take. In the recent London revival, directed by Rebecca Frecknall, the production also shifts the gaze and reframes how we see the women in the story in illuminating ways. Sometimes, queering a narrative isn't just foregrounding the experience of queer characters (though this is important in *Cabaret*, obviously). It's also about looking at it outside the patriarchal, heteronormative gaze. And Moira perhaps got there first before Frecknall's London revival. Within the show, and for *Schitt's Creek* audiences, seeing *Cabaret* through Moira's gaze is also a kind of queer homecoming for the piece. It has had a troubled history with its queerness, with the gay characters, particularly Cliff, being pulled in and out of the narrative, as explored later in this chapter. It's a kind of subtle assurance that Moira would, in her direction, give, finally, a version of *Cabaret* which embraces queerness at its core. Like the show, *Schitt's Creek* embraces queer narratives on television like never before.

Wilkommen . . . Bienvenue: The Emcee and Stepping into Queerness

Finally, but most significantly, Patrick, in his role as the Emcee, uses the show as punctuation in his journey to accepting his queer identity. It is a beautiful use of the musical to parallel his journey in this season: he initially auditions for Cliff, a character who struggles with his sexuality and has a history of either having his sexuality erased by incarnations of the show or remaining in the closet. He was described by the *LA Times* as "left in the closet," a variation on how David describes Patrick a few episodes after his accidental outing with his parents. Pulling the two references together is another in many of the nods to popular culture through Patrick, enabling characters to (finally) be "out" on television. Cliff, then, has had a troubled path through *Cabaret*'s history. Again, as Margaret Gray for the *LA Times* commented, reflecting on fifty years of the musical: "We can track America's attitude toward homosexuality, for example, through the progressive outing of the 'Cabaret' male lead, from the reluctant straight man back in 1966 to unambiguous—if closeted—gay man today" (Gray, July 20, 2016).

In talking about Cliff in the original incarnation, Hal Prince suggests his closeting was due to the times in which it was produced and suggests that the box office success of *Cabaret* vindicates this choice. There are many parallels between Patrick and Cliff, and by default, Isherwood; however, what Patrick gets a chance to do, which Cliff does not, decides to change his life.

Earlier in *Schitt's Creek*, among viewers/fans there was debate over whether Patrick was gay or, like David, also bi-/pansexual. Again, it's an interesting parallel to Cliff's often-changing sexuality. Patrick being rejected from the role of Cliff is also a brilliant nod to the troubled history of that character's depiction on stage and screen. In the film version (1972), he was closeted by the original stage version, briefly, curiously bisexual (or bi-curious at least), and by the Mendes version, at last rewritten and reinstated as a gay man. In Hal Prince's version, they left Cliff in the closet, much to Prince's later regret. He said: "We persuaded ourselves that the musical comedy audience required a sentimental heterosexual love story with a beginning, middle, and end to make the concept palatable. . . . In my opinion, we were wrong" (Prince, 2017, p. 68).

This is a strong parallel to Levy's lamentation that in writers' rooms, people still "count the kisses" (Artiva, January 10, 2019) to determine how much queerness can be shown on screen. Even in musical theatre (a traditional refuge for queer people) and one that is so inherently queer in the broader sense, a bisexual character was considered "too much," indicating the struggles in the through line of telling queer stories. It also highlights the importance of David as a character—bisexual men like Cliff (or pansexual men like David; in short, those attracted to multiple genders) are an even rarer occurrence than gay men. There is something in the perception of threat or deception that has surrounded bi/pan phobia, particularly for men that we see in Cliff and their general absence from TV and film.

It would have seemed an obvious choice for David to become the Emcee—he embodies the gender and sexual fluidity of the Emcee in everyday life. His clothing is gender fluid embracing skirts and other "feminine" clothing styles. Regarding sexuality, his "the wine not the label" approach could have been lifted from the lyrics and staging of "Wilkommen" where the Emcee flirts with his Cabaret "boys and girls."

He also has the performative quality, the performative that has been hiding many other elements. Had the show indeed chosen another narrative direction, Or indeed, had Levy been steered in a more traditional TV direction in which the world David lived in would have questioned these elements of his identity, the Emcee would have been a perfect vehicle for David to demonstrate his gender and sexual fluidity to the town. Other shows might have used this as a means for a character like David to foster acceptance of his identity. However, *Schitt's Creek* works on the default of acceptance and the absence of homophobia. So, despite the surface-level similarities, he doesn't need the Emcee; he's already gone through his metamorphosis of personal acceptance. Instead, the Emcee becomes a much more powerful tool of acceptance, one for Patrick to accept himself.

Season 5 is where we see Patrick reconciling much of what has gone unspoken in the previous two seasons to take him from "exploration" to full acceptance. During his audition, Moira directs, "The thing you must understand about Cliff, Patrick, is that he has been with many women, but he has never derived true pleasure from it." It is a knowing wink to the audience and Patrick himself, who replies, "Think I can wrap my head around that." The clear shift and honest emotion he puts into that scene reading, one which nearly floors Jocelyn, indicates the character's resonance with him. As Patrick has rejected marriage to Rachel, he also has let go of an imagined life, much like Cliff does in his narrative. And while Patrick later talks of picturing his life with "a wife and kid by now," he also affirms he's happy with his life with David instead. This is not an option for Cliff, who sees having a baby with Sally as a path to an (outwardly at least) "respectable" life for them both. Sally responds to Cliff's proposal by singing "Maybe This Time" in previous incarnations of the "win" their heterosexual pairing could offer. With what will ultimately be a shifted version of Sally in Moira's production of *Cabaret*, it's important that Cliff also shift. But more importantly, the show can display the difference between their formerly closeted gay character and Isherwood/Cliff by rejecting Patrick as Cliff. Instead, it gives us Patrick as the Emcee stepping fully into his queer identity.

In his character arc, crucially, a part of Patrick comes to terms with what has gone before, from his first kiss with a man to confronting his past with his ex-fiancé, where he eventually moves toward coming out to his parents and proposing to David. Patrick's story isn't a "tortured gay" story, and he has accepted who he is. Still, the show is careful—particularly in his coming out story—to acknowledge this journey for his character as significant. At the moment, we see Patrick not get the role of Cliff, and it becomes a critical marker on his journey—his road not traveled—much as Cliff was a similar outlet for Isherwood. In Patrick's short-lived stint as Cliff, we see parallels with Isherwood, who wrote in his own journals memoir *Christopher and His Kind*, "Couldn't you get yourself excited by the shape of girls, too—if you worked hard at it? . . . It would be a lot more convenient for you if you did. Then you wouldn't have all these problems." It also is reminiscent of Patrick's "you make me feel right" speech from season 4. When his ex-fiancé is revealed, he tells David, "David, I've spent most of my life not knowing what right was supposed to feel like." As Cliff is Isherwood's voice in *Cabaret* and given the importance of queer cultural through lines in *Schitt's Creek*, this parallel with one of America's most significant gay writers feels important for readings of the show.

That Moira instead casts Patrick as the sexually open, gender-fluid Emcee also plays on these dual levels. On the one hand, she offers Patrick an opportunity to embrace queerness within his storyline (as explored momentarily). But also, in the broader meta-narrative, she is somewhat righting the wrongs of queer stories like *Cabaret*, much like *Schitt's Creek* has been doing all along. In *Cabaret*, Cliff wasn't allowed to be queer; it was too much for audiences, or so they thought. The world wasn't ready for a bisexual leading man. Yet here this show is, with David Rose front and center as a pansexual leading man, while his boyfriend, newly out, gets to play one of the theatre's queerest roles in the story within a story. As layers of queerness go, it's pretty up there.

The Emcee is a person (their gender is fluid and undefined, as is, fittingly, their sexuality) with an ambiguous life and background who finds refuge in an unusual place; as discussed later, this is an overarching theme in *Cabaret*. In *Cabaret*, he is an outsider to Berlin; we never learn his past, where he's from, or much about him other than he's somehow washed up in Berlin seeking refuge. Berlin is a tolerant haven, the Kit Kat Club a haven within that. Again, we can trace Patrick's previous journey: running from a past life, finding refuge in a strange town, seeking refuge and a "do over" from a previous life. He was finding a haven within that town. In addition, the Emcee has an adopted or chosen family. Leaving behind his previous life and fiancé, Patrick finds refuge in Schitt's Creek. And as he notes in "Meet the Parents" (season 5, episode 11) about how comfortable he is with the Roses, he also finds an adoptive family there. While Patrick is more running from himself than any risk of persecution in his previous life, it does seem that the town of Schitt's Creek has become his version of the Kit Kat Club—up until "Meet the Parents" at least. It is a place where he can be his authentic self, without the "real world"—that which he left behind—seeing.

The Emcee also allows Patrick to explore—and embrace—elements of queerness previously unexplored or unknown to him. This is important in our conversations around queer culture and how sexuality, personality, and personal expression aren't linked for some people. Patrick and Reid are the boy next door, which is why, when dressed up in the Emcee's makeup and costume of suspenders and shorts, it is a striking contrast in character and for viewers. The Emcee also imbues performers with a certain sexual magnetism. And it is a fun moment to push Patrick—and by association, Noah Reid—into that role via the Emcee's eyeliner and suspenders. Taking on the Emcee role is a fun moment of seeing both Patrick and Reid in an entirely new light.

That is not to say that Patrick doesn't share some of the Emcee's qualities in other ways. His natural confidence is a central facet of his character—as David says to him at their first meeting, "Okay, you're either very impatient or very sure of yourself"—and in comparison to David's anxious, neurotic persona, Patrick does indeed embody the self-assured Emcee personality. However, while David wears his queerness comfortably and clearly, Patrick is more reserved. And so, stepping out of being someone David describes as a business major who wears straight-leg mid-range denim and stepping into the Emcee's suspenders and eyeliner feels like an exploration which links to newfound confidence in his sexuality. He will not turn into David, but this new element of his confidence will be seen in how he asserts confidence in his relationship and his queerness found somewhat during his time in the Kit Kat Club. This is paralleled by the evolution in his acceptance of his queerness alongside the *Cabaret* plot.

While this conversation around the Emcee feeds into a bigger one around gay actors for gay roles (as discussed in chapter 13) and how much an actor can and should bring of themselves to a part, there's also no escaping that some queer parts bring catharsis, even revelation about themselves, for the actor. This is undoubtedly true for Alan Cumming, who goes on to say of his time as the Emcee:

> I quickly assimilated to this public perception in my own life, I did feel sexy, and I was having a lot of sex. I liked my body, and I felt comfortable in it. I think that is what makes someone sexy; their comfort with themselves. It's another form of authenticity. And if you can feel desirable and know that people desire you, I think you are on a fast track to self-confidence! (Cumming, 2021, p. 174)

It's a symbiotic relationship—the Emcee helps those actors who become him to embody some of those qualities, and actors who need that are drawn to it. But you also need a specific "something" to be the Emcee. In Patrick's case (maybe not in Reid's), he has the confidence of someone like Alan Cumming. It's way too in the show's context; while David's gender fluidity and queerness align him with the Emcee in many ways, he'd lack that natural confidence and swagger that the Emcee—and indeed Patrick—have in spades.

Consider his performance at the store's open mic night—another instance of him onstage and performing—where he openly embraces his queerness publicly in his serenade of David. Much like the Emcee stepping into his onstage persona, Patrick can embrace elements of himself that do not come as quickly in everyday life. In his serenade, it is the sincerity of the emotions for his new boyfriend that they are both having trouble processing. As the Emcee, it is a mix of the other sexual, performative, and identity elements of his newly embraced sexuality that have been unexplored. The Emcee also imbues performers with a certain sexual magnetism. And it is a fun moment to push Patrick—and by association Noah Reid—into that role via the Emcee's eyeliner and suspenders. The taking on of the Emcee role is a fun moment of seeing both of them in an entirely new light.

So Patrick brings a particular element—confidence—to the Emcee, but the Emcee gives him things in return. As mentioned earlier, David would have been the natural choice for the role. In another version of the *Schitt's Creek* story, David Rose as the Emcee would have been a genius move. He's very Alan Cumming–like in character if we stick with the actor who most recently rewrote the role: David Rose is pansexual (like the Emcee and Cumming). While David doesn't assign any particular gender labels to himself, he embraces gender fluidity in how he presents and dresses, much like the Emcee. David knows who he is and doesn't hide it from the world, but his anxious demeanor means while his queerness is front and center, as a person, he lacks confidence (though he hides it). If David didn't have a Patrick by this point, we might have seen him stepping into his mom's production and finding himself in a different but similar way that Patrick does as the Emcee.

Patrick finds elements of his queerness in the Emcee he likely would never have tapped into without. It's not necessary for Patrick to suddenly "perform queerness" in either his dress or his behavior once he comes out. He is a queer man who has missed the exploration phase of queerness and what that means for his identity. While not everyone is defined by their sexuality, it impacts queer people's identity. For many, the exploration of "queerness" as part of who they are, not just who they sleep with, is part of both coming to terms with their identity and expressing themselves as their most honest version. For Patrick, who found a safe space to discover his sexuality in the town, playing the Emcee becomes an additional safe space to explore some of that. During his proposal in the previous episode, he has confessed to spending hours walking trying to figure out his feelings for David and how to act on them. But by the time season 5 is over, he has come out to his parents, proposed to David, and even considered (if rejected) the idea of an open relationship. And while all these are about more than the confidence the stage role gives him in exploring his sexuality, they feel like a neat parallel to stepping into the role. Again, queerness and accepting one's queerness is more than admitting feelings for someone; it's realigning what you thought you knew about yourself and where you thought you fit into the world. Patrick does that in the town's haven, so he also holds off coming out to his parents, but he still has things to work out.

Just as he realized his sexual orientation wasn't as he always assumed (and was assumed) until David "unlocked" it, maybe playing the role of the Emcee will also unlock other things about his personality, gender, and sexuality. Maybe it won't, and that's also fine, but the critical thing here is the Emcee is the first piece of queer culture he's exposed to in any meaningful way since coming out, which is important.

Exposure to queer culture is important for a queer person. As the adage goes, you can't be what you can't see, and while Patrick has been in the world and seen queer people, maybe even experienced queer culture before, until now, he didn't know it was *for* him and *about* him, and that's the difference. In the Emcee, Patrick isn't now seeing another character in a story; he sees a character who belongs to the broader community he's a part of. In stepping into that role, he acknowledges and embraces his part in that community and explores what it means and might mean for him. He will not turn into David, but this new element of his confidence will be seen in how he asserts confidence in his relationship, and Patrick's queerness was found somewhat during his time in the Kit Kat Club. And this is paralleled by the evolution in his acceptance of his queerness alongside the *Cabaret* plot.

The choice of number for Patrick in "Wilkommen" is apt here. It is the Emcee's—and Patrick's—declaration of who he is and the world he inhabits. And while Stevie's "Maybe This Time" will shortly be a declaration of action, Patrick's "Wilkommen" could be considered a declaration of arrival. The "welcome" of the title can be considered his welcome, embracing and feeling part of his queerness. He arrived into a broader "queer community": he arrives as the Emcee, newly happily engaged to a man, a contrast to his unhappy engagement to a woman, and he is out to his parents. They have accepted him, and he now lives in the safe space of Schitt's Creek with his chosen family. This movement feels like a culmination of all that. His stepping out of the "mid-range straight leg denim" and even temporarily into the queerness of the Emcee persona feels like a declaration of Patrick entirely for the first time welcoming himself into that world.

To audiences here, Patrick as the Emcee makes sense. The Emcee is the way into the world of *Cabaret* and, as explored, directs the lessons an audience learns. The Emcee is an all-seeing theatrical dominance defining the production. Patrick, likewise, is an outside eye from the town, so he isn't a Schitt's Creek–specific point of view like Stevie or Roland or the other townsfolk, and he isn't one of the Roses; instead, he offers perhaps everyone else's view on both the town and the Rose family. He also represents all the queer viewers looking at the show and he finds a way to step into what it offers. *Cabaret* is shown a huge part of that experience for the character. This also links to the parallels in which *Cabaret* and *Schitt's Creek* challenge an audience's thinking.

Other Parallels

The musical asks the audience, as the character Fraulein Schneider asks Cliff Bradshaw, if you saw catastrophe approaching, what would you do? And as much as *Cabaret* is a show that deals with queer identity and historical prejudice as a window to contemporary prejudice, it is, of course, equally about anti-Semitism. A small fitting detail likely overlooked by casual viewers sees Ronnie and Bob cast as Fraulein Schneider and her suitor Herr Shultz. Ronnie is a Black woman, Bob is a white man, and Levy is making a subtle comment on the ongoing racism issues in the world, in the same way that *Cabaret* was in the 1970s. Their story was foregrounded in the recent London revival and mirrors how Johnny and Moira's love story is the strongest in *Schitt's Creek*. Remembering that the older character's love stories are just as important is a nice parallel.

Of course, a darker political and social message is associated with the parallels with the Roses. Again, while Levy does not labor the point—not making any direct reference—coming from a Jewish family, incorporating that identity into his show must also have been a factor. The joke about the town choosing *Cabaret* over the "too political" *Cats* has a double resonance. The powerful and still incredibly relevant statements that the musical makes on anti-Semitism are important. While the queer through lines of the show might be more prominent (see chapter 6), this detail shouldn't be overlooked. Isherwood's original stories and Kander and Ebb's musical are unflinching in their depiction of the impact of the Nazi regime, and numbers like "If You Could See Her" offer a powerful confrontation to anti-Semitic viewpoints. For those who know the musical, these details will resonate. For Jewish viewers, the musical choice, out of all the options, sends a powerful message of being seen.

Placing the Roses next to this musical makes a powerful point for anyone who makes the links, knowing not everyone can live in a place like *Schitt's Creek*, and for others, the parallels with 1930s Germany are still more apparent. It is characteristic of the writing approach to guide the audience to this rather than laboring to the point. Again, to parallel *Cabaret*, which does not lecture an audience and merely shows them the chilling consequences of inaction, *Schitt's Creek* offers the opposite: what happens when you remove prejudice?

"What Would You Do?" Significance of *Cabaret* in *Schitt's Creek* as Queer Utopias

While *Schitt's Creek* as a show never goes this dark, *Cabaret*'s approach to steering its audience and the show's approach are markedly similar. The difference being in *Cabaret*, the utopia of the Kit Kat Club is a warning from history. In *Schitt's Creek*, the utopia of a town without prejudice came instead as a way to, in the words of its creator, lead by example. Contrasted against *Cabaret*'s stark warning of the effects of prejudice, Levy's central message becomes all the more powerful. It's a darker "queering" that *Cabaret* has long participated in the "what ifs" in a dark way alongside the queered utopia reminds us that in looking at the world differently, we must reflect on our part in it. The effect of *Cabaret* is the darker side of what *Schitt's Creek* does: holding up a mirror to the audience and asking "what if?" The Kit Kat Club, inside Schitt's Creek, becomes a double entendre, the utopia of utopias that shines a light in the broader world. While *Cabaret* does it through darkness against light, *Schitt's Creek* does it with light, though their approaches are the same.

The difference is that *Cabaret* and the Kit Kat Club serve as a moral warning: not to turn away from reality. That reality will eventually catch up with you. In *Schitt's Creek*, the metaphor is updated somewhat to the show's "lead by example" approach, asking what if we were more like this, more welcoming, more inclusive . . . what if we took that ethos to the wider world. Both are utopias; one (the Kit Kat Club) is blind to the world outside and is a refuge, but also not seeking to stop the onset of prejudice, the other (Schitt's Creek) is a utopia that seeks to change the world by asking, much like in *Cabaret*, "what would you do?"

11

The Wine, Not the Label: Coming Out Stories for Grown-Ups

Coming out stories have always been a core element of queer narratives because they're a core part of queer experience. In *Schitt's Creek*, there are several coming out narratives at work. The most famous is Patrick's: his moving later-in-life coming out has become a touchstone for many fans. It's become a vital story in the canon of coming out narratives for, among other things, its sensitive and honest portrayal. It and other discussions of sexuality on the show also acknowledge the impact of coming out for parents and others. But alongside the "big" coming out that we experience with Patrick, there's the smaller, but no less important coming out that David also demonstrates by existing as a queer character on screen.

"The Wine, Not the Label": David's Labels and Queerness

But Patrick's is not the only coming out in the show. David, too, has to come out, and this is important for two reasons. First, it identifies David as pansexual, a vital element of his character and the kind of representation the show offers. Second, it addresses an important element of life for queer people: they never stop coming out. It's an easy, often lazy storytelling and the cultural assumption that queer people come out once in a blaze of rainbows and/or trauma, and then its resolved and done. The truth is that coming out is a lifelong task. Every new job, new friend, new date, and yes, new town means you have to come out over and over again. Even if people assume—as Stevie does with David—you have to, at some point, confirm or deny. And while the town exists in a bubble away from homophobia and other forms of prejudice, David still has to come out when he moves there. The first time is significant for everyone, but the never-ending coming out is important, as is how it is received. And for David, coming out as pansexual is a particularly significant coming out in TV narrative terms.

David explains his sexuality by saying he drinks all kinds of wine, that he "likes the wine, not the label." This is a phrase that has become a perfect shorthand for pansexuality—which sees attraction to the person, not the gender—and the conversation quickly turns what we know about David on its head. The use of labels, or not, is always important. Saying, "I do drink red wine, but I also drink white wine" is a great way to begin the conversation. The neat summary, "I like the wine, not the label," has understandably been adopted by queer people of all "labels" because it neatly fits any sexual and gender expressions. A wine metaphor is also a lovely updating of something from an iconic queer text: Evelyn Waugh's *Brideshead Revisited*. This is also a story centered on complex questions of sexuality and an "aren't they" in terms of relationships and identity. In the novel, when Anthony Blanche says "I know your tastes" while ordering wine for Charles Ryder (a character whose sexuality is ambiguous across the novel), it is a nudge and wink in the coded language of the novel to Charles' sexuality. The wine metaphor is continued across the novel in various coded discussions around sexuality. Like "I know your tastes," "the wine, not the label" offers another through line in queer narratives within the show.

David's sexuality is important, too, because it is sustained. He is consistently unapologetically and wholly himself. His sexuality doesn't get erased across the series, either. Often pansexual/bisexual characters/people are then, shall we say, "bi until proven straight" or "pan until proven gay." David is not. He references an ex-girlfriend while visiting a wedding venue, which might not be the classiest move (though it is also peak David, he changes, but not that much). Even in real life, bi and pan people find their sexuality erased by being in a relationship—whether a gay or straight couple, they are labeled as such, and not as bi or pan. That David remains vocal about his sexuality throughout the series is important.

David's relationship endgame could have gone either way in the show's early years. At the same time, it was important and the right character direction that Patrick win his heart. Another entirely plausible direction for David would have been finding a woman who fulfilled the same needs that Patrick does—grounding him, loving him for who he is, etc.—and it's a testament to that really simple coming out and use of ongoing reminding the audience that David likes all genders that would have been a plausible and fulfilling character outcome. Ultimately, the right story outcome for where the show sits in TV and queer history was to end up with a man, but it's important that as a pansexual character, it plausibly could have been someone of any gender.

But David also has a coming out story of a more everyday nature. Because queer people don't come out just once, they come out repeatedly, as do their families. As discussed in chapter 8, acceptance of Johnny/Eugene in David/Daniel's coming out is hugely important. When the Roses move to the town, they too are coming out to friends as parents of a queer son, and that conversation, as much as Stevie and David's, is important. David's coming out also includes another overlooked coming out: his parents talking about their queer son. While it shouldn't be directly compared, parents' coming out to new and old friends about their queer children also risks judgment and rejection. The conversations Johnny and Moira have also remind us that those who parent queer children also encounter prejudice, something that, in this small town, Johnny and Moira approach with caution.

Although David uses the wine metaphor but never refers to himself with a label, it's important his dad does give him a definitive label. In the same episode, Johnny says to Roland, "My son is pansexual," and it's significant that Johnny does give a label to David; because queer identities other than gay or lesbian are so rarely talked about on TV, it's important to give the language and labels for them.

Much like the conversation with Stevie, it's set up to make the viewer think it might go another way, as TV has taught us to think. We see Johnny, an older generation of parents, quite uptight to this point, lamenting that his son might still be in a phase and being told otherwise by his wife. We see he isn't homophobic, just worried for his unlucky-in-love son. While this shouldn't be conflated with the experience of the queer person, it's still important. And Johnny, new to the town, already vulnerable because of what his family has gone through, risks confiding in Roland.

Meanwhile, the mayor of this town, until now a mullet-sporting, baseball cap-wearing, unrefined human, is the voice of love and reason. Roland says, "We can't tell our kids who to love" and, in so doing, firmly draws a line in the sand for the show. It is, in typical fashion, funny as much as endearing—Roland is stoned during the conversation and eats barbecue in a typically inelegant manner. But like David's coming out, it also counters our expectations: the rural town mayor is inclusive, welcoming, and wholly unbothered by David's sexuality.

The setup with first Johnny lamenting whether it's a phase seems a well-worn one for parents wishing their children weren't gay, but this is quickly flipped, as is the show's character, by Johnny showing this comes from a place of concern rather than dislike. He confides in Roland that his son is pansexual and wishes his life had been easier. There's a real honesty to Johnny's perspective here. For any parent, however accepting, worrying that their queer child's sexuality will cause them added difficulty in life is an understandable one that comes from love. In the same way, Patrick's parents' response manages to keep the queer person at the center but also acknowledges the impact on their loved ones, and it also comes not from a place of bigotry or discrimination but from love.

"He's My Boyfriend": Patrick and Coming Out as a Grown-Up

Patrick's coming out story is the biggest moment of potential jeopardy for the entire relationship—indeed, the whole series. It is an honest and important moment. Even in this protective bubble of a town without prejudice, things can go wrong. Because in the series, while the town is a safe place, there isn't an illusion that the rest of the world is so, just that this place is somehow a step removed from it—the townspeople know that there are struggles in the rest of the world (with race, sexuality, and more), they just choose not to engage with that behavior. There are "real-world" references reminding us that Schitt's Creek is a town that's part of our real world. And little comments like David's aversion to team sports because we have enough political division provide little nods of awareness to the world's bigger issues. Similarly, while no direct reference is made, there is enough indication that outside the town, homophobia still exists—and this seems to be part of the broader point. Patrick's story gives reassurance and hope to those also going through it.

Patrick's story is a positive coming out story for grown-ups. Most coming out narratives center on teens and young people, reflecting the idea that coming out happens in high school or college, when people have their first sexual and romantic experiences. There's little in media for people like Patrick, who take longer to understand their sexuality. These teen-centered coming out stories are important—it's wonderful that queer teenagers can see themselves represented and find stories to guide them in this way—but they aren't the whole story, particularly for a generation like that of Patrick's age group—thirty-somethings who now live in a world with increasing queer representation but grew up in a time of silence and often fear and discrimination. Whether for personal or broader cultural reasons, plenty of "Patricks" in the world need those stories, so his was a vital narrative.

Interestingly, Patrick comes out accidentally. It's a noteworthy parallel to many queer lives where you may be out in some aspects of your life but in the closet in others. And this is an important distinction from many other coming out stories. It is not always as simple as in or out of the closet. You can live a happy out life in some respects but keep that aspect of life secret from other people or areas of life. This is seen more commonly than perhaps some might assume: people have long lived gay lives out and proud across most of their life but never disclosed their sexuality at work, for example. Similarly, it is very common for young people to move away from home for the first time, for university or a job, and begin living their best queer lives in a new town, but not come out to family or friends at home. And that's exactly what happens to Patrick.

Having lived in the town for over two years, he's comfortable "out." We couldn't define him as closeted in a broader way. He's never had to hide his relationship with David and is clearly—as he says in "Meet the Parents" (season 5, episode 11)—very comfortable in the town and with David's family. What's revealed in that episode is that, however, Patrick hasn't told his parents about David and, by association, hasn't come out to them. How the show sensitively and honestly handles this is a big part of how the show has come to mean so much to many. Patrick's coming out rings honest and true for the experience and the emotion involved from all parties. In the narrative setup, Johnny accidentally reveals to Patrick's parents that David and Patrick are together, and it is brilliantly executed. It begins as comedic, with Johnny saying the wrong thing and Roland making it worse (making a brilliant joke about Johnny's age and being "less progressive" when, of course, in the show and in real life, the opposite has been demonstrably true for Johnny/Eugene). From that, there's a beat where Patrick might be embarrassed by David himself—fulfilling and fitting with David's insecurities. But all that switches in a moment where, after David asks, "They know about me?" Patrick immediately switches things and confesses his fears about coming out. It's the perfect arc from comedic to chaotic to an honest stab to the heart/stomach for anyone at that moment.

The honest, open conversation Patrick and David have following directly after this gets to the heart of what it means to come out. Patrick says his fear is his parents will treat him differently. And that's the honesty of it: every time a person comes out, the fear is that everything will change. This is a fear every queer person, however loved and supported, has felt. He reiterates his parents are good people, implying he has nothing to fear regarding their potential prejudices, but he is still afraid. And, for their part, his parents fear that he will become someone different in their eyes. For someone coming out later in life, that's a particularly poignant element: Patrick's parents have viewed him one way for thirty years or so, and while arguably it shouldn't always be, sexuality is part of how people view us. So, of course, Patrick is worried this will change things. No matter how certain or secure a relationship is, coming out irreversibly changes something for any queer person.

David, too, articulates the thoughts around coming out that are vital, and in his words to Patrick and later Patrick's parents, he offers what perhaps anyone in Patrick's position needs to hear. Most importantly, he says, "What you're going through, it's very personal, and you should do it on your terms." That line feels like an unlocking of something and an act of acknowledgment. So often, coming out stories push the person to come out because that's what makes everything okay, suggesting that queer people can or should feel "wrong" if they aren't out in every aspect of their lives. David takes that and makes it okay for Patrick to not be out in every aspect of his life.

David here takes on the role of a queer elder as someone who has gone through it before. He might joke about "bringing a couple home" and telling his parents to deal with it, but David has been through it, not just the "big" coming out but all the small ones, and he can guide his boyfriend through it. David takes a step back and tells Patrick it's okay not to be out. He pushes aside his feelings—his potential hurt at being hidden from Patrick's parents all this time, any insecurity he brings up—and instead, he makes it all about what Patrick and he needs. Levy gives Patrick, as the one coming out, the agency in the story; he's accidentally outed, yes, but David (and Levy) give him the voice and agency to take it back on his terms.

What's powerful, too, is that Patrick is older than most of the stories we see. Usually, we see teens dealing with it alongside raging hormones and discovering who they are. Patrick knows who he is; he has lived with, grown into, and been one version of himself for several decades. But while he's been in the bubble of the town and the relationship with David, he hasn't had to acknowledge that something fundamental has changed in his life. His coming out to his parents is even more powerful because of this; it's a coming out to himself too. Maybe Patrick hasn't fully reconciled all this yet—and that's okay—but in saying it out loud to the people most important to him, he has to acknowledge it and own it in himself fully.

For an older person, shifting your sense of self is hugely significant. As a result, the decision is as much about him stepping into his identity and his queerness.

It's also an important episode as it acknowledges coming out and sexuality from the parents' point of view. Often in coming out narratives, parents are framed as antagonists or as roadblocks. That's not the case here. And while, rightly so, the emphasis is on the queer person, looking from the parents' point of view is a refreshing and important element. From Eugene and Daniel Levy's personal experience and wanting to incorporate elements of the parents' experience, we see this from a loving but sympathetic point of view for both David and Patrick.

In a way, Patrick is right: there is always a shift in any relationship when someone comes out. It doesn't necessarily mean a lack of acceptance or even a real change in how you view a person, but it is a shift in what you know about them. For example, that his parents might be hurt that their son kept part of his life hidden or that they worry their relationship isn't as strong as they'd hoped are all valid, important dynamics of coming out to acknowledge for parents of queer kids. It's never an excuse for hatred or exclusion of that child—however old they are when they come out—but it is a process for both sides, especially perhaps when it's an older adult coming out. It's so important for Patrick's parents to clearly say that it isn't that Patrick is gay that upsets them but that he didn't tell them. More specifically, he felt he couldn't tell them, making them feel they have done something wrong as parents. It's perhaps to some a small detail, but to queer viewers, it's vital. We wouldn't expect Patrick's parents to have a real issue with his sexuality, but like him, there's a seed of doubt. Instead, his parents are upset because he feels he can't come to them, and that is such a relief.

Is Patrick's coming out an idealized one? To some degree, of course. It happens quickly and easily, with no discernible fallout, neither from his parents nor his boyfriend, both of whom, whichever way you spin it, he misled in different ways. It's also a really easy coming out compared to what many in his position would have. Even without malice, many parents would have questions if their child, after years in a serious heterosexual relationship, came out to them. But in the narrative world of the show, there's no reason those more difficult conversations didn't happen away from what is shown. Maybe Patrick sat down with his parents the next day and explained everything; maybe they asked the awkward questions he hadn't been ready for before. Maybe David told his boyfriend how being hidden from his parents for nearly two years felt. And given the solidity of their relationship by this point—and past mistakes in finding out about Patrick's former fiancé—they would likely have had those conversations.

It's not necessarily the responsibility or interest of TV to show every detail like that. The show is a highlights reel and a way in, not a documentary. And while Patrick's might not be a "usual" or "realistic" coming out for many people, maybe that's also the point? What Patrick's experience shows is important: hope. He shows hope that it can be okay, and much like David being comfortable in his skin, Patrick's "I've never been happier" is a sign to other queer people that this could be them too.

"I Was Worried They'd See Me Differently": Patrick and Late Queer Identity

While coming out later in life is important, *being* out later is even more so. And while in the show's premise, David and Patrick exist in a small town, it might not be an immediate or pressing issue, but it is one Patrick draws attention to. For example, what if they had moved to New York? David would likely fall back on old habits of going to queer spaces he knows, like bars and clubs. How does Patrick feel about that? In a big city like New York, too, they might want to meet other gay friends, or at least this might be David's default again. Not to say that as a straight man, Patrick wouldn't have had gay friends before, but it's likely his friendship group wasn't predominantly gay people; how would he fit in New York City?

Patrick's is a learned queerness that we watch him begin to navigate. Through his relationship with David, he learns to be queer. It's not a unique experience, but as we see Patrick, who has lived his life to this point as a straight man, begin to learn how to live in his queerness, his new identity, that's as important as his coming out. Patrick doesn't change who he is with his sexuality but who he is to the outside world has changed, by both the realization and his coming out,and this is important for queer audiences, especially those who came out later in life. They remain at their core who they are, but their lives and selves are still changed by it (hopefully for the better).

Patrick has lived his life to this point as a straight man—in terms of prejudice and wider identity here, it doesn't matter that he is not straight, but that the world sees him as such—and he experiences the world as a straight man. Where does that leave Patrick in terms of queerness? He's gone through about thirty years of life not knowing the kinds of discrimination and name-calling David specifically but also people like David—perhaps identifiable or at least identified by society as queer but also in living that long without a label—have experienced. Yes, Patrick has suffered from not knowing his labels and not understanding himself, but he's also spared himself the labeling by others and what that brings with it. There will always be elements of David's past that Patrick can't understand, having not moved through his teens and twenties navigating spaces as a queer person. And when he starts to navigate the world that way, it is in the haven of the town of Schitt's Creek.

Patrick is the ideal product of the "town without prejudice." He is the queer person raised in an environment of acceptance. He is allowed just to be queer with no question and no impact on the rest of his life.

But that's not the whole story. Patrick is impacted by his coming out both in repercussions from his past relationship and his coming out, even his (well hidden, but there) insecurities in getting into a relationship with David. We see that even when all the risk and prejudice are taken away: accepting queerness can still be a challenge. And that feels important; it acknowledges that shifting identities and ways of experiencing the world are challenging, even when the world is as welcoming as the one *Schitt's Creek* creates. In Patrick, we see how identity is complex and how sexuality impacts it but doesn't define it. In short, there are several ways to be a queer man.

"The Wine, Not the Label": Patrick and the Labels

Another important facet of Patrick's queer identity is his labels. As much as David never says the word pansexual, his identity is clearly labeled by himself and others. Patrick doesn't label himself, and his identity is important. His parents assume he's gay because he's with a man, but is Patrick's identity more nuanced?

Is he bisexual? Or pansexual? Probably not. His ability to sustain a relationship (and we assume a sexual one) with a woman isn't enough proof of this. It's not impossible, of course—Rachel could have just been the wrong person for him—but given Patrick's thoughts on feeling "right" with David and feeling "things you're supposed to feel," then bi/pan don't seem to fit, despite perhaps Patrick's best efforts there. Because Patrick never did feel "right" with the women he dated and only experienced "right" with David, which indicates, perhaps, an unknown (to Patrick) preference for men. But given it was such a revelation to him when he fell for David, we can also speculate it's more nuanced, it's perhaps not all men—some men perhaps as he also flirts with Ted and Ken the store customer—but more likely too Patrick also needs connection to feel sexual attraction. That's why, until David, a man he truly connected with on multiple levels, he didn't feel sexual attraction to any other man.

Gay seems the most obvious label. But what if there is another, if not a total, sublabel? Things aren't always black and white; an alternative would be fitting, given David's sexuality. What if Patrick was demisexual? The definition of demisexuality is only experiencing sexual attraction with someone you form an emotional bond with. So we can argue that Patrick had never formed a close enough emotional bond with someone before. Because of that, he had never truly experienced sexual attraction fully before, either. What we could also argue is this lack of understanding of himself and his orientation had prevented him from discovering his gayness because he'd also never allowed himself to form such a bond with a man before, not knowing it was an option and not knowing that it would lead to actual full sexual attraction.

The way Patrick describes never feeling "right" before also feels like the way many asexual people talk about their experiences. The idea of just going along with things, of not feeling what you're supposed to, the way they're described in books—in TV even—is a very asexual experience and how when many realize their orientation is also a way of explaining it to others. Patrick *does* feel it for David, and he demonstrates his sexual desire for him. This leads us to the potential demisexual label, and a close connection only triggers his feelings. The two can be linked: his attraction to men overall but only in a very specific circumstance.

In the show, we assume heteronormativity has caused Patrick to never "experiment." But what if he assumed he's not asexual because that's the default? Because what he describes also aligns with demisexuality. Patrick doesn't feel "right" until he kisses David in the show. He doesn't experience "the things you're supposed to feel" until he kisses David. What he might mean is he doesn't experience attraction, or sexual desire, until David. Because this, not just gender, could have been the shift for Patrick. He fell very specifically for David. While demisexual people can also have a gender preference, which also might have been part of Patrick's revelation, the clear element is David himself; falling for David was key. The point is that in Patrick's journey, he wasn't looking to "experiment." Quite the opposite: he admits to being initially unnerved by his feelings for David. He doesn't see David as part of a journey of coming out or a means to explore sexuality; his attraction to David takes him by surprise and while it might open up a revelation of liking other guys, really, he falls for this guy very specifically. That doesn't mean that Patrick doesn't find men generally physically attractive; this is something we see him work through during the series too.

In the conversation about Ken ("Rock On!" season 5, episode 6), David encourages him to "experiment" with another man. Patrick finds Ken objectively attractive, but aside from his teasing of David, he doesn't seem to have been drawn to him. When sent on the date, Patrick declares that he can't do it, perhaps out of his sense of decency and monogamy but also perhaps because he realizes he is only sexually attracted to people he has feelings for. The encounter with Jake inviting them over for a whiskey can support this reading; Patrick goes along with it because it's what David wants to do (or thinks he wants to do). And while asexual folks can and do enjoy sex in casual ways, it can also be an uncomfortable experience. This is the show exhibiting what Patrick felt like pre-David, for years with Rachel and the other women: he dated women because that's what he was supposed to do. These encounters for Patrick show the shades of not only gender but specifically *David* being who/what feels right. And that is a very ace/demi approach.

It's here, too, that the separation of sex and love that Dan Levy has mentioned also supports our reading. In the *Entertainment Weekly* YouTube interviews about the finale (April 9, 2020), Levy mentions that sex and love are separate for David and Patrick. So in his view, the happy ending David receives on the wedding day isn't a threat to their relationship, as their love is separate from any sexual encounter ("Happy Ending," season 6, episode 14). This is also why David gives permission in principle for Patrick and Ken. But this can also support our reading of Patrick as demi/ace. For asexual people, sex means something else: there are sex-repulsed asexuals who don't enjoy any sexual encounter, but many asexual people will engage in sex for other reasons: closeness to a partner, physical pleasure (asexuality is about attraction, not the inability to experience pleasure), emotional connection/expression, and fun. For many asexual folks, the equation of sex = commitment and loyalty isn't the same; that's not where the commitment to a partner lies. So again, with David as allosexual and Patrick as demi/ace, we can see why sex is a secondary indicator of their bond. It's part of what they do for various reasons, but it's not the reason for their bond. So this explains why the happy ending along with Ken and Jake isn't a big deal in their relationship.

Why is it important? First, representation. Even if Patrick was not written as demi, there is so little ace spectrum representation in media that there must be characters viewers can read this way. Lagging behind other representations, ace spectrum folks are where gay and lesbian folks were a generation ago, reading between the lines to find representations. Reading Patrick as demi also doesn't alter his story. He's still a guy who accidentally fell for another guy when previously he hadn't felt like that was an option. He's still the guy who proposed to the man he loved and had a wedding. He's still a guy who had to come out to his parents later in life. Patrick's narrative remains the same, even if we give this part of the queer community a chance to see themselves in him.

Queerness and Identity

David Rose wears his queerness for all to see. For better or worse, his queerness is visible. It's usually held with pride, but he's mindful that it can also be damaging, like when he mentions not wanting to be the victim of a hate crime. David Rose's queerness is pivotal because it is unapologetic and different from queer characters often seen in TV drama and comedy. David's type of pansexual character is also important. He's a femme pansexual guy, one who is coded consistently with femme camp characteristics. First, we don't often see bi/pan men on TV, particularly American TV; male characters must fit in their boxes, gay or straight, firmly. So David is important, first, because he shows that femme bi/pan men exist. There is a sense in society, as with much of the labeling and categories we put members of the LGBTQ+ community into, that bi/pan men are "straight passing." It's also important that he is "camp" or "effeminate" or perhaps the more friendly "femme" because it shows people like David that it's okay to be who they are.

On the other hand, Patrick doesn't align his queerness with parts of his identity. In terms of character, he hasn't grown up aware of his queerness or in a queer community. In the show, they both offer different ways of existing in and being accepted for their queerness.

The narrative that who you sleep with or love doesn't change who you are is something of a double-edged sword. On the one hand, queer people shouldn't be defined by their queerness alone. Like everyone, they are multifaceted humans whose sexuality is but one component. But for some queer people, this is an integral part of their identity. That marginalization, being an outsider, and then belonging to the queer community is vital to them. But the town of Schitt's Creek offers an alternative to the notion that queerness defines a community in the traditional ways. So Patrick stays perfectly "Patrick" but dates, loves, and marries David. He is queer (in whichever label he/the audience chooses) but doesn't change who he is suddenly. On the other hand, David changes with love for Patrick, being removed from the queer scenes he was part of before, and becomes arguably better for it. Rather than an argument against those communities, it feels like an argument for creating and curating the kind of queer spaces that work for you.

After all, the store becomes a queer space—a place where everyone is welcome—the community Patrick and David create in their town is *their* queer community, one that welcomes them, specifically David and Patrick, for them, not some version of performative queerness to be accepted. And that's the overriding message of queer identities in the show. You can be Jake, embracing queerness in all its forms; Ronnie, quietly dating in a small town; or Patrick, unchanged in straight-legged denim, and still be accepted. Or you can be David, loud and proud and visibly queer. The town welcomes all versions of queerness and allows them to flourish.

12 Queer Affection and Sexuality

David and Patrick kiss forty-five times throughout the three seasons (and one bonus kiss the season before) that they're a couple. Dan Levy has spoken in numerous interviews about ensuring Patrick and David's physical affection isn't tempered, that they behave just as they would in real life—it's logical on arriving at work at Rose Apothecary they would kiss, it's logical that they would kiss at seemingly random times to show affection—because that's what couples do. Dan Levy has mentioned the importance of having David and Patrick show affection to one another on screen. In a 2019 interview with *The Advocate*, he noted: "I know that in writer's rooms across North America, there are still conversations about how much is too much when it comes to intimacy between, in my case, two men," he said. "That's an insane conversation to be having. Like, 'How often can we show them kissing on air?'" (Artiva, January 10, 2019).

This was never the case for David and Patrick; they would always be affectionate on screen and be a believable couple. There are parallels in this with Alexis, Ted, Moira, and Johnny. Both couples are affectionate on screen: we see Ted and Alexis kiss, talk about sex, in bed together, etc., just like we would expect from any on-screen romance. It fits with the show's tone; it's not overtly sexual, but also not prudish. They are young people in a relationship; therefore, we see them show affection. In another show, we'd see less affection from David and Patrick. Think about how many kisses we see Ross in *Friends* share with his various girlfriends/dates over the years, whereas Carol and Susan on the same show don't even kiss at their wedding. Or, to take a more recent example, *Modern Family* infamously is progressive in so many ways with their gay couple, Mac and Cam, but they only kissed for the first time on the show at their wedding.

However, David and Patrick have various "incidental" kisses across the series. More so than even Alexis and Ted, their domestic setup working together allows for incidental kissing and also touching. It mirrors Johnny and Moira's expressions of affection. David and Patrick's relationship is affectionate without being overly sexualized. It is a sexual relationship, but that isn't the main focus, and their easy domesticity as a couple, while including physical affection, is hugely important.

The parallels between Johnny/Patrick and Moria/David are highlighted in this way too: if Mom and Dad are allowed to be affectionate, so should their queer son(s). Johnny and Moira are the ultimate examples of a happy, fulfilled marriage. If we are to have David and Patrick as their parallel, then in terms of affection, they, too, should parallel it. There's something radical in both. Johnny and Moira are an older couple, but they are continually affectionate and sexual, but not overly so. We see them regularly kiss, embrace, and touch throughout the series. They do so in a natural way that seems realistic, not the overly polite affection of some TV parent figures who seem so rarely to even touch we could be forgiven for thinking they didn't even like each other. For Johnny and Moira, her taking his arm as they walk, touching his arm, and kissing goodnight or embracing are natural gestures. There is a radical queerness in that too: that we embrace older couples as romantic and sexual beings without it being a joke or something to be mocked. That Johnny and Moira are a romantic, still-in-love, happily married couple in their sixties/seventies is a radically queer TV notion. We often don't let our older TV characters be romantic, still in love, or simply affectionate. But *Schitt's Creek* creates its matriarch and patriarch in that image, and it is an image that David and Patrick follow.

Like Moira and Johnny, David and Patrick are affectionate in a way that subverts and queers the narrative. In the same interview with *The Advocate*, Levy goes on to say "We're going to show them kissing as often as we damn well, please. They're in a relationship. If I'm going to walk into a store that I own with my boyfriend, I'm going to kiss him hello. That's what people do. That's what straight couples do. That's what this couple is going to do" (Artiva, January 10, 2019).

That in itself was important for furthering queer representation. David and Patrick needed to be shown as affectionate, not just in the kisses but across a spectrum of affection. In every scene together, they demonstrate affection in different ways. David is fond of draping himself across Patrick or leaning on his shoulders. Patrick holds David still by the waist or pulls him into his space that way. They stand almost touching together in the store in almost every shot of them there, sit together on the sofa, or lie together in bed; they dance together. We see them quietly, domestically affectionate at every turn, and Levy is right. It's important; it's also an act of queer defiance. Just existing on screen, being happily queer, continues to be an act of queer defiance. But also, Levy integrates this seamlessly—each kiss is not a big deal but it is a big display. So while individual kisses may mean something significant for the plot—a first kiss, a proposal kiss, a marriage kiss—they are the minority of David and Patrick's kisses. The majority are incidental in the world of the show but huge in the wider context because they exist for kisses' sake, not because "two guys kissed." That is a huge leap for queer shows and queer affection.

It is affection, not just sex, that is crucial too. This is not to detract from the radical and important ways sex is a tool for queer representation, rebellion, and politics. For a group whose existence, specifically how they are sexual with one another, is politicized and demonized, representation of queer sex is vital. Indeed, confrontational sex has been a vital tool in theatre: for example, when Larry Kramer proclaimed the dangers of sex in *The Normal Heart* and politically alienated himself from some members of the queer community. TV shows like *Queer as Folk* and *Looking* take sexualized gay culture and put it front and center. *Looking*, one of the most recent examples of specifically queer shows for queer audiences, and one that focuses on gay and bi/pan men, uses sex as the heart of storytelling, politics, and the community it depicts. The characters in the incredibly queer subcommunity of San Francisco use sex in how they relate to themselves and each other. In the show, too-frank conversations about sex are integral. This is a way the show offers up its queerness, and it is a part of the radical identity of the show. Since even *Tales of the City* and the original *Queer as Folk*, this has been part of the fabric of gay stories: the liberation of sex and the need to use sex as part of the narrative and the politics. They were the contrast to the sanitized gay characters of mainstream TV.

Schitt's Creek could be read as towing a safe line between the two. David and Patrick show affection; yes, their sex lives are hinted at but never seen. The same is true of David's other queer sexual encounters; is it keeping sex off-screen? Yes and no, but we don't need to see it to know it exists. As sex isn't erased from the narrative, gay or straight, the show is extremely sex-positive. However, removing the purely sexual from David and Patrick's dynamic is a queering of the expected narratives. It takes a set of characters—the queer couple, and the queer male couple, specifically—and says we won't play by the existing rules. The existing rules were either hypersexualized or not sexualized at all. *Schitt's Creek* says, "Let's go in the middle" and by doing so, radicalizes further because it subverts both expectations.

There is something radical about romance and affection being more important sex. It's something equally wonderfully queer that David and Patrick offer us here: a love story not driven by sex. None of their stories are driven by sex; feelings drive each part of their journey. That is a radical notion for media where "sex sells" internally to the story and externally to marketing the show; the notion of "look at these hot guys" would normally have been a selling point, but it's not the focus here.

Therefore, the incidental touches between David and Patrick are huge in this depiction. They're a visual shorthand for understanding how stable this couple is. How often have we looked at particularly queer couples on TV and seen them kept apart and distant, to the point we wonder if they even like each other, never mind loving each other? For David and Patrick, this is never in doubt. We also get a set of physical touches that lead to their relationship. In the lead-up to their relationship, they are physically distant. Take the first scene where they meet: they're across the room, with a desk between them. They're also in Ray's office, a space that meant nothing to either of them. The next time they speak is by phone, again distant, but David is in his store, inviting Patrick in. When Patrick offers to work with David, he enters the store, into David's space, and stands close for the first time. From then on, we consistently see Patrick only in the store. It's almost as if he only exists in that space in David's mind. As much as the store is a public space, it's also their private space—something that will continue across the series—where they build their relationship. We watch their communication evolve: the trademark teasing and bickering between them across the episodes leading up to the store's opening. We see the hallmarks of romcom moments, with a lingering glance across the store and the episode culminating in a hug—the first time they touch—that lasts too long and is cut short by a flickering light. So far, so romcom, but there's a shift: the store opens to the public, and David and Patrick's relationship leaps with a touch.

When they kiss for the first time outside the motel, they use physical spaces and physical touch as part of the language. They're outside David's new "home" that has yet to feel like home, but they are not quite inside yet; they're tentative, which signals they are not quite there in their relationship either. But the next day in the store, they perhaps have their first "real" kiss. David greets Patrick with a kiss on the cheek—a tentative, sweet gesture that tells viewers we aren't going to have a one-time-thing kiss and that this couple will be physically affectionate. The kiss at the end of the episode feels like the first "official" kiss in some ways, not just because it affirms they are doing this (in TV terms, too, that it wasn't just an end-of-season tease) but that it takes place in their store, in their space.

The physicality of that kiss feels different. It's Patrick stepping into David's space and taking charge. As he'll say later in the series, he's normally a take charge kind of guy ("Meet the Parents," season 5, episode 11). Still, after a long while trying to get David's attention, Patrick steps back on the night of David's birthday, worried he will let David leave without kissing him. We later learn ("The Hike," season 5, episode 13) that he'd been wrestling with his feelings for David, trying to pluck up the courage to tell him how he felt for a while. In "Dead Guy in Room Four" (season 4, episode 1), when he kisses David in the store, it feels like him stepping into those feelings and making a choice. The choice made in their store is also important, public and private, but it also feels like a declaration of commitment.

Patrick and David have most of their onscreen kisses at the store. This feels important to Levy's storytelling—that the store represents home and something bigger to David—but so is the casual affection expressed here and elsewhere. Aside from their kisses in the store, David and Patrick are seen being quietly affectionate almost consistently. This could be Patrick's kisses on David's cheek as he's victorious in baseball, their good luck kiss before *Cabaret*, or David's drunken kiss when Patrick picks him up from the winery. More so than the kisses, it's the casual affection in other ways that's important.

In terms of marketing, juxtaposed with many other TV shows and films, the temptation would have been to put David/Patrick and Dan/Noah in sexy photoshoots: think back to the likes of *Friends* in the 1990s in comedy-land to every high-profile drama where the leads are in a relationship—these often resulted in sexy magazine covers. This could easily have been the fate of *Schitt's Creek* with David and Patrick's relationship. Instead, the photoshoots for the show stayed firmly in character kind for promo purposes from official channels. The media largely focused on the Rose family rather than David and Patrick. This made sense for the "family show" narrative internally and externally, and also that the show's overall narrative is about the Roses and their journey. The only notable exceptions were for the final season. For this, the official promo included shots of David and Patrick outside the Rosebud Motel, including ones of them kissing. Also, for the final season, Levy/Reid did a series of photoshoots for *Entertainment Weekly* (2020). While *Entertainment Weekly* had previously focused on Dan/Eugene/the Roses for the final season, they did a

David/Patrick–focused series with three digital covers based on romcoms. Based on *Notting Hill*, *Sixteen Candles*, and *Casablanca*, these covers were romance-focused, not sexy photoshoots. All this might sound minor, but it is a pretty seismic shift.

Even as actors, the emphasis is usually on sexy photoshoots for leading men (and women). But in gay publications, the male actors are almost always framed in a sexy (usually shirtless) way. That Levy has also cultivated an image focused on his fashion taste, not his looks/sexiness, is also significant. For his personal brand and the show, it emphasizes the work, not how he looks. The show's marketing as an act of activism is further explored in chapter 13. Still, there is something radical about a lack of emphasis on sex-selling and shifting the narrative from sex in queer characters without desexualizing them.

The emphasis is on romance in the external messaging for the David and Patrick narrative. The emphasis on romcoms—and in this case, the very old-fashioned style of romcom in the promotional shoot—gives a degree of old-fashioned romance we've rarely seen for queer narratives. That, once again, is revolutionary and queer. Because there was a sense with queer narratives that they always had to be different, something in there already being "other" meant defiance of the heteronormative values of other stories, of the types of characters seen, and yes, often edgy, confrontational ways of talking about, among other things, sex. All those were necessary, and it is fair to say that sometimes, you must go to extremes to get a seat at the table. But once at the table, maybe the most radical thing to do is go the other way.

David and Patrick aren't desexualized in the way previous characters were. To quote Dan Levy in an *Entertainment Weekly* interview: "This is a couple who has been so open and so honest and has not put sexuality and their sex lives in a box that they can't touch, and it hasn't necessarily defined who they are as people" (April 9, 2020).

This is such a radical notion for queer storytelling. The extremes of hypersexualization and desexualization have been so long that we've grown oblivious to anything in between. But it feels like a revelation when David and Patrick show up, casually affectionate, feeling wholly like a real and authentic couple.

The show is sex-positive, but that David and Patrick's relationship isn't founded on or governed by sex alone is an important conversation and an act of "queering" in itself. Think how many storylines are governed solely by sex, whether someone cheats/doesn't cheat being the make or break, or whether sexual attraction is or isn't there. The list goes on. None of that is a factor for David and Patrick. We assume they're attracted to each other, and we assume they have a sexual relationship. But both are mentioned more in passing because the core of their relationship is different. As Levy says to *Entertainment Weekly*: "For this couple that they're so stable and so steady that these kinds of things like sex that can be so sort of intense for people and you know is such a make or break in terms of putting loyalty onto it. Which is fine for other people" (April 9, 2020).

That's not to say they are sexless or desexualized, just that sex occupies a different, less central space; as Levy continues about the happy ending of the finale, and the perceived indiscretion: it's not make or break, as Levy goes on to say, because this isn't what their relationship is founded on—"it's founded on something much deeper much more substantial much more respectful." Their happy ending as a couple is also that they are stronger than just a sexual bond.

We rarely see gay men in bed together in a nonsexual context. We see David and Patrick on a bed—not in it—in a sexual context only once, and every other time we see them in bed, it's domestic and nonsexual. Far from desexualizing them as a couple, instead it romanticizes them. Dan Levy shared an image of Patrick and David in bed (from season 5, episode 3) and said, "It was the little things that meant the most. Happy Pride" (@instadanjlevy, Instagram). Again, seeing a queer relationship normalized by doing the same things that straight couples do on TV every day without comment was a huge part of the show's importance.

So we see David and Patrick in bed together in nonsexual situations more than in sexual ones. The show also incorporates other kinds of affection, from their morning interrupted by Ray to Patrick recovering from dental surgery. One of the most poignant is the two times we see them in bed together during "The Wingman" (season 6, episode 2), where David wets the bed: when the incident happens and later at the end of the episode. It's powerful regarding the domesticity and day-to-day thread that runs through their relationship. Because it takes the romanticized (not the romance) out of their relationship but also enforces its strength. So Patrick's charmingly no-nonsense approach to David's accident and openness and vulnerability in sharing his mouthguard and snoring device at the end of the episode normalize every day in their relationship. It might not be the sweeping romcom sentimentality of David's (or Dan Levy's) dreams, but what it offers is more powerful—an everyday, honest, and real feeling of the relationship between two men.

We see them in bed together in the morning and evening, talking, and being affectionate. We even see them in bed with David's family all around

("Moira Rosé," season 6, episode 7); Alexis puts it as sharing a room with two brothers who kiss (which they do in response). All of this, particularly the latter, confirm the normalization of their relationship. In the same episode, their relationship becomes even more firmly cemented within the Rose family—with Johnny's talk with Patrick and Moira's with David, even with the "husbands" picking up the drunk spouses from the vineyard. But finally, with Patrick not just in the motel but in David's bed with his whole family around, he's fully part of the family. Still, their relationship is also domestic, normalized, and uncommented on as Johnny and Moira share a bed next door, which feels revolutionary.

All this culminates in their wedding, where they walk down the aisle and kiss like every other straight couple we've seen get married on TV. But the lack of drama around the kiss at the wedding is important. Repeated comparisons with *Modern Family* feel unavoidable when that wedding kiss was such an event, while David and Patrick's wedding was an event, not the fact they'd kissed. The wedding was important, as it celebrated the queer love that had permeated the show. It was an event because it was without drama—we knew they would get married, and their happy ending was never in jeopardy. But that they kissed? Not once but twice, in a way, a nonevent, and in being so a huge event. We're so used to seeing them

Dan Levy and Noah Reid as David Rose and Patrick Brewer in Schitt's Creek, *Season 6, "The Incident."*
Credit: CBC/Not a Real Production Company 2020/Alamy Stock Photo

kiss by this point that it doesn't raise an eyebrow, but they are celebrating their love to end the series—that's the huge event.

There is one sidebar that fans have picked up on in the show: David and Patrick never hold hands. Is there a deeper meaning there? Is that a lack of affection between them? Does it even matter?

Realistically, it probably didn't feel natural in the actors' bodies performing it. Maybe Levy or Reid aren't "hand-holding" people, and it looked and felt awkward. Much of their characters, after all, are based to some degree on their chemistry. For them, the naturalness of the gestures between David and Patrick felt more important—the way Patrick holds David's waist, the way David drapes himself on Patrick, the way David pets Patrick's arm, etc. All this felt more natural than skipping down the street hand in hand. On one level, we probably shouldn't read much into it; hand-holding doesn't feel very David-and-Patrick, and what we have instead is a repertoire of other gestures that clearly show their affection. It also shows affection comes in different forms.

Perhaps audiences agonizing over hand-holding is a heteronormative reading of the situation. What's to say that hand-holding indicates more affection than a hand on the waist, back, or shoulder? Just because rom-coms have conditioned us to see hand-holding as indicative of security as a couple doesn't mean every real-world couple feels it, nor should every fictional one. But if we are looking for a comment, it's a nod to the real world outside the bubble of the show and the town. Maybe David Rose learned the hard way that walking hand in hand with your partner is a recipe for all of the negative things a queer person learns to fear. Maybe he's shielding himself and Patrick from that. It's a leap, sure, but also, we can read this as an example of how deep queer trauma reaches, and how much intergenerational trauma there is. If queer people grow up learning to fear certain elements, it takes time to unlearn them. Maybe this is as true of Dan Levy as David; maybe some fears can't be undone by one town without prejudice or one magical relationship. Maybe, not holding hands is a lesson that not even this wonderful mythical town fixes everything. They kiss freely, and sure, they live their lives. But some things take longer to undo in our past and our queer history.

For now, we might not be quite there. Maybe there are invisible strings of discrimination and trauma still holding us back. We could get the happy ending, the wedding, and all the kisses, but elements are still missing or difficult. It may take more than this one show to put that right. Just like David, maybe we won, but we're still a work in progress, and that's okay. David and Patrick's open domestic affection gives us the next stop on the road. We no longer are without affection and no longer are defined by sex either. We have romance and affection; we can build on that moment.

"A Whiskey or Whatever": Sexual Expression

Queerness is separate from sex but equally tied up with sex and sexual expression. Another facet of queer culture is sex positivity, but also sex out of traditional and gendered norms. *Schitt's Creek* manages to walk a line of being comedic around sex but also nonjudgmental, offering a subtle message on sex positivity. All of these have their roots in very queer sensibilities. Sex within the queer community has long, with varying degrees of success, advocated for a move away from traditional, monogamous, heteronormative ideas about sex. Mostly on TV, we see couples seeking sex as a means to long-term love, slut shaming women (and men), and using usual sexual practices as a joke.

For David and Patrick, their hugely important queer romance is also important for what it says about sex and the "rules" around it. David, in the final episode, gets the happy ending from the masseuse; it's a perfect microcosm of this, and a subtle statement on queer ideas on sex and sexuality. In another TV show, that would have been not only shocking but also a relationship unraveller. On *Schitt's Creek*, it's a hilarious moment inside and outside the show. David joking in his vows "you are my happy ending" is indicative that the moment isn't taken too seriously in the show or their relationship. But like the phrase "you are my happy ending" for David, it also has a deeper meaning in the show's context; their relationship is deeper than a sexual misstep. The reason David assumes the happy ending is okay with his husband is that their rules and understanding of sex/love/trust have been written on their terms; the reason Patrick doesn't let it derail their relationship despite not being thrilled about it is that he knows their relationship is so much more than one sexual encounter.

As explored elsewhere, Patrick's clothes are as important as the Roses' clothes. But that David comments on his "straight-legged denim" as the reason Patrick couldn't be interested in him is as important as the assumptions the world (and audiences) make about David. And that lends itself to the fact that Patrick isn't identifiably queer. He doesn't wear his sexuality externally as David does. He also doesn't know how to. When navigating the flirtation with Jake, Patrick is on the back foot—something we rarely see from him—because he's unused to male attention. With David, it was different; it was an unsure, sparring, and connection with a person. But the difference is that Jake has identified him as queer and deliberately flirted with him, a situation in which Patrick doesn't know how to act. Similarly, when they go to Jake's, the disconnect between "I can be that person" and being that person becomes apparent.

This, or the fact they consider a whiskey with Jake, isn't indicative that their sex life isn't working—quite the opposite: we can assume all that is fine. In queer culture, sexually positive outlooks indicate a sexually compatible and lovingly secure relationship to explore options outside it. This is not to say that David and Patrick will become Jake any time soon, but it's a marker of the strength of their relationship that they could consider it. It's been an evolution throughout their relationship to show how rules of relationships—and sex—don't have to conform to what maybe we think. Patrick, who has previously only negotiated relationships in a very heteronormative way, combines learning "new" rules of queer life with his naturally kind and accommodating nature and accepts it. To borrow another metaphor from the show, when Patrick gives David the framed receipt on their first date/David's birthday, David comments on the solidity of the frame and Patrick replies that he's learning. Both comments could be a metaphor/comment on their relationship. For David, the solidity of the frame is something he's never had before: a solid foundation to a relationship. However, more important is Patrick's now solid frame that he's learned about. The last time he gave David a frame, it was a fumbled gift when he was unsure of where he stood or his feelings. In taking this next step Patrick is indeed learning about a type of romantic and sexual relationship (with another man) that he previously never envisaged. And in doing all that, Patrick learns about himself and his sexuality.

Jake, too, is hugely important; he embodies all things queer and is sexually permissive; as David puts it, he "doesn't care in a good way." And while Stevie isn't wrong that "only Jake is capable of loving Jake," it's not necessarily a toxic trait when everyone takes Jake for who Jake is. He clarifies who he is looking for, and everyone around him accepts that. In another narrative, Stevie tries to force him to settle down to stop his promiscuity. Instead, she leans into what Jake can do for her. Jake's sexual liberation, like his queerness, is accepted by the town, allowing him to be who he is. Such liberation, his "take it or leave it" fashion without judgment or slut shaming, particularly for a queer character, is important in illustrating the sexually permissive approach the show has.

That Stevie is included in this is important, too. In straight sex in the show, there's an element of queer permissiveness too often absent from straight stories around sex. For women in the show, there is also sex positivity. Stevie sleeps with Jake, maintaining a long-term casual relationship with him, and she isn't shamed for it. She is unashamedly sexual in her pursuit of Jake and is a realist about it being purely physical.

Meanwhile, Alexis has had a sex life that is presumably as rich and varied as the adventures that went with it. She, too, is never slut-shamed for sleeping with an (again presumably) large number of men, though she is mocked for the dangerous or weird life choices that went with those dalliances. These women take a certain amount of pride in their sexuality, their effect on men, and enjoying sex.

Celebrated equally are the sex lives of older characters. Roland, Jocelyn, Johnny, and Moira are still sexual beings, as are other characters like Gwen, whose misadventures with poor oblivious Bob are a running joke. But these older characters must be seen as still sexual; this is an act of queer rebellion and sex positivity. From early on, we encounter Johnny and Moira struggling with privacy just as much as David and Patrick later will. While we understand that David isn't exactly thrilled to walk in on his parents in that position at that time in the morning, Moira and Johnny aren't shamed for being sexual at their age. It's a difference between their son saying, "I don't want to see that" (understandable) and the show saying, "Ew, they shouldn't do that." Instead, the show lets them go off to a cabin to have sex, where the jokes are on their inability to follow directions, not their sex life. Instead, Moira and Johnny are seen as having a healthy sex life and attraction to one another, even after all these years. It's truly a rare thing that older characters can celebrate and embrace sexuality on TV and that as much as their loving relationship forty years in is important.

They aren't alone in this; Roland and Jocelyn have what sounds like a fairly adventurous sex life. While it's a running joke on the show, it's not done in a shaming way; the butt of the joke is usually Roland's oversharing, usually to a bemused Johnny. But from their graduation night role-play to a double night-time couple's massage, they seem to be having a good time. And the show's attitude to that seems good for them. There's much sex positivity, and queerness goes hand in hand with that. The inclusivity and positivity around David and Patrick's sexuality and sex life also extend to the straight characters on the show. And while, no, Johnny doesn't want the details of Roland's sex life any more than David and Alexis want to hear their parents through the motel wall, the idea that they are still allowed to be sexual beings is important.

Sex and the expression of sexuality are read through a queer-coded lens in *Schitt's Creek*, and it makes for a refreshing take for both queer and non-queer characters that they're all granted the same permissiveness. (For the slightly more gutter-minded viewer, remembering the motel's name is also slang for either a man who "bottoms" frequently or the impact of said bottoming on a rectum . . . again it could be a coincidence, but it could be a pleasing added extra for those in the know, much like David's massage.)

Queer Characters for Queer Audiences

There is a multitude of ways to show audiences queer characters. As explored in chapter 2, there is a long history of queer narratives on which *Schitt's Creek* stands. These shows largely cater more to showing straight audiences queer life or queer stories for queer audiences. So which is *Schitt's Creek*? On the whole, it's probably the former, which is not an insult; such shows are hugely important, in that they display a straight world how to be around queer folks. This is the heart of Levy's "lead by example" approach; if you show a world without homophobia, maybe people will learn to live that way. Some of the queer messages of the show are geared more toward straight understanding. The wine metaphor is the perfect way to explain to non-queer folks a queer theme. Patrick, coming out, says to his parents, "We understand this is hard for you too" without decentering the queer person (Patrick's) experience. David and Patrick's relationship, too, is, on the whole, very safe and very heteronormative. They end, after all, with a big white (and black because it's David Rose) wedding. They follow that acceptable path, and there's nothing wrong with that—in life or TV—but the more palatable path shows straight audiences, "we're here, we're queer, we're just like you." This is generally considered a way to get those audiences understanding. There's nothing wrong with that; it's a hugely valuable tool. It's not doing what many queer shows for queer people do and speaking in the language of the community.

Or is it?

In an interview with *The Advocate*, Dan Levy said, "We've come a long way" from when show creators "categorized" queer characters to make us more digestible for straight viewers (Artiva, January 10, 2019). And while on the surface, *Schitt's Creek* is a show that explained sexuality to and gave queer romance to a mainstream audience, there's a lot more bubbling under the surface that tells us Levy was preaching to the choir in subtle ways.

The attitude in the last episode to the happy ending is also telling. Crucially, as Dan Levy says in an interview with *Entertainment Weekly* (April 9, 2020), it's a separation of love and sex; as he says in that interview, we assume all that is working okay, but that is separate from their love and how they feel about each other. For many people, particularly straight audiences, that's an alien concept, synonymous with infidelity and the end of a relationship. This doesn't break up David and Patrick because they have a queer, in the wider sense, attitude to sex and love. So while Patrick wasn't "raised in queerness," he has perhaps a combination of innate understanding and has been slowly educated by David that things are not as they have always seemed. It isn't a betrayal in David's eyes to get the happy ending because a sex act without feelings doesn't alter how he sees Patrick or feels about him. While this completely goes against many dominant sensibilities, it makes perfect sense for those with queer attitudes in the broader sense. It's also something that can be fairly common in queer relationships—formal and informal non-monogamy exists, and monogamy isn't seen as essential for a successful relationship.

This is where Levy has been clever. It's a funny joke, it's perfectly David and Patrick, but it's also part of a wider tapestry of nods and references that say, "I see this community; I am part of this community." On the one hand, it's a bit of comedy-drama for the wedding episode that doesn't jeopardize them too much. But on the other, it was a big leap in hinting at something more, that perhaps David and Patrick are *less* of a mirror to straight society than we think.

We can initially bring this back to David's sexuality. The unashamed fluidity of David's pansexuality and his gender expression, without being a figure of fun, were revolutionary for queer shows, especially ones on mainstream networks. As Dan Levy describes: "People in the queer community have always sort of existed in a rather fluid world," he concludes. Having David come out pansexual brings explicit visibility to that fluidity. "To not have to define yourself or categorize yourself, I think, is beneficial to everyone. I think the more we can understand that people just exist and that as long as we're doing good in this world, we don't need to bother or worry about defining or classifying people, the sooner we'll be in a better place" (Artiva, January 10, 2019).

Not to reduce all queer stories to sex, but this is a key indicator in terms of attitudes and one that shouldn't be ignored. Sex and sexual expression, sexual politics, and their differences from straight people are important to the queer community. David and Patrick do, in principle, on the surface look like a couple conforming to heteronormative standards of queerness with their big white wedding; there's a lovely little nudge there to something more. It's more, too, in their attitudes. David sees nudging Patrick toward experimentation for the wider good of their relationship, first breaking free from the heteronormative way in which many of us—including Patrick—are raised. Again it's using Patrick's later coming to terms with his sexuality as a tool in that he didn't "grow up" queer in the sense of having an awareness of the community, so he's learning lessons, perhaps along with viewers. Dan Levy spoke to *GQ* about that episode and asked if an audience could understand that opening up a relationship for some people makes them stronger, or their large family-based (and perhaps the unspoken "straight") audiences might be alienated by the idea. It led Levy to ask if all those bigger ideas could "live within our little show that was a comedy, but also a little dramatic"? Levy, naturally, decided it could because, "We always wanted it to be real, never to cut corners when it came to depicting this couple as realistically as possible" (McGurk, November 17, 2021). Levy incorporated that essentially very queer attitude into their "little show," and it's one of the most telling, most delightfully queer moments that let *that* audience know "we see you" and says, "this show was made for you too." As a queer fan, that's important. Straight viewers tend to gloss over this as funny or ridiculous moments. But they're the most honest to the queer community. Not all of the queer community is heteronormative, reflecting straight values. In including these, Dan Levy is giving us a peek behind the curtain, going, "Yes, this passes for straight viewers, but I made it for you."

Those queer shows that speak the language of the community in ways the community understands are generally the more uncomfortable for straight audiences. They often rely on sexually explicit content or present different ways of life that have historically made straight cis audiences uncomfortable. From trailblazers like the original *Queer as Folk* showing explicit gay sex and gay men having babies with lesbians to keeping their main protagonists happily unattached. All of these themes challenge the heteronormative ways of being in society. Take another Russell T. Davies–penned series, *It's a Sin*, which concentrated on responses to AIDS in the United Kingdom: it was sexually explicit, to the point of detailing hygiene practices before sex in ways that straight audiences are unlikely to be familiar with. These small and large rebellions are ways of telling a queer audience they are seen. Some shows like *Queer as Folk*, historically *Tales of the City*, or, more recently, *Looking* wear it on their sleeves, a "queer show for queer audiences" first. Straight viewers are welcome, but they're a guest. Those shows differ from the *Will & Grace* or *Modern Family* model, aimed at a wider audience, inclusive and progressive, but not quite as *from* the community. On the surface, *Schitt's Creek* seems, in that model, the queer show accessible to all. But several nods across the series indicate Levy is conscious of making sure his queer audience feels truly seen.

Some straight people might not understand the weight of this. Maybe from that perspective, David and Patrick's romance isn't interesting enough. It's too lowkey, too without drama, too "vanilla" for some, perhaps. But it is also their drama-free everyday romance that makes it important. It's strangely important after generations of representation of gay characters on screen being fueled by drama, tragedy, and sex to see the day to day, to see the very dull, by some measure, moments of Patrick and David. Seeing David come in and kiss Patrick's cheek in the store feels like a revelation to those who grew up clinging to every tiny gesture and hint of something like that.

And the healthy, fairly painless relationship is vital representation. The relationship without the constant fear of "who is going to get killed off/ written off." Straight people have never known that "please don't kill off my favorite character" in this specific way. They've never had a relationship become canon and endgame so comfortably that you didn't have to worry.

Schitt's Creek does both. It's a mainstream show that gives knowing nods to queer viewers. It's a queer show that includes subtle elements that queer audiences will align with and allows a straight audience. It's a tricky balance. As a queer fan, that's important.

13 Queer Romance for Grown-Ups

In *Schitt's Creek*, there's a balance of that unrealistic romcom story and an often humorous but down-to-earth element. And when we talk about "queering," we also talk about updating. The whole show feels like the writers are taking all that they loved about the genre—the comedy/drama genre from TV—and giving it an updated twist.

The Courtship

David had ended a season 2 with a kiss outside the barn with Jake, another failed dalliance, which meant the Patrick storyline had the potential to go either way. But from the start, the chemistry between Dan and Noah was clear on screen, and hopes were high from viewers by the time we reached the end of season 3. What we get across that season is a lovely slow burn of a friendship into romance without a feeling of jeopardy.

The key with David and Patrick is that they're hilarious while heartwarming. Because there's rarely any real danger to their relationship, and because of the show's ethos of being overall "good people," the comedy it creates, particularly in their early days, is lovely. Essentially, they play on the classic "odd couple" pairing: David is loud, big in personality, and slightly chaotic, while Patrick is quiet, organized, and assured. Their foibles rub each other the wrong way, allowing Patrick to tease his new business partner and David to flail mercilessly. The comedy comes in not knowing who Patrick is interested in. Is he flirting with Alexis? With Stevie? Wait . . . with David? The details of the slow revelation that Patrick might be into David, which become more apparent in rewatches, are charmingly funny. The comedy comes from the wonderful revelation that they're both terrible at this. Neither of them knows how to start a romance for different reasons, and it's heartwarming as much as it's often hilarious.

We see the shift, with Alexis and Stevie teasing David about Patrick's interest and him dismissing it. As discussed, playing on David's engrained preconceptions mirrors the audience. But this lovely slow burn reaches its charming—and still funny—peak when in "Friends and Family" (season 3, episode 11), David makes a few inappropriate remarks ("Just as long as it doesn't get hard" at Patrick. At the same time, they bicker and tease each other over the opening of the store. Then, at the episode's close, there's a hug that lasts just a fraction too long, and it's only interrupted by a flickering light. It is a classic romcom trope used to full effect. We're still unsure where their relationship is headed.

The Kiss

Levy doesn't make us wait too long, and in the season 3 closer, "Grad Night," he gives us a kiss between David and Patrick and a date (once David knows it's a date). On David's birthday, Patrick offers to take him to dinner; David doesn't think it's a date and invites Stevie. But once Patrick's gift is revealed, she bails and leaves them to the romance.

It is one of TV's most lovely first steps to romance. Patrick gives David a framed receipt from the first sale in their store. It's at once an in-joke after David made fun of the frame Patrick bought for the business license and a sweet, meaningful gesture, marking their success with the store and how they met. Wonderfully romantic but awkwardly delivered, it is on brand for the two. Patrick is on the back foot on their date, nervous and fumbling, where he is usually self-assured. Because of this, Levy flips the script (literally in that he'd previously written another version) and has David kiss Patrick in the car at the end. It's perfect because, for all of Patrick's confidence and posturing, he needs David to take the lead.

It's a sensitive portrayal of what it feels like to have any first kiss, but particularly as a queer person—as a new queer person in Patrick's case—it's a leap. It's something straight viewers will never understand, as assured Patrick is of David or their mutual attraction; this is a point of no return. As much as Patrick has analyzed his attraction, gone over it, and waited for the right moment if he takes action, then it's done, he's taken a step, and you can't ever go back. Levy's writing and Reid's performance at that moment do this sensitive moment justice and deliver the right balance of its weight, charm, and humor.

That Patrick thanks David for "doing that for us" (that is, the kiss) indicates the weight of the moment beyond just a kiss for Patrick and the show. For Patrick, it's the thing that has allowed him to leap into being someone else—or into being himself. It's also a comment on what the show is doing: Patrick is, in effect, the queer audience, saying, "Thank you for giving us this as well."

Luckily for everyone, the chemistry between Levy and Reid was there, and Patrick stayed. Their romance continues in their established style of funny-charming-sweetness. It's never too sentimental to be unrealistic, and they remain true to the characters. David is still very David, and while love might change him eventually, it doesn't change him overnight. In the early stages of their courtship, they navigate Patrick's newness to a relationship with a guy in charmingly awkward—and ultimately very funny—ways. First, David wants to sleep over because of a dead body in the motel, and Patrick's panic that David wants to sleep with him is dealt with in funny but authentic ways. It addresses that Patrick isn't ready to go from kissing one night to sex the next, and David respects that (he does want a place to sleep that doesn't have a corpse in it). Elsewhere sex is a funny, authentically played strand in that David and Patrick lack privacy, so they do their best in the backroom of the store, until Stevie offers them a room, which is gatecrashed by a visit from Jake. Nothing runs smoothly in their courtship entirely, but the roadblocks are small. They're stumbling through and offering that rarest of things: a drama-free queer romance.

The Best

One of the defining moments of David and Patrick's relationship comes when Patrick sings "The Best" to David. Setup in true Patrick style, with him teasing David over the open mic night, the scene is beautiful—and Noah Reid's arrangement and song performance makes it so. Beyond a serenade—which could go very wrong in many respects—there is much more to the scene at play. There are two people showing not just each other but publicly declaring that they are in something together. This feeds into an ongoing theme of Patrick and David's ability to have what they have being tied to the town and what the town gives them as a safe space to grow and be with each other.

In the scene, we see Moira initially skeptical of the performance as David is—she offers to pull the fire alarm. But as soon as Patrick starts singing, she is swept away.

The emotional vulnerability of Patrick to do what he does, but also for David and his response, is a powerful moment for audience and characters. For the characters, it's a huge leap; Patrick struggles with expressing his emotions differently to David, but neither of them quite has the language for it. So Patrick does it through song. It's a bigger leap for either of them than the "I love yous" that will follow later. Of course, Patrick doesn't massacre it, and it's a beautiful moment of romance between them. The fact that it's a man giving a serenade to another man, being emotionally vulnerable on screen, on TV is a beautiful and rare thing, another rare thing.

In TV terms, it's a wonderful piece of storytelling as they're across the room from one another the whole time—we never see them touch or show physical affection in this scene—yet it's one of the most romantic scenes in the series. Despite the importance of David and Patrick's physical affection as outlined previously, this for different reasons is equally powerful. In a much more traditional "romcom" way, Dan Levy's writing shows the power of romance isn't just in sex or physical affection. There is a deleted scene in which they kiss after Patrick sings, and fans have been hungry to see it, but Dan Levy refuses to release it. Levy is right to withhold this deleted scene; there is such power in the open mic night scene, and it's held in the distance between them. It's a scene about the unsaid or unsayable. At that moment, neither has the language for their emotions. So they find another way to say it. That they're falling in love at that moment across the room is a beautiful way to express it for two people who don't yet know how to be in love. We don't need a kiss to say that.

The Stumbling Block

Of course, it couldn't be that easy for two characters in a romantic TV arc. And as much as we as an audience want a happy ending for David and Patrick, for dramatic purposes they need some stumbling blocks. The encounter with Jake sets up their first stumbling block: Patrick's ex, Rachel. While Patrick gets annoyed at two of David's exes in a room, he also carefully skirts the issue of his exes. It comes crashing down when she turns up during Patrick's first official meeting with the Rose family at a barbecue. We discover the girl who came to town to get her fiancé back is Patrick's fiancé, and David is heartbroken. It's the first time Patrick is anything less than a perfect guy, and for a handful of episodes, it shifts what we think and, indeed, where this might be going.

While Patrick is the villain of Rachel's story, and we feel sorry for her, and Patrick's communication skills could use some work, we can't blame him. While there is a reading of "man secretly gay hurts woman," that's a damaging way to read Patrick's character and goes against the progressive nature of the show. The show's message would indicate we can feel empathy or sympathy for both of them while undoing some damaging past narratives. Are there women out there who might identify with Rachel? Of course, their hurt, if they were in a relationship with someone who turned out to be gay, is valid. But the important thing is that this is not their story. *Schitt's Creek* is not Rachel's story; it's David and Patrick's.

We have told too many queer stories from straight points of view, where the minor detail to straight audiences of perspective comes in. We don't see Rachel's point of view in the story because it's not about Rachel. Levy's storytelling is sympathetic to her and gives credit and respect to her as a woman while not making it about her. The subtleties are important. It's respectful and important to women's stories on TV that Rachel isn't just another "jealous woman" coming in to wreck a relationship. But that doesn't mean it's about her or that she's entirely in the right. Again, the subtitles of flawed characters are doing the work here.

Traditionally, the "gay back to straight" narrative rests on the queer person "seeing sense" or "doing the right thing," or it is a moment of trauma for them in which they are pulled back into their own life or a chasm opens between them and their new partner. In other narratives, this would have broken up David and Patrick. Instead, it helps to seal their relationship. While giving a realistic rift in them, we see Patrick as the person learning about his queerness and a healthy relationship. David is learning what a real relationship is, actually learning and growing from this. The shift comes when we see, rather than the woman "wronged" by it, the queer person (Patrick) healing from it. What we get with the door shutting on the chapter with Rachel is Patrick's journey to accepting his queerness fully.

The narratives around queer stories, particularly in American literature and TV/film, go one of two ways: a queer person dies or reverts to being straight. That was, for a time, the only way to "pass" a queer story. As explored elsewhere, the "bury your gays" trope has become depressingly familiar and a reason for the importance of the "happy ending" emphasis in *Schitt's Creek*. But another equally damaging trope is the queer person returning to being a straight trope. For example, the erasure of the queer identity is "just a phase" or "an experiment." Equally damaging are shown that emphasize the hurt of a straight character in the process of the queer person finding or demonizing the queer person for finding themselves.

The storyline is also honest: sometimes people get hurt when they discover their true identities. In a way, Patrick's hurt toward Rachel is the softest, kindest version of this scenario it could be. They are already broken up, there's been at least a little distance there, and while she still harbors hope, Patrick does nothing wrong. He doesn't cheat on her with a man; he hasn't led her along knowing he was gay. He broke up with her (several times) when it didn't work. Their mistakes are mutual and human—they got back together because it was easier, and, in a way, Patrick's being gay does Rachel a favor: it sets her free from holding onto a relationship that was never going to work.

The Best (Part 2)

While Patrick is continuing that journey, David ends up owing him an apology. It's a great bit of storytelling: while Patrick did hurt David, he ends up not the only one to blame. David handles the apology badly, and in fact, they go through a very silly but grown-up way of resolving things all at once. No blame is assigned in their love story, which makes it refreshing; they both make mistakes and make up for them differently.

The Rachel incident also brings out the best in their relationship, even at a low point. David is vulnerable with Patrick in ways he hasn't been with anyone, and Patrick does the same. Their conversation at the barbecue is one of their most open and honest. David is learning to be open, saying how hurt he is, that he feels like "damaged goods." Patrick, for his part, tells David all he's done for him and reveals how he feels about his sexuality for the first time. When we hear Patrick tell David, "You make me feel right," it's a sign he's here to stay, too—even if David can't see it. The parallel of Patrick running from Rachel all those years yet staying in front of David, imploring him to listen, is powerful too.

The way they make up—a little oddball, a little queer, and incredibly moving—is so uniquely them, but it also shows there are ways to make romantic gestures outside of the norm. David decides to lip sync "The Best." For Patrick, singing at the open mic was a way to express his commitment to their relationship, to show they were moving forward from dating to something more. David soon after uses it as an apology, as his olive branch ("The Olive Branch," season 4, episode 9). Anyone else would take Patrick's suggestion of taking him to dinner, return the favor of buying him gifts, or any of the usual approaches to an apology. David Rose is, of course, anything but usual. So instead, he lip syncs to Tina Turner. But his choice of olive branch also marks this relationship with Patrick as something different.

On the surface of it, the moment is funny and charming, a suitably quirky apology for the characters and the show. The scene becomes incredibly moving, both in the commitment to Levy's performance and giving David by default the true commitment to the moment (that Levy and Reid drank a bottle of prosecco at lunch before doing the scene is another story). On the one hand, the idea he's willing to risk making a slight fool of himself, coupled with the acknowledgment that the song means something to them now—it's become a shorthand of something between them—is undeniably incredibly romantic, in an unconventional way. Neither of them is good at saying what they feel directly, and David, particularly who has been so burned romantically, needs the song as a buffer to this. David's dance is him telling Patrick he's as all in as he put himself out there to be. Patrick says, "You know people can see you, right?" And David does, but he's willing to put that embarrassment aside to prove his feelings.

And Noah Reid's reaction—Patrick's reaction—to David's dance is to be amused, but also Reid plays the love that is now there. The arc from Patrick's first declaration with the song, through the rocky moment in between and the potential unraveling of their relationship, only to be cemented by this moment of real vulnerability from David, is incredibly moving. It's moving, too, because it shows the unconventional ways to be open and vulnerable in love. Those declarations can take all forms, as can romantic bravery. So, while yes, the act of the lip sync was brave, what it stands for, David committing to Patrick, and putting his feelings out there, is even more so.

The Anti-Romance

Of course, we also get the anti-romance of David's (and Patrick's) story. Refreshingly, there are few true roadblocks in their narrative, but we do have the fun stumbling blocks of Jake and later Ken in the narrative. Both of these serve other elements—depictions of sexuality in the show for a start—but also add to the feeling of this being a show for queer grown-ups who grew up without queer stories. In this, Jake's identity is important.

Jake is the other pansexual/sexually fluid character on the show. Jake is, as David puts it, "Everybody's ex and nobody's ex." While in an often-comedic way, he represents many of the preconceptions of pansexuality: that pansexual and non-monogamy, or sexual promiscuity, are synonymous. And while it is in some ways impressive that in a small town he manages to find quite so many exes, he is also an important (if comedic) facet of the show's representation. Jake is sexually fluid and non-monogamous, and the show presents his choices without judgment. The parallels of David and Jake are a nice subtle exploration and exposition of that: David's sexuality is accompanied by his insecurity around romantic relationships, a lack of confidence, and a need ultimately for Patrick to come along and prove to him long-term, settled relationships are possible.

Jake is effortlessly confident and seemingly content in his ongoing ever-fluid relationships. And when Patrick and David decide not to partake in that, the joke is very much on them and their lack of "adventurous spirit." In the same way, it was on David and his lack of inclination to form a "throuple" in an earlier encounter. The point remains that Jake's and David's takes on sexual fluidity are valid.

As an important aside, Jake and David aren't conveniently bisexual or pansexual for a storyline and forgotten about. In Jake's case, little has changed in three years when David and Patrick accept his invitation for a "drink." Meanwhile, David consistently mentions exes of both genders—or without reference to gender—across the series. One particularly lovely touch in reminding the audience of his pansexuality is when he mentions an ex-girlfriend during their tour of a wedding venue ("Smoke Signals," season 6, episode 1). It's a small thing, but for bi/pan viewers it's important; in marrying Patrick, he isn't erasing his pansexual identity, and there isn't a refusal to acknowledge his exes of both genders. In that respect, David's past is treated equally to Patrick's. Somewhat comedically, David replies, "We've all been with a bunch of other girls" to Patrick when he tries to defend that he hasn't just been with David ("Rock On!" season 5, episode 6). And that they've both been with women in their past isn't used to erase their sexuality; Patrick now views himself as gay ("Meet the Parents," season 5, episode 11), but David's sexuality remains unchanged even as he commits to Patrick.

The distinction is important. Patrick's sexuality is altered by his relationship with David, at least in how he understands it, talks about it, and labels it for himself. The show could have left it open-ended that Patrick falls for David while having dated women in the past. But they make a very clear distinction that those same-sex relationships are what feels "right" to him and that he labels himself as gay in coming out (as does David when talking about him, which indicates it's a discussion they've had at some point). Meanwhile, David could fall into the classic category of pan/bisexual people being labeled concerning their relationship. David doesn't become gay because he's in a long-term relationship with a man. His marriage to Patrick doesn't erase his attraction to all other genders. And for representation, for bi/pan people, that is of monumental importance.

The Proposal

Of course, we get an "I love you" from Patrick (first, of course), then David soon after. It's typically them as well, with Patrick slightly trolling his boyfriend, but also with David offering a heartfelt leap with his in return. Patrick teases him, slightly springing the revelation on him but knowing secretly that's the best way in. He teases him for his record of "once at a Mariah Carey concert" and lets him go to process it all. After a heart-to-heart with Ted, David realizes he needs to leap too and confesses his love to Patrick.

This sweet, quirky romance sees them through to the next milestone: Patrick's proposal. Again, it's delightfully quirky and unromantic on the surface, which makes it so rewarding. They spend the whole time bickering in the episode ("The Hike," season 5, episode 11). Patrick foolishly thought a hike was a good idea for distinctly indoorsy David, but it turns into one of the most romantic TV proposals written because it is very particular to David and Patrick. When they get to the top of the mountain—David having piggy-backed Patrick up the last bit—Patrick proposes with four gold rings. Dan Levy remembers thinking of that moment: "And I was in the middle of trying to fall asleep, and I thought to myself, *He gives David four rings. He gives David gold versions of the rings that he wears every day.* And I started weeping in my bed, alone, in the dark. It was very sad for me" (Meslow, November 13, 2019).

It's emotional because it is a person truly seeing another person, truly knowing them. That is more romantic than any grand gesture. As Levy continues, it's "the idea that Patrick would be so in tune with David, and study him, and care about him, and know so much about him" (Meslow, November 13, 2019).

Context, too, is key; these are two slightly damaged people (David maybe more so than Patrick) who have figured out something—and someone—which makes it work. Patrick truly sees David, as Moira says to him early on, and as much as David protests, then "hopefully not all that I am," it's actually the seeing all that he is that is the romantic thing.

And they're imperfect in that they frequently misunderstand each other as couples do, or bicker as couples do (bickering arguably being their love language too). Even their "perfect" moments are imperfect. Patrick's proposal is indicative of that—he's planned it to the letter and yet it goes wrong, because a hike is not David's idea of a fun day out. So while they bicker and sulk at respective intervals, it also becomes the perfect day and moment. David manages to look after Patrick when he needs it (after stepping on a thorn) and Patrick turns around David's huff at hiking, at being forced out of his comfort zone with a heartfelt speech. In fact, it's a perfect metaphor for their relationship: Patrick forces David out of his comfort zone and offers safety and love, and David steps up and steps in and looks after Patrick when he needs it. And both in the process will get things wrong but it ends with love and respect for one another.

We focus on David at this moment—he's, after all, gone from "damaged goods" to saying yes to a marriage proposal—and his happiness is important. But what Patrick says at that moment is incredibly powerful for any queer person. Patrick talks about walking this route while trying to figure out his feelings for David, then says, "This just felt like the perfect place to ask you to marry me." It's a moment filled with such hope as a queer storyline that you can go from not knowing who you are to being in love. You can hide things from your family but also move on to ask someone to marry you. Almost every queer person has had a version of Patrick's walks, doubting, wondering, and being scared, so the bookend of it actually all working out, and being okay, is important.

You Are My Happy Ending

The wedding is a hugely important moment in narrative and TV terms. For the latter, any happy ending for queer characters is still something to be celebrated. It was also significant that it was without drama or real risk for the characters. Tumultuous and traumatic stories usually define queer characters; to have the most drama be a rained-out wedding is a relief. That David sits up and asks, "Is Patrick dead?" on his wedding day is a nod to that from Levy, that we can't possibly have got this far and everything is okay, that we are tragically used to tragedy for queer characters. Of course, Patrick isn't dead, all is well, and they get married in the town hall of the place they fell in love and call home.

It's a beautifully simple ending to their story. It's also one that is so very them. Patrick quietly takes charge when things go wrong, making everything "right" for David. While David quietly freaks out but not in the way he used to, he's quietly certain of Patrick—and ultimately, all is well. The whole town turns out to celebrate David and Patrick's day, with the Jazzagals singing them down the aisle to their song. More importantly, though, it's a celebration of family, old and new. Patrick's mom and dad are with him at his wedding—his dad is his best man—showing they are embracing their son's happiness.

Meanwhile, Stevie, as David's maid of honor, walks down the aisle on Johnny's arm and then stands with her best friend. The Roses are suitably chaotic, with Alexis buying a wedding dress to walk David down the aisle (a lovely nod to the town sign declaring "it's his sister"). While, of course, Moira makes an entrance in her pope attire.

However, their heartfelt vows stick out, which are perfectly them but also show how much they've grown. As quiet and straightforward as he is, Patrick sings his vows. It's a counterpoint to the relationship and wedding with Rachel that could never be; he's now so assured and proud of his love that he can sing it from the rooftops. It is a throwback to several key beats in their relationship; he says David knows he'd climb a thousand mountains for him, a reference to their proposal spot, and his singing is a reference to what feels like the first "I love you" at the open mic night. Of course, Patrick sings "Always Be My Baby" by Mariah Carey, who is the only other person outside his parents David ever said "I love you" to. Patrick is straightforward as a man; he's not given to flowery declarations, so saying it through the song again works for him; it's a way to say it in the most heartfelt way.

David, meanwhile, talks a lot but struggles to say what's in his heart, so it feels significant that he does say it at this point, not only to Patrick, who, despite knowing that David loves him, may have never heard the words out loud in this way. David's speech is important because he says it to Patrick, his family, and the whole town. The scared, anxious young man who was "damaged goods" can finally stand up and say how he feels. His words are important too: "I've never liked a smile as much as I like yours; I've never felt as safe as I do when I'm with you. I've never known love like I have when we're together."

David is acknowledging his past, insecurities, and heartbreaks, and he's marking this as a moment to go forward. Even in his "I love you," he's rarely been able to acknowledge what Patrick means to him. David declaring it again, this time in front of the whole town—the town that has taken him in and offered him a safe space to be truly himself—feels like an important declaration to them as much as Patrick.

David Rose and Finding Himself in Love

David's sexuality plays into the show's broader commentary about looking to the inside, not the outside, and about accepting everyone. But it also takes TV expectations and turns them on its head. It's right in the wider TV history element that David married a man, but it's a testament to his character that in an alternative timeline he may have married a woman and that is also an equally significant and plausible option. Important, too, is that David's pansexuality is never an issue between him and Patrick. Many narratives involving bisexual and pansexual characters contain some elements of suspicion from their dates/partners or jealousy. Dan Levy's narrative for David is consciously avoiding that; it's never interrogated on screen between them. But also, it might imply that David is the person to help Patrick negotiate who he is because of the difficulties and prejudices he might have encountered. Likewise, as someone attracted to all genders, he's in a position to help Patrick work out, when he's ready, where his labels, preferences, and everything else might lay. Given that David doesn't care how someone identifies in terms of gender, it's not a leap to also consider him accepting the labels his partner does and doesn't choose to adopt (we hear Patrick described as gay by his parents, but he never uses a label directly himself). Indeed, David himself never uses "pansexual" to describe himself either, showing that the idea of "the wine, not the label" is fairly universal—it doesn't matter to David how he's labeled more who he is with.

Beyond that, David is a sensitive, sweet, and ultimately vulnerable queer character who isn't a caricature and isn't defined by his sexuality. For Dan Levy, playing David was a cathartic experience; writing what he didn't have in terms of queer characters, he says David and his unfiltered way of being made him "bolder in terms of owning my feelings" (Picardi, September 17, 2019).

Creating David was then, for Levy, a rewarding one personally and for what he could do as a character and for audiences. He went on a huge journey as a character, as Levy told *Variety* in 2020: "I feel like David is an incredibly protected person—I think you see it in the way that he dresses, you see it in the way he speaks, you see it in the way he operates; he's a very closed-off human. And it was important for me that we get let into the inner workings of his mind and how and why he is the way he is" (Turchiano, January 14, 2020).

But above all, David's journey with his relationship and its impact on him as a person was the main takeaway from the show. He went from a socially awkward, afraid of intimacy, and self-sabotaging man to someone able to accept and feel comfortable in love and being loved. David's story isn't a story of love fixing everything; moreover, one of the powers of love. The fact Patrick loves him doesn't make the business a success or even their relationship a success; both take work. But the safety and security of Patrick's love allow him to step up, step into it, and grow up too. He was not growing up in the sense of not being a grown-up without a relationship, but more growing into himself and who he was capable of being, all while showing him he was worthy of being loved. That's a lovely arc for a protagonist. It balances his growth, change, and people's power to change a person's life. He goes from not feeling worthy to being fully loved.

David's arc is important for many queer viewers who have perhaps felt unworthy of love for simply being who they are. For not having "Davids" on TV who get to love out loud and get their happy ending. The adage "you can't be what you can't see" applies here, and David is important for giving viewers precisely that: someone like them to show they can have it too.

You're My Happy Ending

It's also important that the final episode felt like a celebration—it centers on David and Patrick's wedding, and it feels like a true celebration. Unlike many TV weddings, there is little drama around their wedding. There is *drama* in the sense it's David Rose's wedding, but there is never any danger it will go wrong. The biggest obstacle to them getting married is rain (which feels like a 1990s Alanis Morrissette call-back), but the audience never doubts that they will make it down the aisle and have their happy ending. Instead, the episode becomes a celebration of their love, the love of their family—of all kinds—and the love of the town.

The only other moment of jeopardy becomes one of both high comedy and curiously touching in a way only *Schitt's Creek* can do. When David gets a wedding day massage that ends in a "happy ending" of the other sort, it's both ridiculous and utterly on brand. The sweet twist comes in that Patrick gets over it; there's no sense that this will derail their relationship or their wedding because their relationship is built on stronger foundations than that. Their wedding is one final, subtle lesson in both the person who makes you feel "right" and it sometimes does work out through a typically left-field example. It's subtly progressive and wonderfully queer, too, disrupting just enough heteronormative ideas of a wedding day with a happy ending from a masseuse just going to be a "really weird story one day" rather than relationship-ending drama.

Giving David his own "happy ending" was a form of catharsis. "I wanted him to live in that safe space where he can let his guard down and be vulnerable and be loving and warm," Levy says. But even though he hasn't found his relationship version of a happy ending, he's found fulfillment that very well may open himself up to whatever the future brings. "When I was developing David as a character, I thought back to a time in my life that I've long since moved past in terms of personal growth and self-worth. We had a shared world—a past where you give yourself away to people and overlook your own needs to keep others in the mix" (Dresden, February 12, 2018).

The important thing about their relationship is that it is treated with the same kind of ease as straight romances have been treated with on TV for decades. It feels subversive and rebellious and, well, very queer because it is. To have it so uneventfully peacefully queer feels like a true rebellion against the plethora of gay love stories rooted in death, sadness, trauma, or abuse. The push-back of a happy story of two men falling in love without fear is so simple and rebelliously queer. Because the community is so deprived of seeing themselves happy onscreen, it's a real rebellion to have a happy ending instead of always seeing queer love as a gateway to trauma.

The show takes those big romantic gestures—like the proposal Patrick is planning when he complains of David's ridiculous standards—and makes them an offbeat version of the romcom ideal. Patrick's proposal is a perfect example of that; we expect an organized, sure-of-himself Patrick to do something well-executed and pitch-perfect. Instead, he misreads his boyfriend's willingness to try new things and gets a stick stuck in his foot. It's ultimately charming and romantic and a lovely play on the big *Notting Hill*–like gestures of a perfect romance.

The Politics of a Happy Ending

14

On the surface, *Schitt's Creek* is not a political show. Certainly, it doesn't engage with real-world politics. Given the era it is in (2015–2020), that's probably for the best as trying to commentate on a tumultuous era everyone was still focused on living through would have been touchy. It also doesn't take the approach of some sitcoms (and dramas) and attempt to make current references incorporating politics. Nothing dates a show faster than a "witty political comment" that has lost context before the show airs. However, even in 2020, when it aired, if you choose to include queer narratives in the show, by existing, you become political. It's a sad indictment of the wider state of television and the world, but it's also true. And so, really, by default, the show became political. But by a strange quirk of how such things play out, the refusal within the show to be political made the show all the more activist just by existing.

Pushing Back against Discrimination

It's important that the final episode felt like a celebration. Unlike many TV weddings, there is little drama around David and Patrick's wedding. There is *drama* in the sense that it's David Rose's wedding, but there is never any danger it will go wrong. And the audience never doubts that they will make it down the aisle and have their happy ending. Instead, the episode becomes a celebration of their love, the love of their family—of all kinds—and the love of the town. The wedding itself is a moment of pure joy but also a political moment, a statement of queer defiance in joy. The whole town turns out to celebrate David and Patrick's day. Singing them down the aisle to "their song" cements the idea of a blissful queer utopia where prejudice doesn't exist.

Schitt's Creek was able to exist and further push the way TV tells queer stories because of all that went before it, and existing and pushing those boundaries is a part of paving the way for what comes next.

What is further needed, however, is the need to reframe romcom storylines for queer audiences. The queer life experience is different; queer cultural experience is different. That's also what "queering" means: to disrupt, reframe, challenge, and question how it's always been done.

Why is this important in TV terms, and why is what Levy did important?

What it feels like *Schitt's Creek* is doing, then, is a combination of righting some wrongs and offering something that has been missing. It seems still surprising to millennials of Dan Levy's age that a sweet, gay narrative can exist where being gay isn't the punchline and nobody dies. While it is (thankfully) no longer the only show with a positive representation of queer characters, it is not the kind of show Levy's generation grew up with. Levy takes what he set out to do—show a gay relationship on par with all straight ones—very seriously. His challenging of networks, possibly to the detriment of what his network considers good public relations, shows a commitment. It also shows that not just the content of the show but how it is talked about is important.

An important note in this trajectory of gay stories—on TV and beyond—is the kind of "interrupted history," particularly for gay men's stories due to AIDS-era storytelling. AIDS unavoidably and tragically diverted queer storytelling. Suddenly, for over a decade, all the storytelling around gay men got channeled into AIDS stories. And this was vital in many ways: AIDS stories were a form of activism and memorial, and they were vital in raising awareness and the collective grief that ran through the community. It's also not a huge leap to see the moral associations made by such approaches. But equally, political reclaiming is happening in the post-AIDS narratives that offer a happy ending. And the idea of happy endings in gay stories is also a political undoing of wider moralizing of gay love (and by default sex) stories. So, while *Schitt's Creek* isn't necessarily trying to be a post-AIDS reclaiming romantic and sexual stories for gay men in being part of that wider canon of gay stories, it is, and that's important.

It also feels very post AIDS, a marker of moving on and healing, that Patrick and David exist in a narrative where HIV doesn't have to be discussed. For a while, in any gay narrative, that felt like a conversation any characters had to have at some point. And in part, this fits the "anywhere nowhere" and "town without prejudice." It's okay that the show doesn't address HIV/AIDS because the world of the show sits just enough outside the real world to do that. And while, yes, HIV is a continued important issue, and one that the gay community does need to have conversations about, it's refreshing that not every conversation, every story, has to incorporate that now. We can have stories about love (and sex) and not tie them to AIDS/HIV.

In that light, the story of David and Patrick becomes important because they're a romantic pairing but also a sexual one. And while *Schitt's Creek* is not an overly sexualized show, the characters are fully sexual beings—of course, if we encounter Alexis talking about her sexual relationships or see David with a female partner in Stevie, then Patrick and David must talk about sex too and are seen as sexual beings. But in a post-AIDS drama, there is still a political element in any gay men having sex. That David and Patrick have a (from what we know) healthy, well-adjusted sex life is important. Also, slightly political in this context is their sex life being open, at least to being outside the bounds of heteronormativity. While they aren't Jake and his suggestion of a "throuple" in earlier seasons with Stevie and David, they discuss non-monogamy in various ways. David suggests Patrick goes on a date with a guy who hits on him, and while Patrick declines, that door is left somewhat open. They also discuss and go some way to have drinks with Jake and open up their sex life to non-monogamous encounters. And finally, on their wedding day, the masseuse gives David the other kind of happy ending; the sexual element there is treated separately from their romantic love and isn't a deal breaker—it's barely an issue.

Beyond the related way of looking at content, it's also an important re-steering of narratives for audiences and creatives. For thirty-something queer people, AIDS was, as children, this scary monster under the bed. And as they grew up, it became a marker of the "bad things" that happened to queer people; there's a certain amount of internalizing that fear and shame that comes with those narratives being the first cultural exposure to "what gay men are like." Consciously or subconsciously, that has impacted a generation through culture. Out of those ashes, the writing of, and the need for, a counterpoint, a set of gay happy endings, isn't surprising. And again, consciously or not, *Schitt's Creek* fits that cultural shift and reclaiming for its creator and audience of the same age. For older millennials of Levy's age, growing up in the 1980s and 1990s, the dominant narrative around being gay was AIDS, from adverts on TV to all the stories about gay men—both in press and fiction—centered on AIDS and death. And while the writing of *Schitt's Creek* might not be a direct response to that, it is part of a wider cultural need from that generation to reclaim happy gay stories, not just from AIDS but from wider history.

Adding to the homophobia encountered directly or indirectly, it's easy to see why this happy ending has become so important to queer audiences. There's a speech in Larry Kramer's play *The Normal Heart* which begins "I belong to a culture" which goes on to list gay men who have impacted culture: Walt Whitman, Herman Melville, Tennessee Williams, Byron, E. M. Forster, Lorca, Auden, and so on—itself a call-back to Oscar Wilde's speech at his indecency trial, which comments on "great works of art like those of Shakespeare and Michelangelo," among other references. Both are about the debt of those who went before and a hidden culture being made visible. There is a through line of queer culture that becomes interconnected in its hidden histories and struggles. And *Schitt's Creek* is part of that through line. But it also provides another step along that long path so that people might continue to say, "I belong to a culture," but that culture is no longer hidden.

In centering, as part of its final season in particular, a gay relationship as the show's central or endgame relationship was, in TV terms, still a bold move in 2018/2019. It was bolder, somehow more "activist" in that it chose not to make a "statement" out of it.

Schitt's Creek was a vital moment in TV history, being a romantic-comedy-drama that ended with a gay wedding. It's a great moment in Canadian TV history and broader TV history. It has been a long road for LGBTQ+ representation on TV, one far from over or won, and one that owes a debt across TV and queer culture.

This cracking open into the mainstream came with a sense of responsibility and an opportunity to do more beyond the show. The cast, led by the example of Levy, embraced activism in various ways. There was activism innate in promoting in talking about the show, but many involved also used the platform and message of the show to take that beyond the show. For Levy, in particular, being a force for good is something he has embraced and taken beyond the show itself in an almost meta "lead by example" moment.

Promoting a Happy Ending

Outside the town of Schitt's Creek itself, the act of talking freely on mainstream TV platforms about a queer TV show and talking about a gay relationship still feels radical. Networks know they'll get complaints; if you look at interviews closely, some avoid engaging with queerness in their questions. This is perhaps subtle, yet it's still there and insidious; the fact that many still avert their eyes from queerness shows there is still a way to go.

In promoting the work, Levy has become an activist: on every talk show that allowed them to promote the show, and every time he was able to mention being gay (which, in watching over the years, you can see him clearly make a conscious effort to do), he is an activist in talking about the inclusive themes of the show. It seems like nothing to straight audiences (of the non-bigoted kind). He's promoting a show. But to have a show with promotional images of two men kissing looks like a piece of activist art from the 1980s or 1990s.

Let's not pretend either that being queer isn't a risk still to career and beyond in terms of discrimination, thwarted career options, and other forms of outright abuse. As an artist, no doubt Levy has struggled to get queer stories heard by powers that be. As an actor, in being "out," he risks having limited roles passed his way. This feels like something from the 1970s or earlier but remains an ingrained part of the Hollywood machine today. As a queer person in the public eye, he no doubt deals with all manner of homophobic abuse at various points, both online and in person. One could hope he escapes the worst forms of it, but such abuse remains insidiously present.

So yes, even from someone beginning at a point of relative privilege, Levy making queer art is a form of activism. That his chosen form is writing and TV also doesn't make it less revolutionary or even activist either. As noted earlier, most people in their thirties and older remember the first "gay [insert activity here]" on TV. This was also the days before streaming services and prolific broadband, and all of these were viewed on TV late at night or smuggled in on VHS and DVDs away from roommates or parents, because on mainstream TV, there were very few queer people. And, as we have seen, even in these "gay series," things as seemingly simple as a happy ending for the characters are lacking. So Levy's happy ending becomes truly poignant for that reason.

The show has illustrated that championing LGBTQ+ causes isn't only the responsibility of LGBTQ+ creatives. How the cast talks about equality when promoting the show indicates what they've learned about allyship. Annie Murphy talks about sibling allyship in the context of the sibling relationship: "David's sexuality is so far from her mind at all times" (*The Advocate*, 2021) and she "wants him to be happy." Catherine O'Hara talks about how she "loved how they handled Patrick's character" and his coming out along with the show being a "world I want to live in" for its equality (*Gay Times*, 2021). And Noah Reid talking about playing Patrick and that "I never felt the need to play Patrick a certain way based on his sexuality—I sort of approached him as if he were me and he was attracted to somebody" (*Irish Independent*, 2021). These are all small but cumulatively important acts of allyship. Noah Reid will likely be asked about Patrick for the rest of his career, and that he talks of the character fondly, intelligently, and with compassion and support for the LGBTQ+ community is a vital piece of allyship.

There is an innate sense of activism around the show. In the most basic sense, this is apparent every time any cast or crew, particularly Dan and Eugene Levy, spoke about the show and foregrounded its acceptance of gay relationships. The emphasis Eugene puts on his acceptance of Dan's sexuality in interviews and Dan on his father's acceptance of him was an act of activism, particularly against an increasingly right-wing backdrop in the United States (the show began during Obama's presidency and ended during the fourth year of Trump's presidency, after all, while their native Canada remained more left-wing).

Outside the show itself, talking about it is an act of activism. In 2020, going on a talk show to promote a TV show shouldn't be an act of activism, but it still is. To go on mainstream (particularly some North American) TV platforms with a "gay" TV show talking about a gay relationship is still a radical idea. Again, it's perhaps a subtle thing that queer viewers pick up on: avoiding the direct question and avoiding naming the thing. But it's there, and it's insidious in some sectors.

The show developed a strong relationship with various supportive press platforms. *Entertainment Weekly* is one of these. The show was regularly promoted in online and print publications. And being a huge platform with incredible reach and a certain amount of cultural clout, this was important. For the show's final season, *Entertainment Weekly* ran several interviews and articles, most focusing on David and Patrick's story. This feels incredibly supportive, progressive, and "activist." The pinnacle was their "digital covers" to accompany the end of the series and the associated interview series. Noah Reid and Dan Levy re-created scenes from classic romcoms as the cover shoot for this digital issue. They did a version of *Sixteen Candles*, *Notting Hill*, and *Casablanca*. What they did on the cover of *Entertainment Weekly* was queer the romcom.

This photoshoot, which resulted in three covers reenacting romcoms and several video interviews with Reid and Levy for the magazine's YouTube channel, is important for several reasons. First, *Entertainment Weekly* putting the show on the cover was a marker of its success. For decades, the publication has been the leading entertainment magazine in North America and is considered a marker of quality in the shows it endorses. As a publication, *Entertainment Weekly* historically supports LGBTQ+ performers and culture. Its Pride covers are ahead of the curve in terms of the American press, and they have long offered interviews and platforms to LGBTQ+ performers and celebrities. But this cover series and accompanying interview felt like they cemented *Schitt's Creek*'s place in cultural history and did it in a fully queer style. They're also an incredibly beautiful set of covers/images—the *Casablanca* shoot, in particular, gives a true air of old-school Hollywood to Levy and Reid. But the beautiful romantic and fully gay photoshoot for a huge mainstream magazine feels very much like the stuff of younger Levy's dreams, particularly in that it lets him queer the romcoms that he loves and in that it feels like final punctuation in the activism talking about the show in the press performed.

In those interviews, the pair talked about the impact of the show's ending and the power of showing David and Patrick's story: "I think the way that we've handled sexuality on the show has been incredibly nonchalant, and that's been very deliberate so not to make the queer storylines stand out in any way because we don't want them to," says Levy. "We want them to be presented with the same kind of casual ease that we present straight storylines." Reid adds that, "There aren't a lot of examples of same-sex relationships on television that are treated just like any relationship would be treated. I know that's something that Dan and our whole writing team have been really [cognizant of]. These guys are just like anybody would be in a couple, and that's how it absolutely should be represented on television. It feels like it's really hitting home with a lot of people who don't feel like they've seen that represented on screens a lot" (*Entertainment Weekly*, April 9, 2020).

On the same day that Levy/Reid did the *Entertainment Weekly* shoot, they also visited a special billboard in downtown Los Angeles. And this was perhaps Levy's most personal piece of activist action in promoting his show. The final season's promotional images and video promos saw the Rose family, Stevie, and Patrick dressed in formalwear in front of the Rosebud Motel. Among the fairly standard set of pictures of the Roses in their glamorous attire outside the motel was an image of David and Patrick kissing. Combined with the previous, this was filled with activist elements just by existing. But Levy (and the network) had bigger plans. The Patrick/David image was used for a series of large billboards. This included one on Sunset Boulevard. Levy wrote on Twitter, "Fuck yes, we did. Shine bright, friends. Very grateful for Pop TV and CBC and their support on this campaign that my teenage self would never have dreamed of being true" (December 18, 2019). That in itself shows the activist angle to this: Levy giving his younger self what he needed to see—visible queer stories and queer love stories; also important was Noah Reid's vocal support of the billboards, stating on Instagram that he was "proud to be part of this moment" (Instagram, December 19, 2019).

The only usual gay posters seen around Los Angeles or any other big city are sexual health ones, which perhaps link back to where the show sits in creating new narratives around gay relationships. Most importantly, though, unapologetically putting the show's gay characters as prominently as possible was an important statement. Levy was quick to praise the networks for getting behind them, which was also important. The show's official Twitter sent out some of the billboards' exact addresses, encouraging fans to take a selfie with it and tag them. And hundreds of fans did, often taking selfies of them kissing their partner too. And while, yes, it was a brilliant marketing campaign, what a wonderful opportunity it provided for today's teenagers. And it was also an opportunity for people like Levy, who didn't have that kind of representation as a teenager, to be able to take that selfie now. That is as activist as the billboard annoying homophobes as they drive by.

Throw into this mix that Levy was promoting this show with his dad; Eugene Levy sat next to Dan on talk shows, accepted awards alongside him, and talked about the gay love story at the end of their show. Eugene Levy was a role model for all the dads of queer people, showing them this could be done. That familial vocal support on a public stage was possible and admirable. These have fed the wider conversations the show has helped produce. So in seeing someone like them—whether you are Eugene as the father or Dan as the son—seeing their easy acceptance can change things. Among the questions they were regularly asked was about Dan's own coming out. And while there is an argument for not forcing queer creatives to use their history and trauma when talking about their work, there is also importance to give queer creatives a platform to do so. In this case, the power of a supportive parent, a man in his seventies, being able to show what supportive parenting of a queer child looked like was a political move.

Eugene, who hasn't been overly political his whole career, quietly takes a standby position in being part of that conversation. Eugene and Dan Levy have always talked about their relationship. Still, in virtually every interview together, Dan talks about his parent's acceptance of him as a gay man—a subtle and important element of the politics and activism of the show. The show's message of "lead by example" extends to its creators. While it's no secret, and Levy is very much "out," there is a kind of activist, political side to people like Levy who choose to be actively out. Some actors who have come out—of which there are still too few who are comfortable enough to do so—rarely comment on that part of their lives unless pressured to do so. And that is their prerogative, just like any other area of their lives. But some take their being out and in the public eye as an opportunity to raise visibility. And that kind of visibility is vitally important.

If visibility is key to the show's activism, then the icing on that cake came with the show's Emmy wins in 2020 and another gesture like the billboard. On the night of the Emmy awards, the CN Tower in Toronto lit up gold in honor of the eleven Emmy wins the show brought home. In a fitting parallel to their selfies in front of the billboard, Levy and Reid took selfies in front of the hometown landmark, celebrating this little Canadian show that put a gay story at its heart—it was celebratory, as much as an activist. But things can be both. And in wondering why the CN Tower was gold that night, maybe some other people also opened their minds based on the show.

The ripples continued beyond the show, with the impact of the show being felt long after it ended. This became apparent in one particularly moving interview with the UK TV show *This Morning* in 2021. In what was Dan Levy's first UK TV appearance, he was interviewed by Philip Scofield. The presenter—a staple of UK TV for over three decades—made headlines in 2019 when he came out as gay. In the interview with Levy, Scofield spoke movingly about what the show meant to him. *Schitt's Creek* being part of that bigger cultural conversation has been hugely important in those shifts. And Levy, as an out and proud queer creator, is intrinsic for those shifts.

Even in 2020, choosing to include queer narratives in a show made the show political. It's a sad indictment of the broader state of television and the world, but it's also true. By default, the show became political in its existence, even in its gentle way; the refusal within the show to be political made it all the more activist just by existing, simply as it was always meant to be.

Gay Actors and Gay Roles?

The issue of "gay actors for gay roles" is an ongoing subject of debate in telling queer stories on screen and stage. With Patrick's coming out storyline and David and Patrick's romance being posited as a huge milestone in queer screen representation, it seems an inescapable discussion to have in relation to *Schitt's Creek* given that while Dan Levy is gay, Noah Reid is straight and conversations about whether straight actors should play gay roles still divides the LGBTQ+ community. *Schitt's Creek* casting Noah Reid, a straight actor, as one of its key queer characters naturally enters into the debate. The key arguments around queer actors for queer roles center on two main elements: the ability to authentically depict queer experience and a "reclaiming" of queer history and culture through a "stories for and by us" approach. While there are certainly instances where a lived experience as a queer person would inform a character's portrayal, there are times when it would be vital (the casting of trans characters in trans roles being an example of this). We can also see reasons why Reid's portrayal of Patrick works, in part because he's a straight man.

Schitt's Creek sits outside of these parameters in some ways. The "town without prejudice" element and how we view gay characters may challenge this external factor. Parking Reid for a moment, let's consider the other two canonically queer characters in the show: David and Ronnie. In the case of Ronnie, she is almost "incidentally" queer. It's not a factor in her character beyond two direct references. And while she is coded as a queer butch woman, none of this influences her character and storylines. In terms of the character, there is nuance to be played with; at the start of the arc, we don't know how Patrick identifies, and the inference is that perhaps neither does he. He might be "very sure of himself," as David puts it on their first meeting, but in terms of sexuality, the very point seems to be that, at this point, he is not. He discovers this through his chemistry and relationship with David.

There is something to be said for casting a non-queer actor in Patrick's role. If we are following the argument of actors bringing personal experience to the role that is used *for* only casting gay actors in gay roles, then Reid, having lived his life as a straight man, brings that to Patrick's experience. As a straight man, he then plays Patrick's wrestling with his feelings for David and, ultimately, the shift in his life because he has that in mind. And if we're taking the literal route there, this too is important, as that would not necessarily be the experience of a queer actor. It's an imperfect science because it is extremely relative to each character and each performer. Levy, for example, makes David's pansexual past believable despite personally identifying as a gay man; there's enough queer crossover in experience to make that authentic, even if he doesn't have the lived experience others might demand.

This is also a debate about lost stories and a chance to tell stories from the community affected. Historically, the only way to get a high-profile queer story in mainstream media was to put a high-profile actor in it. But because to be a high-profile actor, many had to stay in the closet, we get a catch-22 of queerness. There are no queer movies with high-profile actors and no queer high-profile actors, because there's no representation (and other complex factors). Wrapped up in this is a sense of appropriation: straight actors are getting acclaim for "bravery" in playing queer roles. This was the case with examples like Tom Hanks in *Philadelphia* (1993), where he was praised for his bravery in playing a gay man with AIDS. There are also moments where there is a clear line: Eddie Redmayne should not have played a trans character in *The Danish Girl* as it crossed a line of appropriation and fuels the idea that trans women are "men in dresses." For each of these examples, there are perhaps grayer areas: Colin Firth in Mama Mia, where the gayness of the character isn't a central plot, for example, might not feel as inappropriate as, say, Andrew Garfield playing an iconic queer role as Prior Walter onstage. Firth's respect for being separate from the character differs from Garfield's declaring he "watched a lot of *Drag Race*" to get into character, and it upset the community, too. Context and tone are important in what is not a black-and-white debate.

In the case of Reid, it is more nuanced. He isn't a famous actor doing it for "gay points." His character, too, is nuanced: Patrick's sexuality is complex, as explored in earlier chapters; he is straight presenting and even assumes himself straight when we meet him. The other side of the gay actors for gay roles debate is that there are limited opportunities for gay actors to portray themselves on screen, and that's one where, yes, we must concede that it may have been better to, in what would become an iconic gay romance, have given that role to a gay actor. However, in a complex world where nothing is clear cut, we can also concede that Reid, a straight man, played the role with respect and nuance and, beyond the show, acted in a clear sense of allyship and LGBTQ+ support.

That Reid wasn't famous helped, in part, the power of Patrick's character and Reid's performance; it is likely most of the audience had no preconceptions of him as an actor or about his personal life. This also feels like an important side of the debate. When Patrick Brewer/Noah Reid first shows up in Schitt's Creek the town and *Schitt's Creek* show, nobody knows anything about him. This is ideal for the character. And while in the internet age, finding out about Reid's life probably didn't take fans very long after his first appearance, pre-*Schitt's Creek*, he didn't have the profile that meant he came with a lot of public domain knowledge about his life. The average viewer also wouldn't have known the actor's sexuality, and that in an ideal world is what we should strive for: a kind of *Schitt's Creek* attitude where it doesn't matter because we've reached a plateau of opportunity and acceptance. This is another nuanced factor whether a queer team is leading a show (or film or play). There is a huge difference between a heterosexual director, showrunner, or producing team making these casting decisions and a queer person/team doing that. Given that Dan Levy had (presumably) the final say in Reid's casting, based both on the need for chemistry with him as his love interest and from a strategic point of view as the showrunner and creator. As a gay man, there is a certain element of respecting his decision regardless of people's stance on this issue. This goes for both his decision as the person in charge of the show and his personal decision as a gay man having the power to make these decisions. It is a decision that comes with weight, and we should also be asking about the impact of the emotional labor on our queer creatives. While it's not a debate that has raged around *Schitt's Creek*, particularly in challenging any non-queer actors in queer roles, we also put the weight of that debate on the queer actors, writers, and showrunners when we constantly ask their opinions on it. They, no doubt, feel the weight of the decisions and the judgment around them.

It's a difficult conversation to reflect on when you cannot imagine an actor doing a better job. When the human behind the role has also been unquestioningly, unflinchingly an ally, it comes down to a personal decision by showrunners, especially if those showrunners like Levy are the queer people whose stories they are trying to tell. That's not to say the difficult conversations shouldn't be had for those showrunners, viewers, and actors.

The show has illustrated that championing LGBTQ+ causes isn't only the responsibility of LGBTQ+ creatives. How the cast talks about equality when promoting the show indicates what they've learned about allyship. Annie Murphy talks about sibling allyship in the context of the sibling relationship: "David's sexuality is so far from her mind at all times" (*The Advocate*, 2021) and she "wants him to be happy." Catherine O'Hara talks about how she "loved how they handled Patrick's character" and his coming out along with the show being a "world I want to live in" for its equality (*Gay Times*, 2021). And Noah Reid talking about playing Patrick and that "I never felt the need to play Patrick a certain way based on his sexuality—I sort of approached him as if he were me and he was attracted to somebody" (*Irish Independent*, 2021). These are all small but cumulatively important acts of allyship. Noah Reid will likely be asked about Patrick for the rest of his career, and that he talks of the character fondly, intelligently, and with compassion and support for the LGBTQ+ community is a vital piece of allyship.

15

Lead by Example: Dan Levy and Personal Activism

When cast and creators of a show, especially a popular show, engage in activism, it provides a platform for the issues they highlight. Some actors choose to champion LGBTQ+ charities as patrons, as Ian McKellen has famously done for thirty years as part of his involvement with Stonewall, or like actors requesting birthday fundraisers donate to funds like The Trevor Project. As for *Schitt's Creek*, creator Dan Levy has used his platform to promote the show in various ways. This has included mentioning his sexuality in most interviews, a simple but powerfully political act that supports other actors, creators, and, crucially, audiences in being open and accepting about their sexuality. He also engaged the wider cast and crew in visible activism, attending events such as the GLAAD awards and marching in Pride parades. This kind of visible activism beyond the show is something many actors/creators now lean into. It is important for queer audiences to feel like those who create stories about them also support the community in real-world terms. *Schitt's Creek* managed to become a uniting of the political angle of the show and creator, promoting the support of queer people around the world and numerous similarly themed charitable causes from fans.

Activism beyond the Show

The platform *Schitt's Creek* gave Levy has allowed him to integrate broader activism into his work and life. Stepping beyond the obvious LGBTQ+ rights elements of the show, the cast and creatives are highly politicized, which has spun out into fan activism (as explored in the next chapter). So from elements such as speaking out against racism in the industry from head makeup artist Lucky Bromhead to localized activism around Toronto

Catherine O'Hara speaks on a panel with actors Dan Levy, Eugene Levy, Annie Murphy, Emily Hampshire, and Noah Reid during Schitt's Creek Live *at the theatre at the Ace Hotel, September 23, 2018, in Los Angeles, California.*
Credit: Patrick Fallon/ZUMA Wire/Alamy Live News

homelessness from Noah Reid to (fittingly) animal rights activism from Dustin Milligan, the activism linked to the show runs a broader spectrum than just a gay show talking about gay rights. The timing of the end of the show during worldwide lockdowns also turned much of the "publicity tours" into fundraisers for various charities will also be discussed here—few if any shows have turned their "victory lap" into a focus on "good causes" alongside award wins.

As one of the many facets of activism associated with the show, the cast has attended Pride marches. In 2018 they were invited to march in Toronto Pride 2018; this was important for many reasons. This visibility of queerness for Levy and the others at LGBTQ+ events, especially Pride, cannot be underestimated. In the video for New York Pride 2020, he talks about hearing about Pride while still in the closet. As a gay person, someone who once was in the closet, Levy might have looked at Pride as this perhaps unattainable thing, but he was now marching in a parade, being a Grand Marshall of one of the biggest Pride marches in the world. It's a wonderful thing on a personal level, but it's also a beautiful activist moment.

Not too many years ago, certainly in living memory of people Dan Levy's age, straight actors would not be seen marching in a Pride parade for fear of being associated with the queer community, for damage to a career, or similar. It's so easy to forget how recent history it was that this would have been unimaginable. But also, even now, so many queer actors are not out and would not march in Pride themselves. Having this show with actors wearing their Pride on T-shirts (T-shirts that say "The Wine Not the Label") is an important act of visibility.

The activism from Levy in and around the show is a powerful tool for queer visibility. Activism is at the heart of queerness for many people, which becomes a facet of the queer iconography in the show's fiction. How Levy conducts his activism in his work and life is admirable and powerful. The show's popularity has given him leverage in studios to tell the stories he wants and the world needs. Beyond that, the platform that the show has given him has allowed him to use his voice as an individual for good.

The platform *Schitt's Creek* gave the cast and creatives has allowed for much good in their careers, from Eugene Levy and Catherine O'Hara enjoying renewed status as everyone's "TV mom and dad," to the inevitable career success of younger cast members like Emily Hampshire and Annie Murphy, to Noah Reid being able to pursue his music career alongside acting full-time. And, of course, Dan Levy looks set to become one of TV and film's most successful writers. But with this success also comes a platform to do some good—be an activist—and for Dan Levy particularly, given the activist drive inherent in his writing, this has been important. In keeping with a very *Schitt's Creek* mentality of "leading by example," the rest of the cast also have embraced using their platforms for good.

The ongoing activism was as important for the fans as the creator. Keeping with LGBTQ+ awareness, the cast has drawn attention to Pride marches, as discussed, with the cast marching in Toronto Pride in 2018 and Dan Levy being made Grand Marshall of New York Pride in 2020. The march in Toronto Pride is important for several reasons. First, it shows the hometown support for the LGBTQ+ community, with the show being filmed in Toronto/Ontario and Toronto being the hometown for Dan and Sarah Levy, Emily Hampshire, and Noah Reid. Prominent local performers/celebrities need to be shown supporting Pride causes and their local organizations. It also felt like a bit of a "money where your mouth is" moment for the show as well, which was quietly doing activism by existing; actively turning up at a Pride march made a real statement. As the maxim goes, "Pride is a protest," and the origins of Pride marches and Pride movements are in protest, taking a stand against injustice. And so, it felt right that in 2018 the *Schitt's Creek* cast, having drawn a line in the sand with the show, showed up for Pride.

That straight actors in the show—Noah Reid, Annie Murphy, and Sarah Levy—also marched is significant. Writers and crew as well as the stars of the show were also important in showing—presumably with those individuals being a mix of queer people and allies—that the show is made inclusively and stands for inclusivity. Reid is also a fantastic embodiment against ideas of toxic masculinity; not only has he never talked or dwelled on the notion of playing "against sexuality" as if it is any issue, but he's also a counter to many a toxic masculinity trait in his attitude. From things like his tactile easy nature in real life with Levy (and we assume other male friends), to his use of "I love you" for Levy on various social media posts, to being outspoken about the need for men to express emotion in interviews. And as much as there are conversations about straight actors in gay roles, straight actors in any role being outspoken against toxic masculinity, in championing men's mental health, is also activist. In a similar vein, Dustin Milligan has a similar attitude, perhaps most famously embodied by his appearance on *Drag Race Canada*—as a straight man visibly and unquestioningly embody "feminine" and "gay" traits showing he wasn't embarrassed or afraid to be shown as either, and that straight men can also be feminine. Obviously *Schitt's Creek* fans firmly embraced and supported this too.

In the video for New York Pride 2020, for which Levy was Grand Marshall (to the virtual event after Pride was canceled for the first time in fifty years), he talks about hearing about Pride while still in the closet. The importance of Pride is in the visibility of an event that queer people can feel "one day" might be for them. Add to that the idea of a young teenager, like Levy describes being, knowing Pride exists, and then seeing a group of actors from your favorite show participating. For queer young people, that is a hugely inspiring thing. But older queer people, who have maybe spent their lives hiding part of who they are, feel validated by that visibility. Pride is incredibly important to the LGBTQ+ community, so the show's engagement with it was also monumentally important. For Levy as a gay person, someone who once was in the closet looking at Pride as this perhaps unattainable thing, but now marching in a parade, being a Grand Marshall of one of the biggest Pride marches in the world, is a wonderful thing on a personal level, but also a beautiful activist moment. The phrase "it gets better" has become cliché and even a parody—so much a parody that Levy himself took part in a skit about it during his appearance on *Saturday Night Live*—but in the circumstances like that, it also rings incredibly true.

The appearance of and vocal support of the straight actors from the show to LGBTQ+ causes is important to the show's broader message. All cast members, not just Dan Levy, attend LGBTQ+ organization events.

Also, all of them talk with passion and sincerity about the queer themes of the show in interviews, and this is vital. There is much debate—as explored in the section on coming out stories—about gay actors in gay roles. But to flip this conversation into a positive spin, to have a straight actor like Noah Reid talking about his role as Patrick in interviews not in the vein of "in this role I play gay" but to join in with the conversation about the relationship, the comedy, the success of the show, and not dwell on the sexuality he is playing, is equally important.

Dan Levy's Activism with the Show

Dan Levy has, in his work, already been contributing to that activism and equality through *Schitt's Creek*, with its celebration of love and deliberate absence of prejudice.

The "politics" of Levy and his cast members—being vocal about things at a national level (like the 2020 American election) to a local one (homeless camp evictions in Toronto)—was at the heart of a lot of their charity and activism work while with the show. The format was different across 2020. Naturally, it was very social media and online platforms heavy due to the pandemic. But the spirit of activism is similar, that is, using the content, the art, and the platform that led a show to have an audience for good. This kind of activism combines profile and consciousness of using the work and the art for good. Led by Levy at the show's helm, he has demonstrated his commitment to using his profile for good in his continued championing of important causes.

"Come Learn with Me": The University of Alberta Faculty of Native Studies

Levy illustrated this particularly across 2020/2021 with his advocacy for the indigenous people of Canada, particularly in the education of settlers of indigenous history. In the summer of 2020, he brought awareness to the University of Alberta's "Indigenous Canada" course, an online, free course that had been running for a few years. In a tweet, Levy asked fans to sign up to learn with him and started taking the weekly online lesson himself. He also ran weekly virtual discussions with academics from the university and other guests (still available on YouTube) in which he discussed his learning on the course with First Nations academics and experts including Dr. Paul Gerau and Dr. Savage Bear (Dr. Bear actually created the course for University of Alberta). That Levy spent several hours a week—taking the course, meeting with the academics, and planning and hosting the discussion—is a level above traditional "celebrity" activism. There is also a certain element of those from minority groups—in Levy's case, LGBTQ+ people—using their privilege, when they can, to elevate other groups out of shared solidarity, intersectionality, and recognition of what it is to be on the outside of something.

Levy's presence in the discussions did far more than bring viewers as well—numbers may well matter, but what will outlast that is the impact on the quality of the discussion Levy had for those listening. What was vital was Levy's engaging way of discussing the topics from a learner's perspective before giving the platform to the experts to guide everyone listening. And by leading by example, Levy flipping the difficult elements onto his worldview allows those listening to think about doing the same. We need those ways in, that nudge in the right direction.

A phenomenal amount of people took the course and watched the live streams (again, it's unlikely any of these academics had previously spoken to an audience the size of the, on average, five thousand people per stream). Levy's Twitter and Instagram followings number in the millions, so a hundred thousand is but a fraction of his audience. But this isn't designed as a comment on a lack of success or importance of the course—quite the opposite, the course was a huge success—but this shows that the audience for this and Levy's reasons behind it supported the greater good. His commitment across three months inspired the people who came to the course because he shared how much he cared about it, kept people engaged, and furthered that learning. And that, frankly, is the most honest use of any platform I know of.

Using whatever platform you have for good and for change has to be positive. One key takeaway from one of the discussions for me was using the platform. It's just one act of activism, but the powerful sense of using a platform for good seems central to Levy—and, by extension, the rest of the *Schitt's Creek* family. But it's also an indication of the way the fans of the show think. The cause of the University of Alberta and education around indigenous people was adopted financially with two fundraisers: one directly following the course, to which Levy also donated fifty thousand dollars personally, and the other around his birthday (for which, as noted earlier, fundraisers by fans are usual). In all, around $150,000 has been raised by these big fundraisers, with a large number of fans holding smaller fundraisers or opting into individual giving.

This drive for fundraising for interesting and under-supported courses and supporting education illustrates a wider sentiment and pull toward activism in how Levy leads his life and conducts his work.

The 2021 Met Gala Theme: "In America: A Lexicon of Fashion"

The Met Gala 2021: outlandish fashion rises again post pandemic. Dan Levy stood on the steps of the Met at his first Met Gala wearing the work of artist and AIDS activist David Wojnarowicz, an artist whose life was cut short by another pandemic, an artist whose identity was part of his work but left him ostracized from the mainstream. Levy is now enjoying mainstream success off the back of his wholly queer TV show *Schitt's Creek*, wearing the queer art of another queer artist on his body.

Designer of the outfit Jonathan Anderson called Levy a "superhero for us all." Some superheroes in queer culture raise their voices and make a stand, resurrecting a form of activism from the past along with the artist who created it. To look at Levy as a gay man, proudly embodying that, says that Levy was participating in a through line of queer culture and queer activism. Embodiment is key here too: Levy wore the work on his body, the work of an artist whose body and what it stood for, at a time when AIDS and queerness were feared.

Levy's outfit collaborated with Jonathan Anderson, Loewe, and Cartier. It was custom-made with styling by Erica Cloud, who has helped shape Levy's distinctive style in recent years. Coupled with designer Jonathan Anderson's reputation for playful but astute fashion, Levy's Met Gala outfit truly understood the assignment. In addition, Levy's outfit for the afterparty from Loewe's new collection gave more than a nod to queer culture and kink—the entire night was testament to telling a story with the clothes you wear. And that story was a queer one.

Anderson told *Vanity Fair*: "Dan is our gay superhero. Through his comedy, he can knock down cultural barriers. We wanted to make something that allows him to make queer love visible, and we found that through the seminal works of David Wojnarowicz" (Evans, September 13, 2021).

The outfit Anderson designed for Levy to wear at the Met speaks to a bigger conversation on clothing, identity, art, and more. Levy's outfit was made from a re-creation of "Fuck You Faggot Fucker" with the central image of two men kissing emblazoned on his chest, the rest of the picture—the world map—wrapped around his torso and the rest of the outfit. The title image—a pencil drawing, re-creation/image of some graffiti—was on the center of his back. The pants replicated the map so that Levy wore the entire world as in Wojnarowicz's artwork.

This work was one of Wojnarowicz's first to tackle homophobia and gay-bashing and embrace same-sex love directly. Its title comes from a scrap of paper containing a homophobic slur that Wojnarowicz found and affixed below the central image of two men kissing. These anonymous men are archetypes, stand-ins for many personal stories made with one of his stencils. Using photographs taken at the piers and in an abandoned building on Avenue B, Wojnarowicz includes himself and his friends John Hall and Brian Butterick in this constellation. Maps like those in the background here often appear in Wojnarowicz's work; for him, they represented a version of reality that society deemed orderly and acceptable. He often cut and reconfigured the maps to gesture toward the groundlessness, chaos, and arbitrariness of man-made borders and the divisions between "civilization" and nature.

The piece is dreamy and beautiful in the pastel colors of the map it's made from and the soft embrace of the men it depicts, but it's also confrontational. It uses homophobic graffiti alongside images of gay men, contradictions, and beauty. The map itself—of North America on the torsos of the men and worn on Levy's torso in the outfit, commenting what Wojnarowicz referred to as "this killing machine called America"—seems as hauntingly apt today as it was in 1984 when he made the work.

Kudos belong to Levy for not using asterisks in his Instagram post to cover the work's title, as the documentary of the same name did (2020); like naming the artist and how he died, these things matter.

Aesthetically, the outfit leaned into its camp, with giant puffball sleeves on the top, layered over a neat, tailored white shirt. The sleeves echo 1980s women's dresses and power suits, in a nod to both gender fluidity present throughout Anderson's designs and, indeed, Levy's style. But it's also a nod to the decade of the artwork. Gold studded on black leather boots add an air of kink couture (as did Levy's afterparty look).

The positioning of the designs and where certain elements fell—from the kissing square on his chest to the sequin details at the crotch—all resonate with symbolism, the alignment of art, and the body. In particular, the choice for the purse, indeed to include a purse, was striking with this artwork. "Fuck You Faggot Fucker" was used as the influence for the outfit and an untitled piece of work as the clutch purse Levy carried. Giving a man a purse shouldn't be revolutionary or noteworthy, but it still is. All at once, Levy's Met Gala outfit is a warning from history as much as a celebration.

Of course, at a celebrity event, we must confront the discomfort of a grass-roots-activist-artist turned outfit for a high-end design house. There are questions to be asked about how that fits. How do we reconcile it?

Parallels of Activism

Queer politics or activism isn't limited to strictly queer issues (or, to put it another way, queer issues are not just about sex, sexuality, and gender). Levy illustrated this particularly with his advocacy for the indigenous people of Canada, which has a surprising parallel to some of Wojnarowicz's work.

Intersectionality was a hallmark of ACT UP's activism and Wojnarowicz's. ACT UP has never limited itself to AIDS activism as an organization and as individual artists and activists, campaigning, most recently, for COVID research and vaccinations, for example. For Wojnarowicz's part, he often critiqued America for its "one-tribe nation" in *Knives*. He also touched on elements that seem incredibly current, from fighting police brutality toward people of color to fighting for abortion rights. His intersectionality in the 1980s and 1990s was ahead of many of his activist counterparts. He took his own experience of prejudice as a gay man and he turned it outward, seeing the impact on others of different kinds of prejudice and using his experience fighting his own to counter it for others too.

"Long before the word intersectionality was in common currency, Wojnarowicz was alert to people whose experience was erased by what he called 'the preinvented world' or 'the one-tribe nation.' Politicized by his sexuality, the violence and deprivation he had been subjected to, he developed a deep empathy with others, a passionate investment in diversity" (Laing, February 13, 2016).

Fashion activism on the steps of the Met: it feels very Dan Levy, but it also pays tribute to the artist and the legions of others who went before.

Queerness, Legacy, and Through Lines

The work the outfit is inspired by is from 1984, the year after Levy was born. Wojnarowicz was thirty-eight when he died in 1992, a couple of years younger than Levy at the Met Gala, bringing something poignant to a lifetime's difference between their experiences. The freedom Levy has to wear this outfit while being a gay creative, making work within the mainstream, has resonance. Because the work Levy has done—and will do—is part of a queer legacy, a history that Wojnarowicz and many like him paved the way for.

It's an important and uncomfortable (as such things often are) conversation. When discussing AIDS, we're talking about gay men's bodies. And wearing AIDS art as clothing on the body of a gay man means something. It's a physical link, almost artwork to artwork and body to body across space, acknowledging that link, personally, artistically, to someone who went before, bringing that work into the present, not just within the queer community but putting it on the world's stage and challenging them to have a problem with it.

Many of the groundbreaking activists of Wojnarowicz's time were either never acknowledged as part of that history in their lifetime or didn't have a life long enough to make as much impact as they might have. There's a weight of expectation to a degree, often unspoken on today's creatives, like Levy, who can make their mark while owning their identity. This weight of expectation exists because their work, consciously or not, is part of a queer legacy. Gay men's work, too, is part of a post-AIDS conversation. Levy's generation came of age in the long shadow of AIDS, the disease that took Wojnarowicz and so many other artists.

It is hard to explain to a younger generation just how tragic and seismic the loss of our elders was, personally and artistically, to a generation of queer people and queer artists. The loss of those elders was felt first-hand in communities that relied on that handing down of knowledge of chosen families. Beyond that, the generation of artists lost—not just the world-famous ones, like the Freddies and the Rock Hudsons, but also the grassroots artists, those embedded in communities, making work on the fringes whose work was lost is marked by acts of activism and solidarity like Levy's. This looked like many things. It looked like new freedoms to be themselves, come out, marry, and be free from the fear of AIDS. But it was also to grow up with the long-term impact of the AIDS epidemic, the fear and panic around queerness it caused, the idea of a "doomed life" it created, and the loss of a generation to guide the way.

Walking the Met Gala in that outfit, Levy owns that story in a way that, during the 1980s and 1990s, Wojnarowicz could not have. It's likely that even a decade, maybe less, ago, he could not have.

That moment was also a standing up for generations of queer people watching. For those who remember the era of Wojnarowicz and those who don't. The younger generation is looking up to Levy as their "superhero" who will now google a part of their history because of the piece he chose to wear, who will feel connected to something bigger because of it, and who will still have the stories of their elders, even if they aren't here to tell those tales.

Cynics might argue that it's just an outfit. That's as reductive as arguing "it's just a painting," whether that's one of Wojnarowicz's or any other in the Met. Much like a painting, it doesn't matter if you like Levy's outfit aesthetically. It's not there to be worn to a wedding or on a date (though if someone rocked up to either, points to them). It's about the story of the piece. Art has power—the power to move, to inspire. And art is activism. That's what Wojnarowicz stood for, the power ACT UP harnessed, and it's what Dan Levy's outfit inspires us to consider.

Other Approaches to Activism

In business, it's worth noting that Levy aims for ethical and charitable goals. His eyewear company, DL Eyewear, founded pre-*Schitt's Creek*, also incorporates giving, advocacy, and activism into its brand. Since 2021, they have been part of the Local Initiatives Support Corporation. This organization assists small businesses—prioritizing those owned by women, people of color, members of the LGBTQIA+ community, and entrepreneurs—located in historically disadvantaged communities. In this way, the growth of Levy's business ensures that others can advance, as well. The company motto is "see with love," which they seek to actualize through marketing campaigns that incorporate teachers as models, as they did in a 2021 campaign. These are a few simple elements that illustrate Levy's ethical and charitable ethos across platforms.

Why is this important? In part, it remains in today's climate still noteworthy when those in the public eye are work for good, not questionable, activities. But also it ties back to the show, this element of "practice what you preach" and "lead by example." During the show, the cast's charitable, advocacy, and activism elements reflected doing the lead-by-example thing. However, they've all managed to continue it after the show has ended. Levy curated a cast of individuals who reflected his values and the values of the show he created. Or perhaps the show spurred that on in them, too, in that they were influenced to continue in that vein. That Levy continues to engage in activist acts like the Met Gala outfit but also lower key events like the Indigenous Canada course shows that this kind of activism is ingrained in him.

Levy's engagement and intersectionality in his choice of activist action indicated using cultural spaces for activism and leading by example in activism off the back of a show that facilitated that elsewhere. Of course, a huge part of Levy's activism is around LGBTQ+ rights, and that activism still carries some risk to his career and some risk of homophobic backlash, and these are all risks a person like Levy, even one who comes from a place of privilege, has to consider. That Levy chooses to still engage in acts of activism small and large is important.

So yes, even from someone beginning at a point of relative privilege, Levy making queer art is a form of activism. His chosen form is writing, and TV doesn't make it less revolutionary or even activist.

Beyond that, it also shows something instilled in queer activism, aligned closely with the kind of work Wojnorwicz engaged with; it's intersectional, even bipartisan, activism. It is taking the work beyond the bubble of just fellow queer people into the mainstream, in Levy's case, where straight society both as allies and enemies might engage with it. And taking ownership of that identity like Levy did here in wearing the outfit—literally putting queerness on his body—that's an activism that's truly queer.

This activism ties into the queer people—both younger people and adults—using their fan interests to connect with other queer people or to explore their sexuality through these like-minded interests. Discussing queer-themed shows with fans has led people to explore or be more open about their sexuality or, in discussing a character's experience, find parallels with their own. This, combined with the community and support of fan culture online, has supported many fans to accept their sexuality or explore their understanding of gender. This next chapter will discuss the importance of this fan culture around queer TV for fans and queer people to find their "community" in the online space.

Dan Levy's queer activism was recognized in 2023 when his was awarded the Order of Canada, which is an award that is part of the Canadian honors system and is the second-highest in the country. Awarded since 1967, annually a number of awards are given out to Canadians of note. In 2023, Dan Levy was honored "For his trailblazing advocacy of 2SLGBTQI+ communities, and for advancing Canadian television as a critically acclaimed actor, writer, director and producer" (Order of Canada, 2023). He's in good company: Eugene Levy also previously received the Member of the Order of Canada (2011) and later the Companion of the Order of Canada (2022) for his services to TV. Catherine O'Hara was awarded for her work in TV (2018) and specifically her work furthering women in comedy. While Dan Levy's TV work also was a reason for his award, it's significant that his activism, his work beyond his work, played a factor. Poignantly, Dan Levy was awarded in the same year as academic Dr. Savage Bear, who created the Indigenous Canada course Levy took and promoted. Dr. Bear was awarded the Order of Canada in 2023 for her contribution to Indigenous studies and community activism. The recognition for Levy's activism also shows that he is garnering a reputation for this as much as his TV work, and that the two indeed go hand in hand.

16

"Once at a Mariah Carey Concert": Fans and a Love of the Show

Dan Levy has often cited the support and power of fans as intrinsic to helping the show grow and reach a bigger audience. The small but dedicated fan following was vital to the show's continued success in the early years. They were at once brilliantly supportive and engaged in all the weird and wonderful things that fans tend to do, as Dan Levy recalled to *Variety* in 2020: "The fans of the show have been such a crucial and integral part of the success of the show. So much of it is word of mouth. So much of it is the memes and the GIFs that are being shared over social media, and the wonderfully curious creative output that has been put out by these fans. People were putting Noah's face on potatoes—I don't even know what's happening! I try not to be on the internet too much" (Turchiano, January 14, 2020).

The fans were key, and the dedicated core was responsible for raising the profile and supporting the team even before the widespread success. When the show started to take off in its final two seasons, attention and fandom grew. This also included many celebrity fans who talked about the show publicly and a huge fanbase of casual and more dedicated fans. The show's fans are loyal and passionate and have created a community around the show. What, then, is it that inspired such devotion to the show? The show has been hugely significant for many viewers, however much a "fan" they class themselves as or how they engage with that. For this book, a range of fans were interviewed across late 2021 and early 2022, almost two years after the show began and completed its final season. In speaking to them, there was a sense of the show doing a lot for them while it was on the air, and continuing, be it through the themes in the show or the community around it, to serve them, support them, and be a positive force in their lives.

Fan Events

There have been several official and unofficial ways for fans to meet up throughout the series. These ranged from unofficial to official, both large and small.

The biggest unofficial event was SchittCon, a fan convention organized in 2019. Entirely volunteer-run, a group of fans met in Toronto before taking a trip out to Goodwood, where the show was filmed (at that point in its final season). The fan event took on the usual form of conventions for part of the weekend, from episode viewing parties to cosplay competitions to quizzes and other activities. It was also probably the first time most fans met up with a large group of fellow *Schitt's Creek* fans. SchittCon became extra special because they could travel to Goodwood while filming the show and meet with many cast members, including Dan Levy, Noah Reid, and Eugene Levy. The images on their website also show fans posing with parts of the (dressed) set, rather than the empty town that most fans get, and interacting with the cast. This was, of course, a reasonably unusual event. The groups were just small enough to be manageable. It seems the crew/Dan Levy embraced the event in the spirit it was intended: the fans who had supported the show for so long getting a chance (at last for many) to visit the locations and see the cast. The crew embraced the fan event—Levy thanked them on his Instagram stories, too, an acknowledgment of the fan support that got them to that final season.

Events like this are important for fans; even without the bonus of meeting the cast/seeing the locations, the chance to interact with fellow fans is always important for groups. Another way they got to do this was in the New York Pop-up event, an official event in December 2019. In the run-up to the premiere of the final season in 2020, sets from the show were re-created and fans could visit, take pictures, and meet other fans. It was, for many fans who could get there, a particularly special moment.

The biggest of the official events for fans was the "*Schitt's Creek* Up Close and Personal" tour, which ran across 2019 between seasons and was scheduled for another tour for the final season in 2020. After many postponements, however, they decided to cancel this farewell tour. During these events that toured multiple cities in the United States and Canada, the principal cast would talk about the show panel style, led by Dan Levy and interspersed with interactive moments with the audience and

*Eugene Levy onstage at the "*Schitt's Creek *Up Close and Personal" event, 2018 in LA.*
Patrick Fallon/ZUMA Wire/Alamy Live News

performances of "The Best" and "A Little Bit Alexis." These were the most significant fan events for the show, and the second tour was set to be a fitting farewell celebration with the fans had COVID-19 not intervened.

Another farewell (at least for now) moment to meet up in person for fans came in 2020 when Noah Reid took to the road for the first time with his concert tour. His "First Time Out" tour, where he played songs from his debut album *Songs from a Broken Chair* and his forthcoming follow-up *Gemini*, were primarily populated by *Schitt's Creek* fans. The tours, while primarily, of course, to support Noah's music, also became unofficial fan meet-ups. While there's always a push-pull for artists and fans with this kind of crossover in interests, Reid's concerts are fond memories for his fans. In addition, Reid's Broadway debut in *The Minutes* in 2022 offered a similar kind of experience: a chance for fans to meet up in a *Schitt's Creek*–related context while watching Reid in the play. Many fans created unofficial meet-ups around this.

A partial substitute for the farewell tour came in November 2021 with two book events in New York and London to mark the publication of the *Schitt's Creek* official book *Best Wishes Warmest Regards*. In New York, Eugene and Dan hosted a live-streamed "in conversation" event, replicated by Dan in London.

Noah Reid at his "First Time Out" tour in LA.
Courtesy Leonie Woolf

Attending the book launch events meant a great deal to many fans. Nicole said, "The opportunity to finally meet people I've been talking to for a year and a half online during a pandemic felt good." Mads adds, "After canceling other fan events due to the pandemic, I just wanted to

Noah Reid at his "First Time Out" tour in San Diego.
Courtesy Leonie Woolf

be in that energy again. It's intoxicating and soul-warming." Sharing that experience with the people who share that same love for *Schitt's Creek* was, of course, a huge draw. Abi comments, "It felt so joyful to be in a room full of people who have had their lives touched by the show in the same

Noah Reid tour poster.
Courtesy Leonie Woolf

Dan Levy at the Best Wishes, Warmest Regards *book event.*
Courtesy Leonie Woolf

way that I have." Grace adds, "To be together with the other 2,195 fans was something I will never forget."

As Rebekah puts it, "As a *Schitt's Creek* fan, one thing sticks out to me: the safe space offered by the show and the community of fans it has created. That same sense of a safe space existed on that night in the theatre."

One of the lovely things about the show, and fans' love of it, is how it aligns with real life. Samuel shares, "*Schitt's Creek* was one of the earliest shared interests for my boyfriend and me, so when I saw Dan Levy appearing in conversation, we both leaped at the chance to go." This is a lovely sentiment; may they look back on that date in years to come, too. Wouldn't that be an extension of the show's queer joy?

The nights also provided the rare chance to hear from someone you admire and form a human connection with someone who brought

Dan Levy at the London book event.
Author's collection

something you love to love. They were also a fitting tribute and footnote to the show's end, offering fans some perhaps closure events for those lucky enough to attend. Of course, where fans put their energy after the show ends is also important.

Dan Levy watched over by Johnny Rose at the London book event.
Author's collection

Fans who produce fan artwork are an integral part of their fan experience. They will likely continue, particularly if, in terms of writing or artwork, it is not particularly dependent on "new" content. Fan fiction is one element that will become important for fans as they seek to expand

Dan Levy waves goodbye at the London book event.
Author's collection

the universe even when the show is over, as discussed in depth in the next chapter. For now, at least for many, *Schitt's Creek* lives on through community, creativity, and its impact.

Fans at the London book event.
Courtesy Leonie Woolf

Creativity and Fandom

There is an element of creativity often associated with fandom fan art, and fan creativity is more broadly integral to fandom for many. Even for those who don't create themselves, fan art is an important element of engaging with fandom.

Not long ago, fan art was the stuff late-night talk show hosts showed actors and creators to make fun of their fans. Before that, we had the eras of massive disclaimers on fan art and promises we weren't breaking copyright laws or trying to profit. Levy has flipped that on its head, including a selection of beautiful fan-made works in the *Schitt's Creek* official book. He took these works from out of the closet (so to speak) and endorsing them, thanking fans for the labor they engaged with to produce them and the support to the show creating them demonstrated. There's something wonderfully pure in that, and while there are commissioned pieces in there, by and large, they are works that fans made for themselves and fellow fans for fun. They weren't trying to catch the creators' attention aside from a "hey, I love what you do, so I made this" kind of way.

Artists have produced many works inspired by the show. And so impressed with the quality of fan art out there, Dan Levy decided to include some of it in the official *Schitt's Creek* book. He picked a selection to showcase in that book as a lovely tribute to fans' hard work and creativity. The array and styles of work are hugely varied. Many artworks focus on David and Patrick, but many created paintings and other art of the Rose family and even the town's buildings.

Fan Art by Maddie: Moira in her wedding outfit.
Courtesy Maddie

Fan Art by Maddie: Dan Levy's Met Gala outfit.
Courtesy Maddie

Other examples of fan art that started simply as a way to express love of the show include NoContextJana (@nocontextjana), who makes custom Funko Pops. While others do this (and across other fandoms), it's fair to say Jana's are unrivaled in their detail and specificity. She has made episode-specific ones and ones featuring Dan Levy's outfits and ones for the Emmy awards and for Met Gala. She even made Dan's beloved dog, Redmond, and his best dog friend Julio (and the dog of Dan's good friend Trevor Ballin). The works are incredibly detailed and a labor of love, as much fan art is.

"I never collected Funko pops before the *Schitt's Creek* ones were released. Once I had the Rose family, I wanted a Patrick to go with David. Around the middle of 2020, I looked up some custom options on Etsy and had a 'I can totally make that' moment. It was a pandemic, after all and I

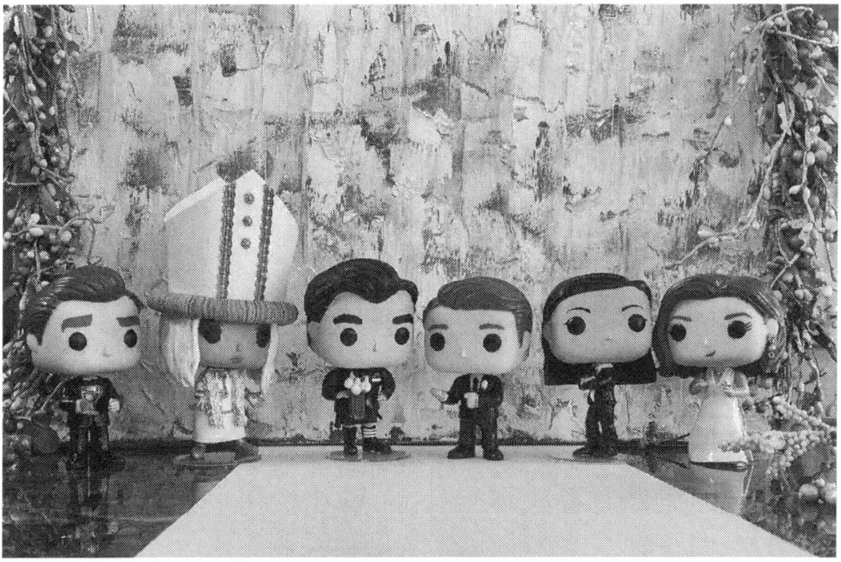

Funko Pop artwork: The wedding.
Courtesy Jana Parker

Funko Pop artwork: Moira Rose.
Courtesy Jana Parker

had already mastered sourdough bread. I watched about 40 hours of YouTube tutorials and made a list of every supply and tool used" (Jana Parker, personal interview, 2022).

Funko Pop artwork: Baseball David and Patrick.
Courtesy Jana Parker

For Jana, it certainly worked, and she now has about a dozen different designs and a waitlist so long for commissions that she's worked on nothing but that since 2021. Thanks to her Emmy awards design, this brought much attention. As she says: "I accidentally went viral on Twitter. I showed my 200-ish followers the Emmy's Night Dan Levy I had created for a friend in London and within 2 hours Dan replied to my tweet. Twenty-four hours later I had 11,000 likes on my tweet and 60 orders in my dms" (Jana Parker, 2022).

It's a real labor of love, with Jana watching each episode around thirty times for a single Funko to get the detail right. But she enjoys the process, even completing photoshoots (with backdrops designed by her husband) for each. As she says of that process: "I love that my husband paints all my backdrops and is so supportive of my art. It's been a highlight that we have so much fun working together even though he has never watched *Schitt's Creek*" (Jana Parker, 2022).

While Parker says she enjoys seeing the *Schitt's Creek* cast acknowledge her work—she's had tweets from Dan Levy, as mentioned, but also responses from Riz Ahmed (Ray), Noah Reid, and Trevor Ballin (a good friend of Dan Levy). But the wider connection with fans has made all the difference for Jana. As she says: "The real-life connections it has brought into my life are invaluable. I treasure the people I have come to know and love that I was able to find because of the show" (Jana Parker, 2022).

As will be a running theme in talking about and to fans, this sense of community, as well as a chance to engage in creativity, keeps fans making work and sharing it with others. Other fan artists are across Etsy, Tumblr, Instagram, and more. Sometimes they make work and sell it; other times, it's just for them. Creativity is hugely important, and fan art, collections, and even tattoos are important to fans. The way *Schitt's Creek* fans have expressed themselves creatively and enthusiastically share it is a huge part of the community feel and a way to feel connected beyond the show.

Cross-stitch inspired by Schitt's Creek*: "I will not feel shame about the mall pretzels."*
Courtesy Anna Burger

Cross-stitch inspired by Schitt's Creek *"Simply the Best."*
Courtesy Anna Burger

Creative ways to engage with the show don't stop at making art either. Collectors like Joe Black, quoted in an earlier chapter, who collects David's outfits, are another creative way to engage with the show. As he said about getting started with the collection, it was the creativity in the show that inspired him: "I watched the show from the very beginning as it aired and after each episode, I became more and more obsessed with the wardrobe, . . . especially David's. I've worn black exclusively for many many years but seeing it so elevated with proper designers and styling made me DROOL! It was murder waiting for the next episodes to see what he would wear next" (Joe Black, interview, 2022).

For Joe, his private collection led to engaging with the fandom. He recalls: "For the longest time the only people who even knew about it were a few close friends and my husband Jeff. Then one day I decided to share a few photos on Twitter and that's when I really engaged with the greater fandom" (Joe Black, interview, 2022).

This personal creativity can lead people to be part of something bigger in the fandom. The same happened with "Schitts Sheets," an account which logs statistics and other information from the show in incredibly detailed spreadsheets and corresponding Instagram posts. This account started as a result of a friend asking a question. As they recalled in our interview: "A friend of mine wanted to know all the ways that David wore his rings, but she didn't have a good method for keeping track of it. When she told me that, I knew exactly how I'd keep track of the ring configurations. To me, a spreadsheet seemed like the perfect tool for the collection of this data. That idea got me thinking about a couple other details in the show that I had noticed and wanted to track, and the first spreadsheets were born!" ("Schitt's Sheets" interview, 2022).

It's a labor of love, and it's an ongoing project: "Now I'm nearing 400 spreadsheets, and my list of ideas for new spreadsheets doesn't ever seem to dip below 200" ("Schitt's Sheets" interview, 2022).

For them, this led to being an incredibly popular fandom account and being included in the official *Schitt's Creek* book by having more factual information at their fingertips than the actual show creators! Schitt's Sheets are an example of a real passion project that by their admission, is a niche interest spiraling and being something other people connected with. They say, "To my joy, I've found other people interested in this type of analysis too." This encapsulates fandom and creativity—the way doing something you love connected to something you love brings connection to others. Whether making art, collecting items, or collecting statistics, they are all ways of bringing fans together, and this continues to be important in *Schitt's Creek* fandom even after the show has ended.

Positivity and Fans

Despite some inevitable tensions, the show has been a considerable power for good in queer visibility, changing the hearts and minds of those with prejudices. This, of course, extends to the fandom. The show has created new allies in the community. Dan Levy has always discussed the show's ability to lead by example. While the fans quoted here were hardly part of the "problem" before the show, the show gave them ways to change the world for the better person by person. Three allies here talk about how the show impacted them.

Karen tells us, "I just love seeing how the show has lifted so many people in the LGBTQIA+ community. Those of us not in the LGBTQIA+ community need to allow them to tell their stories and share their experiences without stepping over them as an outsider."

Melanie adds: "As an ally, I feel *Schitt's Creek* has provided a beautiful forum for me to discuss topics involving love, sexuality, and inclusiveness with my children. I don't know what the future holds for my son and daughter regarding their romantic relationships. Still, I am hoping them witnessing how much I love and support the relationships in the show will let them know I will support and love them regardless of who they choose to love."

This was also famously seen by the "Mama Bears" letter, a Facebook group called Serendipitydodah, which was set up as a support network for the parents of LGBTQ+ youth. They often send letters of gratitude to people who make the world better for LGBTQ+ people. As part of the *Schitt's Creek* documentary *Best Wishes, Warmest Regards*, Noah Reid read out their letter at a round table of some of the cast. In it, they said: "Your willingness to explore, inform and educate about LGBTQ people and their relationships in an entertaining but respectful and positive manner sets a tone that is often missing" (*Best Wishes, Warmest Regards*, 2020, and Serendipitydodah Facebook group, 2020).

They talked of the show's importance for queer viewers to see themselves represented and how the show would be a catalyst for change. They said that Levy helped make the world safer and kinder. They closed by saying they were a group of lifelong fans. Levy and others cried when they heard the letter, and it has become a marker of the power and impact of the show on people's lives. As shown by fans surveyed for this book, so many people have a story, large or small, about the positive impact it had. As for the Mama Bears, *Schitt's Creek* offered a window into how to be an ally and invited fans to step up to do that, which so many of them did and continue to do.

Allyship and Education

We've seen how queer fans value the show and how engaging with fanfiction supports that. For queer fans, this can be similar to what Dan Levy did in making the show, taking ownership of who they are and their stories. Fanfic can be an important part of that both in reading and writing, as Lemon explains: "*Schitt's Creek* fic has taught me a lot about what it means to be queer. It's helped me think about sex differently, but also the ways that the world really oppresses everybody for their gender and sexuality. It's made my world a little bigger and helped me take up more space in it (which is saying something, I take up a lot of space already!)."

A selection of allies explained how their reading and writing fic helped their understanding and allyship with the LGBTQ+ community. For Liz, it feels like education about the good and bad in other queer representations:

> I think it's helped me understand my own privilege, and it's also led me to realize JUST how poorly LGBTQ+ representation is handled in books and TV. I just read a book where a female character came out as gay, and the differences between SC/SC fanfic and how her story was handled were jarring. Same with another book. The characters weren't allowed to just be gay. It had to be A Whole Thing. I always knew the representation was lacking but seeing how it can be otherwise made it clearer to me.

These messages of tolerance, acceptance, and seeing the world through another lens shine through in the *Schitt's Creek* fandom, and there is a sense of wanting to replicate, in their small corner, the messages of the show.

Fandom Negative Experience

Mixed up in all this for *Schitt's Creek* is the particular relationship queer fans have with the show and the incredibly personal impact it has on them and their lives. From the many who used the show to understand their identity, come out to family and friends, or feel seen for the first time. All of this is particular, and its important to discuss different experiences with non-queer fans of the show. Mixed in, too, in the world of fandom, are sometimes tensions. The idea that straight fans—especially in larger fan dynamics or conflicts—may be appropriating, even fetishizing the queer relationship in the show and what it stands for. For queer fans, no matter what queer utopia the show has created, relating to it in the wider world is always complex.

Most of this is the usual that we expect and ultimately cannot avoid in any online community. There are, of course, many communities within fandom, and some fans will be blissfully unaware of drama or individuals in other areas of fandom. But to paint *Schitt's Creek* as a utopia fandom would be wrong. It can also be highly dependent on what platforms you choose to engage with fandom on; as one anonymous respondent said, "that's what the block button [on Twitter] is for." Different spaces can create (and hide) different levels of toxicity. There is anecdotal evidence that Facebook groups can foster some unpleasantness. Again, a fan wished to remain anonymous but said of their experience: "The fans in one Facebook group are unpleasant. The moderators have to post the rules about respect frequently. They're rude to LGBTQ people who ask for respect."

This can negatively affect how a person engages with the fandom; as this fan added, "My experience on Facebook was brutal, so I'm wary of engaging with others." And perhaps most surprisingly, but also as an indication that there is still work to do even in the world of *Schitt's Creek* fans, as another added anonymously: "I am not central enough to be involved with drama, but homophobic or generally bigoted people would often post on the Facebook group I was in." One element firmly at play in *Schitt's Creek* fandom is that much of it takes place on social media platforms (Twitter, Instagram, Facebook). As seen in the exploration of charity work, this is often a force for good. But also, the intersection of personal and fandom identities can be problematic. Previously, in fan culture, pseudonyms and fan-specific spaces and platforms, LiveJournal, Forums, AO3, and Tumblr gave a separation between fan identity and personal identity. While it's possible to do that on social media—by having a separate "fan" account, again under a pseudonym—there is still less of a boundary. This lack of boundaries can also play into some unpleasantness regarding the show's creators, which some fans expressed discomfort with. Michelle Penny comments: "I think any time I see a video of people kind of disrespecting any of the actors' space or saying awkward and cringy things on social media concerning their significant others, who they think they should be with, I have a hard time with that. There have to be boundaries."

Another anonymous fan confirmed something similar, saying: "[Fans] Trying to track where and when the actors in the show are IRL at any moment and putting that online is deeply worrying. I had to stop following SC-related hashtags on Insta because of this—an example is the lead-up to Noah Reid's wedding. The obsession with details was way over the top to me, and I wouldn't want that level of scrutiny in my life just because of the job I do."

There have always been "big name" fans in fandoms, whatever medium the fandom uses, and these, by default, become gatekeepers, whether intentionally or not (though yes, many times it is intentional). Also, cliques and factions naturally form with either allegiance to elements of the show or to fan groups or fan leaders.

In the case of *Schitt's Creek* fans, this became a factor in terms of interactions with cast members—specifically Dan Levy—on social media. In part, this stems from the fact that in the early days of the show, Levy was much more accessible on social media—his following was smaller, and he had a fan group that was loyal and vocal. He was able to engage with them. This was emphasized by how the show ended in 2020. With the world in lockdown, thanks to COVID-19, Levy (and many other cast members) had much more time on their hands (much like fans). Also, the cast was online and engaging with fans for promotional purposes. This is also a marker of Levy's value to the fans that supported the show. But that strange period in 2020 perhaps gave fans unrealistic and slightly competitive views of what being a fan meant. There began a kind of scorekeeping of the kinds of interactions that fans had with Levy primarily but also with other cast members. In public and private, whether Levy viewed someone's Instagram stories, liked a tweet, or replied somewhere has become a low-key competitive element between fans. Some view those with more interactions (or those who claim them!) as higher up a food chain. There is, of course, nothing wrong with enjoying the interactions on social media; it's a lovely thing, of course, for fans and creators to connect. Perhaps it's a fair comparison that once the Roses stopped thinking about how they looked externally, about who was talking to them and valuing them, they found true happiness. For fans, too, rather than worrying if Dan Levy would see their Instagram story or how many followers they have, they should concentrate on the friends they'd made through a shared love of the show instead.

While it's important to acknowledge that *Schitt's Creek* is not immune to such things, most fans report the fandom as friendly, welcoming, and relatively drama-free. What's more, the show and the fandom/friends they had within it were something hugely important to them.

Queerness and the Fandom

Other elements of the negative are tied to the queerness of the show. With any fandom, some individuals cross perhaps boundaries of appropriateness, specifically with "shipping" Dan Levy and Noah Reid in real life. This brings into the issues of queer baiting and fetishizing queer stories and queer men on screen. First, of course, Noah Reid is straight and, while filming, he married a woman. So despite Dan Levy being gay, there is no more reason to think he would be in a relationship with Reid than Dustin Milligan or Tim Rozen (to cite other straight-identifying actors on the show). But of course, romance on screen translates to fan rumors (or wishful thinking) on the internet. It is a compliment and testament to their chemistry as a couple on screen, but still a line of respect for actors' private lives that shouldn't be crossed by fans. Many an on-screen couple has been dogged by rumors about their private lives off screen. Why does it seem to go to extremes in this case, and why does it sit so uncomfortably?

This "shipping" of Reid and Levy is an extension of that and is often taken into public social media spaces. This is where it becomes an uncomfortable element of fan culture. Because whatever one thinks of "real person fic," it's also a creative endeavor, knowingly fictional and kept to very specific spaces. This, of course, then blurs into the uncomfortable elements of any fetishization of actors. And while we might brush it off as it happens anywhere, we might also ask, if *Schitt's Creek* is a place/show that strives to do better, maybe we should be asking that of the fans too. So while an aesthetic appreciation of the cast members is expected (and probably somewhat enjoyed by the actors in question), some lines are often crossed. This is dependent on the space the conversation takes place in. While not to everybody's taste, conversations in semi-private and dedicated fan spaces, such as Tumblr, Discord groups, and even Facebook groups, are expected and part of "normal" fan discourse. Of course, we'd expect fans to be respectful but perhaps freer in these spaces. However, as much of *Schitt's Creek*'s fandom activity is centered on social media—a fairly new thing in fandom—many of these comments are out in the open. Here, collectively, as a fandom (and not unique to this one, though it is prevalent), there seems to be a cultural blind spot. Some are aware of this problematic behavior and don't participate, perhaps sometimes actively trying to stop it. However, those newer to fandom do not register this as a disconnect or inappropriateness.

Why, in particular then, does the "shipping" of Reid and Levy in such a public, often explicit way sit so uncomfortably? Yes, because they are real people with private lives who should not be brought into this fan discussion. But also, it goes against the grain of what the show achieved. The show gave us a romantic but not overly sexualized depiction of gay men in David and Patrick. Fans make it the opposite in their "shipping" of Levy and Reid. The uncomfortable truth is that it's often gay men (or, in this case, one straight, one gay) being sexualized for a straight audience. On the one hand, it's part of the joy of *Schitt's Creek* that it's not just a "queer show for queer audiences" but something that reaches a much broader audience with queer stories. The problematic side to this coin is when straight audiences fetishize queer characters.

It's an uncomfortable truth that many straight fans don't want to admit that, for some, the show and the characters are something that feeds either a sexual or emotional fetishization. As discussed in the fanfic section, that doesn't have the same overall effect when it's David and Patrick because straight writers and readers adopting and engaging with the story is precisely what the show is about. It doesn't matter if it's overtly sexualized because at heart what remains is an extension of the story: love (and okay sex) between two characters who happen to be gay. When fans make it about the real-life actors (one of whom also happens not to be gay), it becomes about those gay actors/characters being "objects" to the audience.

This also raises the question of how queer and straight fans experience queer media and fandom around queer shows. For a queer fan, *Schitt's Creek* is a refuge, a place to see themselves reflected, a place they don't get in most mainstream media. While the tide is turning, the fact remains that queer fans consuming media will see themselves reflected far less than straight fans. So in being a fan, there is a certain amount of territorial and protectiveness from queer fans that might be interpreted as negative by straight fans. But also, if we flip this from the queer fan's perspective, this show was not "made" only for queer audiences. Still, it is more for queer audiences than straight fans, who have many media to choose from. So can we blame queer fans for getting slightly territorial?

Why is it important to acknowledge this? Because shows like *Schitt's Creek* and the fandom associated with it become an important refuge for queer people. Unintentional harm, therefore, is done by straight fans at times. The show, and its fandom spaces, should be a safe space for queer fans. However, suppose queer fans enter a space where gay men are predominantly fetishized. In that case, this will affect the show's feeling of safety and their previous fan spaces. In the context of this particular show and, more broadly, this feeling of safety for queer fans in fan spaces matters. This leads to several factors, including the queer fans being excluded and feeling their voice isn't part of a conversation they were once part of. As a result, queer fans can feel like they are not the right kind of "queer." For queer women, trans people, non-binary queer people, and those who aesthetically don't fit the neat "cute/hot gay men" demographic, the behavior of fans focusing only on the "my precious gays" element can alienate those whose queerness does not fit a neat box or look like those characters. It's also quite clear that someone's queerness does not exist only for someone else's entertainment.

There is a subsection of fans reported as "thirsty," as the internet says. Their primary focus is on the physical attributes of David/Patrick and Dan/Noah. A bit of healthy appreciation and sexual expression isn't a bad thing. Some lines shouldn't be crossed, and while, on the whole, *Schitt's Creek* fans are respectful in terms of not approaching cast members with these comments, there are always exceptions.

There is also an element of queer that is only acceptable to some of these fans because it comes in an aesthetically pleasing package. Is it only acceptable because they can look at "cute" pictures of David and Patrick and/or make "sexy" fan works? It's a question that will have crossed some queer fans' minds. Also, the idea that their identity, in this case, becomes a commodity—the "cute gay boys" being something to be used for entertainment, partly because of their gayness—is sometimes an uncomfortable space for queer fans. While they want to celebrate the representation, sometimes the representation feels like it is being used for other people's satisfaction or gratification alone.

Is there a middle ground? Absolutely. Of course, people indulge in conversations about actors and may wish to do so in a sexual way. But there are pockets of *Schitt's Creek* fans who do this in semi-public arenas, which isn't appropriate, both in terms of the actors themselves and other fans who do not wish to engage in seeing it. The solution should be a "closed doors" policy that fans can and will discuss what they like in private chats, but this mentality of explicit discussion falls outside the realms of appropriate behavior.

Seeing Yourself in the Narrative

Seeing versions of themselves or their lives on screen was huge for queer viewers and allies. Sadly, it is an unusual thing for many fans. Those who had grown up with the same shows Dan Levy did, as discussed in the early chapters of this book, or even those older, are not used to seeing themselves on screen in this way.

For many fans, the show and the fandom also aligned with a shift in their experience or understanding of themselves. This makes the show forever significant in their lives. Like Nicole, who shares that she is, "Still trying to place where I identify, but *Schitt's Creek* has made it acceptable to question things about myself and be okay with those questions." And Janny says, "I realize now that pansexual is probably the most accurate identification for me and for the first time in my life—I'm 64—I am fully proud and comfortable with that." For Mads, "It's shown me that I am deserving of love and that special someone to love and respect me, no matter who I am or what I identify as."

Kelly shares the impact the series had on her life: "Through the characters, especially David and Patrick, it helped me to realize who I was—demibisexual—and it made it feel okay that it took me a few years to discover who I was and that there is no timetable for any of that. I'm so appreciative of the show for that. *Schitt's Creek*—and my supportive friends—also gave me the courage to come out to my partner and my mom, and I am forever grateful."

For others it was simply seeing a version of their identity on screen in a positive way, as Kayla commented: "Seeing a gay love story on TV is very special as it opens the door to the community. It's awesome that David and

Patrick's love story is almost seen as normal in the show and is displayed as not a big deal. This is how it should be!" Or as Helen reflects, it was about the broader inclusivity: "I am a lesbian. I absolutely love the relationship between David and Patrick. I aspire to have a healthy relationship like that. I also love how the town and family and friends support their relationship. I love that they are a part of the SC community."

It is a show that has been so important in helping people have those kinds of conversations with themselves and with their loved ones. Abi says, "I cannot overstate how much the show has meant to me as a bisexual person. The first time I came out was when I was watching the show, and, seeing my family's reaction to it, I knew only good could come of me telling them. I will be eternally grateful to the show for giving me that moment."

The series, and the portrayal of Patrick in particular, feels like coming out stories for grown-ups, and these stories show just how important that is. The idea the show presents of "lead by example" goes beyond the show itself. It is about showing different ways of living queer lives, showing people they are welcome, and showing that they too can be part of that community. Even those unable to be there have such an important place. As Rebekah observes:

> *Schitt's Creek* is important because it's a story of love and growth with a happy ending written by a gay man, with a queer relationship central to it. Dan Levy's attempts to create an inclusive world, without homophobia or discrimination, with authentic queer characters speak of a better world, one we all want to live in. As someone not out to my family, watching—and rewatching—Patrick's coming out and being accepted comforts me and makes me feel seen in a way that little other media has.

What if the show's power affects how people saw themselves, shifting them from allies to realizing they are part of the community? Wouldn't that be a beautiful thing? It's happened, even in this small cross-section of fans, as Magalay shares with us:

> I have always considered myself an ally, but it wasn't until I saw this show that I actually dug into learning more about the meaning of each letter of the LGBTQ+ community. In my research, I finally found something that fit me: asexual. When I read that, I cried. I felt like this weight had been lifted off my shoulders. Even though I am married to a man, the only sexual orientation that has truly made me feel right was identifying as asexual. Therefore, Dan and this show has given this to me, at 36 years old, and there will never be enough thank yous that I can give to them except my undying love and allegiance.

Or it has been a part of their journey with queerness, as it was for Nicole F:

> Seeing *Schitt's Creek* and their representation made me realize that I can see myself a bit in Patrick's journey. Not realizing that not being interested in romantic relationships, not imagining myself being sexual, and learning that it's okay to not want any of that. Also not LGBTQ+ related, but the express statement of not wanting kids is a big plus for me. I don't like kids. I don't want them, and seeing David not want them and it not be a make or break in a relationship is spectacular. I mean, I'm still coming to terms with the fact I'm on the asexual spectrum, but it's a journey.

Even for those LGBTQIA+ folks for whom the show didn't offer a revelation about themselves, it was no less important because the representation it offered mattered. It's easy to say abstractly that "queer stories matter," but it's important to hear from those it matters to. As three gay men tell us here, the portrayal of David and Patrick was impactful and significant. As John says:

> Seeing the way David and Patrick's relationship was written and portrayed has been a blessing. I haven't been the victim of much overt discrimination over the course of my life, and I've been married to my husband for 30 years. So, we're basically David and Patrick 30 years in their future, but David and Patrick had the advantage of starting their relationship in an environment free from homophobia. For us, it has always been there and is still there, and I probably didn't realize how gut-wrenchingly beautiful it would be to see a world devoid of it until I watched *Schitt's Creek*.

Joe considers himself an older fan—or, as he puts it, "a gay man from the Jurassic era"—but this was important in seeing representation on TV: "The fact that the main love story was a same-sex male couple was something I'd never seen before on television, and the total lack of homophobia of any kind was revolutionary, to say the least. It did my ancient stone heart a lot of good!"

"For me," adds Samuel, "the depiction of David and Patrick's relationship made me realize that I didn't have to fix everything about myself to be in a relationship and that if the relationship was right then, I could be just as I am, baggage and all." For others, the show's appeal is about the message it sends in a broader sense. Mads simply puts it this way: "It's shown me that I am deserving of love and that special someone to love and respect me, no matter who I am or what I identify as." Above all, much like the overarching message of the show, the queer joy it brings is what brings fans to it and coming back to it as fans over and over again. For Heather, it's taking that fear out of it, which is important: "It's just a big sigh of relief to engage with a completely LGBTQ+ affirming space. I never need to worry about the tendency of terrible or tragic things to happen to queer characters because it is just not that type of show or environment. And while there's a place for exploring darker themes elsewhere, it's nice to have this totally safe space."

Quite simply, it's a feeling of hope that the happy ending instills, as Adam Rogers-Salus eloquently puts it: "Dan taught about the community through David. Noah played Patrick perfectly by tearing down labels. It makes you believe the happy ending can come."

What made the show special, particularly for queer fans, was the idea that they would have their happy ending and, more importantly, that they were worthy of it and the love and acceptance that the town and the show gave them.

Many fans feel the show changed their lives in various ways. While the show has been a force for good, we must acknowledge the less positive experiences and potentially problematic elements within the fandom. Therefore, this section celebrated fandom but took a step back to see the broader issues. Much as the show asks humanity to keep learning and doing better, we can do the same for fandom: celebrate the positive but ask what more fans can learn from the town and the show.

That is where the fan impact goes beyond the show's bubble—creating fans in unexpected places, spreading the message, and, equally importantly, the show's joy. For Levy, that the fanbase endures beyond the show is also important, because ultimately, it means the show and its message live on:

> The incredible thing about this show is that it has built a community of fans that have become so supportive of not just the show and its messages but also of each other. They have rallied behind fundraising initiatives, they have rallied behind each other, and I think it's an incredible thing to know that the show is now finished, but we have this community that has been formed by way of the show that will continue to live out the philosophies and promote the messages of the show long after we've wrapped it up. (Levy in Conway, November 20, 2020)

17

Community, Fandom, and Fanfiction

There's a long and important history and community around fanfiction, and *Schitt's Creek* fans are both a part of that lineage and a departure from it. As well as being an important element of fan expression and creativity, historically fans used fanfiction to fill in the gap in both stories they wanted to see and for queer representation.

Firstly, what is fanfiction? This definition from the Fansplaining podcast is succinct: "stories involving popular fictional characters that are written by fans and often posted on the Internet—called also *fanfic*."

More broadly, fanfiction is fiction based on an existing story, character, fictional world, person, or scenario that the author got from somewhere other than their imagination and which retains some meaningful connection to that originating material rather than simply using it as inspiration or any work of fiction that takes inspiration (characters, events, etc.) from a preexisting work. It is written by fans for other fans. It's generated by not-for-profit and shared on online platforms. The Organization of Transformative Works, which hosts the world's biggest fanfiction site, Archive of Our Own (AO3), was set up in 2009 and currently hosts around seven million stories across some forty thousand fandoms. Not all of them are queer-based, but a high percentage were in the last census of the site. AO3's informal 2013 census found that the average user's age is twenty-five. They also found that only 38 percent of respondents identified as heterosexual, and more people identified as genderqueer than male. Traditionally, fanfiction, particularly of the "slash" variety (same-sex pairings), has operated to "fix" elements of missing LGBTQ relationships on TV or to "ship" characters who can never get together in the real world of the show. So, for example, you could write a version of *Buffy* where Tara lives or a version of *Supernatural* where Cas and Dean can be a couple, not just queer-baiting the audience. From its now-infamous origins with Kirk/Spock fic, there is a long and very queer history in fanfiction.

The specifics of *Schitt's Creek* fanfiction are interesting for two reasons: first, they are working with a canonically together queer couple, and the canon reflects the "shipper" wishes of the fandom. As a result, David/Patrick fic largely follows canon: it explores different aspects of their relationship but sticks to the outcomes of the series. The parameters of their relationship might shift with authors, and we see them meeting in other circumstances, but the endgame is the same. Again, because there's nothing to "fix," fans tend to write within the parameters of what is already there. There are, of course, more extremes of exploration in fic, whether that's thematic beyond the stories of the show, things happening to the characters (divorce, death, other life changes), or in the realms of more sexual explorations, which run the gamut of what we'd expect in fanfiction.

Schitt's Creek is a mainstream show that is also queer. It's a show with a special place in queer audiences' hearts for its portrayal of queer characters, but it also has broader appeal with straight audiences. The combination of these two is the show's real power: it demonstrates that you can resonate strongly with queer audiences while bringing these stories to straight viewers and having them take them to heart—the TV dream and the queer narrative dream. However, when fanfic has been a refuge for queer writers and readers, is this more than feeling like taking something away from their space? There's a clear difference between the *show* being accessible to all, a space queer viewers want to welcome straight audiences into, and the space of fan labor and the impact of straight audiences there.

Schitt's Creek and Queer Fanfiction

Fanfiction is hard to track because it constantly changes, so any statistics will immediately be outdated. Also, while AO3 is the principal repository for fanfiction, it is not the only place it exists; fans will also write short-form fics on Tumblr or social media sites like Facebook and Twitter. But for a brief statistical overview, at the time of writing in 2022, AO3 lists 8,394 works under the *Schitt's Creek* tag. Of those, 7,108 are listed as David Rose/Patrick Brewer centric (the / indicates the romantic plot or "slash" across different fandoms). So 90 percent of the stories center on a David/Patrick romantic (or sexual) plot. Unlike many other fandoms, fanfiction aligns closely with canon in *Schitt's Creek* fan works. As Jenkins writes, "fan writers do not so much reproduce the primary text as they rework and rewrite it, repairing or dismissing unsatisfying aspects, developing interests not sufficiently explored" (1992 [2013], p. 162).

Tumblr user Mostlyinthemorning compiled a list of fanfic statistics for 2021 (and dating back to 2019), and these offer a good snapshot of fandom and fanfiction. They list 2,706 fan works on AO3 under the *Schitt's Creek* tag written by 483 authors. They calculate this is around 18.7 million words, showing that fans aren't slowing down in their writing even a year after the show ended. An interesting statistic pulled out by this research is that 25 percent of writers were first-time fic writers (at least on AO3) in 2021, showing the fandom was still bringing in new writers.

They also calculated the top ten authors by word count, with Pandoras-Daydream at 635,520 in a massive lead ahead of the following most prolific for the year SoonerOrLater at 416,734. doingthemost with 414,073 was ahead of the rest of the top ten by two hundred thousand words on average. Of course, these are prolific exceptions and likely writing under the effects of continued limited social lives given the timing. Indeed, the year before, averages were around the fifty-thousand-word mark, so the impact of COVID-19 and life likely accounts for some of this. This is similarly reflected in the number of works produced by authors. The most prolific by number of stories in 2021 was Rosey_Peach with 109 stories followed by doingthemost with eighty-one.

AO3 uses a tagging system to help readers find the fic they want. The statistics compiled by mostlyinthemorning on Tumblr are enlightening for figuring out tastes/trends in *Schitt's Creek* fic. They cite "fluff" as the most common tag (511), with the post-canon second (484). Canon-divergent is much lower in the list (223); some of the more "fun" tags also creep into the top list with the adorable "husbands" (169) as a full ten tag. This list shows that most fans favor a style of fluffy sweet stories that stick close to the canon in both content and tone. This further supports the idea that *Schitt's Creek* fic is different; we aren't trying to "fix" the show but continue living in it. Unsurprisingly, David and Patrick rank as the most popular tagged relationship by a substantial amount—over two thousand compared to less than one hundred for the second most popular (Stevie and David).

Fanfiction allows writers the space to simulate aspects of their own lives, think through fraught issues, and to even "try on" different scenarios that could comprise their future. It's a modern-day take on an ancient and essential impulse: imaginative play. It's well known among psychologists that play is crucial for developing social and emotional skills; kids aged three and four who spend more time pretending score better on social tests

Fan art: "Stevie and David."
Courtesy Nanayjeans

measuring how well they understand other people's thoughts and beliefs; young writers often write stories about bullying or not being popular, and about dealing with things like sexuality.

Of the *Schitt's Creek* fans interviewed for this book, a lot had read fanfic before in other fandoms. Those listed included *The X Files*, *Harry Potter*, *Supernatural*, *Star Trek*, and even *The Office*. Some even were into real person fanfic or bandfic (about boybands). Several respondents included their fandoms and ships like this from Rebecca Humphreys-Lamford, who said:

> Other than one piece of *Supernatural* Dean/Cas fanfiction that I wrote, I exclusively just read fanfiction. I've read Sherlock Holmes/John Watson (BBC *Sherlock*), Arthur/Merlin (BBC *Merlin*), Steve/Bucky and Clint Barton/Phil Coulson (Marvel Cinematic Universe), gen Harry Potter, Yuuri/Victor (Yuri!!! On Ice), Castiel/Dean (*Supernatural*), a little Red, White and Royal Blue fanfic too. ⋆checks fanfiction.net bookmarks⋆ Also, (shamefully) some *Twilight* Saga and (less shamefully) *Wicked* (musical) fanfic, Christian/Syed (*EastEnders*—god, they were the first gay couple I ever saw on TV and I was obsessed with them) and 10/Rose (*Doctor Who*).

From Rebecca's list alone, we can see the array of fandoms and ships (pairings of characters romantically or sexually) that can exist for even one person! And those who responded saying they'd engaged with/written fic before had similar lists.

Queer fans have long been leaders in adopting online culture as a way of engaging with TV and finding communities there. Age-wise, while Gen X were early adopters of online culture, millennials now represent one of the biggest demographics in fanfiction. Having at once the biggest experience of being short changed in queer representation, they were among the first to "take it into their own hands" and write what TV wasn't giving them. Now as they are older, TV has finally caught up to what they dreamed of while a new generation of viewers, fans, and, yes queer fic writers enters behind them.

This approach to writing has a much longer history. The act of "queering" narratives has been a recognized literary approach for many decades. Sometimes this involves rereading the author's works through a queer lens—the queer reading of *Brideshead Revisited* insists that Sebastian and Charles are lovers—or reading a queer author's work—however heterosexual in its themes—through a queer lens. So, we might queer *The Importance of Being Earnest* knowing Oscar Wilde's sexuality or see *A Passage to India* in a new light because of E. M. Forster's sexuality. Or even when an author's sexuality isn't the focus (at least for most), we can "queer" their works, as often demonstrated by Shakespeare.

It's part of the bigger conversation about how we "queer" narratives or reclaim them (or both). But it's also about that gap in the literature, in culture, many queer people feel. For many, many years, they have chosen to write their narratives. It's often a formative part of growing up and coming out for many young people. But it also continues to be an important part of life for many people as they grow older and grow up. So yes, when I teach fanfiction, it's usually through the lens of "queering literature" and how people have used fanfiction for decades to see the narratives they are missing elsewhere. On a very basic level, when they make Merlin and Arthur gay or they make the Doctor's companions fall in love with each other and run off and save the world instead of waiting for him, it's because there aren't enough gay narratives on TV.

What does fanfiction look like? What kinds of stories does it tell? They are almost too numerous to list—as with books, films, or yes TV, there are as many subcategories of fanfiction as there are genres of anything else. We will explore their key areas with the examples in this chapter, but broadly speaking, fic falls into two main categories: canon-compliant and canon-divergent. This means stories that stick to the "rules" and stories of canon—the show itself—and those that don't. The canon-divergent category can mean slight divergence in the plot (so, Kirk and Spock are gay now) to alternate universe (Kirk and Spock run a coffee shop now and are possibly gay too). The alternate universe is the biggest area of canon-divergent fic. This can mean many subsets like historical, fairytale, magic, and high school. What does this mean? It means David and Patrick from *Schitt's Creek* are, for example, English gentlemen from another era, baseball players, actors, firefighters . . . anything that they aren't in the real show. If a fic sticks to the show's world, it will only be canon divergent to "fix" or expand existing stories.

As Rebecca expands on her list with reasons for writing it, she says: "My biggest urges to seek out fanfiction have usually been because of a cliffhanger in the source material . . . just to see what could happen to the characters next whilst waiting months or years to find out what actually happens."

Within all this, a multitude of tropes, genres, and even things become "canon" even within the subworld of fanfiction for a particular show. Sometimes fans convince themselves something is realbecause they've read so many fics with that detail. Fanfiction is a rich and varied world in which novel-length and published-quality work coexists happily with short form, silly, and, yes, sexually explicit work. Many fans also use fanfiction as a "sandbox" or "training ground" for other writing in their lives, or as a way of trying out styles or ideas in a lower-stakes environment. The writing quality can vary, but often it is of a high standard. The key is fans are creating work for their own, and other fans', enjoyment.

The specifics of *Schitt's Creek* fic are interesting for a couple of reasons: first, they are working with a canonically together queer couple, which reflects the "shipper" wishes of the fandom. As a result, David/Patrick's fic largely follows canon—it explores different aspects of their relationship but sticks to the outcomes of the series. The parameters of their relationship might shift with authors, and we see them meeting in other circumstances, but the endgame is the same. Again because there's nothing to "fix," fans tend to write within the parameters of what is already there. There are of course, more extremes of exploration in fic, whether that's thematic beyond the stories of the show, things happening to the characters (divorce, death, other life changes), or in the realms of more sexual explorations, which run the gamut of what we'd expect in fanfiction.

In terms of the breakdown of pairings in fic, the fandom naturally skews toward David and Patrick. That is not to say that other pairings aren't written about. Ted and Alexis get a decent share, even their own stories, and are elements of David/Patrick-centric stories. Even Moira and Johnny get some of their own stories, either exploring their past or future post canon. Similarly, Stevie and either Amir or Jake feature in a range of stories, giving Stevie a range of original characters as partners. This shows that *Schitt's Creek* fans, too, are using their writing to explore the world, to quite literally continue living in the town with these characters, which also speaks to the strength of the show. The love fans have for the writing, including, rarely for a queer "ship," the central romance and how it ended.

What Are *Schitt's Creek* Fans Reading?

When asking fans what they enjoyed in *Schitt's Creek* fanfiction, the response was overwhelmingly toward David and Patrick's stories. Given theirs is the key or endgame relationship in the show or the "main ship," this isn't surprising. Some have particular interests and styles they like to explore within the world of fic, usually coming from previous experience in fandoms, such as: "Hurt/Comfort (primarily physical)—favorite trope since the time I first discovered fanfic. Sports/athletic AUs, as it has opportunities for H/C and generally high emotions are involved (the tension of winning/losing). Missing scenes to allow characters to react/process things that happened onscreen while they were not around during the canon events" (Surreal).

Many want to exist longer in that world: "Mostly David and Patrick pairings. I enjoy early relationships and first-time stories for all the delicious energy that happens at the beginning stages. I like all the tropes, low or no angst, AUs. I enjoy good writing in Fic in genres that I wouldn't read in traditionally published books. I think my attachment to D and P has a lot to do with falling into the fandom/fic world just as covid happened. They're my comfort and my escape" (Red Panda).

This is also shown when fans comment on their other reasons for reading different kinds of fiction. Much of it involves a deeper dive into the show they love that much: "I enjoy so much of what I read in the fandom, but my favourites are longer, involved storylines with great character development, imagery, and dialogue. I love when a writer can put David and Patrick in a world of their choosing (or a canon version of SC), but they still resonate as the characters we fell in love with on the screen. I'm impressed when a writer can weave dialogue, themes, etc., from canon seamlessly into an AU, and it feels like a natural part of their storyline" (Ashley).

For queer readers, this is also often linked to wanting to see more stories representing their world. As Rebecca Humphreys-Lamford commented: "I mostly read David/Patrick fics because, as a queer person is beautiful to be able to continue to share in the joy of a queer relationship that is full of love and care and has a happy ending. However, I'll pretty much read anything *Schitt's Creek* related: alternate universe, canon divergences, fluff, angst, you name it, I've read it!"

There is, of course, a clear divergence from more "traditional" reasons for fanfiction in the *Schitt's Creek* universe. These fans aren't seeking to "correct" any "mistakes" from the original creators; instead, they simply want to spend more time in the universe. One other traditional reason for reading fic holds equally strong: sexual content.

Sex and Sexuality in Fanfiction

The elephant in the room is that fanfiction often involves a lot of sexual content. Fic can range from nonsexual to extremely explicit. In the case of David/Patrick (and other queer ships), straight women are writing the sexual content, for whom, for obvious reasons, the experience is not a lived one and more a "learned via another fanfiction one." Does it matter that the sex is not factually accurate? Probably no more than any other writing. Does it perhaps stray into issues of appropriation and fetishization? Possibly. But for *Schitt's Creek* fans, fanfiction is an almost unique world, one where they're celebrating, not trying to "fix" the queer ship.

The show alludes to sex between its characters and, as discussed previously in this book, is an incredibly sex-positive show, but little is shown on screen. Sex is implied and referenced on multiple occasions, often, as we'd expect, with humorous intent, such as when David interrupts his parents (season 1, episode 5) or when David receives a "happy ending" from his masseur on his wedding day (season 6, episode 14). But we also get indications of healthy sexual relationships between straight characters (the Roses, Stevie and Jake/Amir, Twyla and Mutt, Alexis and Ted) as well as unhealthy queer sexual encounters (David and Sebastian Raine) and healthy queer relationships (David and Patrick). Mostly these are in "missing scene" or "fade to black" format, where we know sex has happened or will happen, but nothing beyond a kiss is shown on screen. This isn't so much an issue of the show being "prudish" or "censored" more, as discussed earlier in the book; it's simply the nature and audience of the show.

So fic sex scenes, in many ways, are an element of fans exploring the world of the show, in the same way extending any other scene might be. Importantly, not all fanfiction contains sexual elements. And when they include these elements, authors do not expand on them with the same detail or importance for the story. Fanfiction allows contributors to have more taboo aspects in their stories as there are fewer restrictions than on traditional broadcast media, which must comply with broadcasting standards. The sex scenes are not simply a description of the sexual acts (though, of course, this comes into play) but usually an expression of both storytelling—so perhaps expanding on Patrick's exploration of his sexuality or character development, and perhaps exploring David's learning how to be in a trusting relationship. Of course, there are incredibly explicit, kinky scenes out there, though these are a minority, serving their purpose for the writers and readers.

For *Schitt's Creek*, a recurring element of fic rested on the show's plot of a lack of privacy for David and Patrick (mentioned in season 4, episode 2, and season 5, episode 3). This element of the show, which hints at the sexual nature of their relationship, is often included in fanfiction, particularly fanworks depicting the early days of David and Patrick's relationship. The creative ways—as well as the romantic and sweet ways—they overcome this is central. One particular "fanon" element (established within the fandom as "fact" or like "canon") is the two of them driving to the motel Johnny later wants to buy as their place to be alone. Fans also devise other "buying trips" for the store and other road trips to give them alone time. Another part of this arc for most fans is exploring Patrick's feelings about being with a man sexually for the first time and all the physical but emotional elements of that. Equally important is David's response to being in a loving sexual relationship. For both men, exploring the emotions attached to sex is a massive part of fanfiction for *Schitt's Creek* fans.

In terms of sex, there is explicitness that can be engaged with in fanfiction that cannot be included in broadcast television. There are often realistic elements in fic where the characters talk about preparation, protection, and even logistics of what is going where. Fans are free to include what pleases them, in a literal sexual and romantic manner. To deviate from the source work, authors can incorporate sex scenes in their stories with varying degrees of detail. As Jenkins writes, "fans actively assert their mastery over the mass-produced texts which provide the raw materials for their cultural productions and the basis for their social interactions" ([1992] 2013, pp. 23–24). Free from broadcasting rules, fans tell stories based on their knowledge and experiences, which can include sexual elements. *Schitt's Creek* does not show explicit content, and including these scenes in fanfiction illustrates Jenkins' quotation.

Erotic scenes are not simply added to the story for the spectacle; they also construct a relationship between the characters depicted. As Jenkins later points out, "[t]he focuses is often on sensuality (especially the stroking and sucking of breasts, the fondling of flesh, the massaging of backs and feet) rather than on penetration and ejaculation (the most common images in traditional pornography)" ([1992] 2013, p. 192). *Schitt's Creek* fic examples further this observation as the intimacy between David and Patrick is not only present during the intercourse; it also surrounds it. Sex scenes also allow authors to show their cultural knowledge of fandoms, tropes, and stories told in fanfiction. These scenes explore David and Patrick's relationship and illustrate their trust and love toward one another, adding extra characterization for both David and Patrick in a setting absent from the source work.

The sex scenes in many ways are an element of fans exploring the world of the show, in the same way extending any other scene might be. Importantly, not all fanfiction contains sexual elements. And when they do include these elements, authors do not expand on it with the same amount of detail or importance for the story. Fanfiction allows contributors to include more taboo elements in their stories as there are fewer restrictions than on traditional broadcast media, which has to comply with broadcasting standards. The sex scenes are not simply a description of the sexual acts (though, of course, this comes into play) but usually is an expression of both storytelling—so perhaps expanding on Patrick's exploration of his sexuality or character development, or perhaps exploring David's learning how to be in a trusting relationship. Are there extremely explicit, kinky scenes out there? Of course, though these are a minority and serve their own purpose for the writers and readers.

And yes, they are a motivator for readers too: "Love me a good explicit fic because David and Patrick together are hot" (Anon); "David/Patrick stories. And for some reason, I like the sexy ones" (Heather Rice).

Sexual content has long been an element of fanfiction and to a large degree is a positive expression of, quite often, female sexuality. In mainstream fiction and society women have largely been discouraged from engaging in sexual practices in an open sense, so fanfiction has become a place to express that in a healthy space. Many responded that it's had a positive impact on their own personal sexual self-expression: "I think reading fics with explicit sexual content has helped me become more confident and vocal in my own life in terms of 'connecting' with my husband" (Purple_Sunflower). Or open up areas of sexuality previously unexplored like Steph E explains: "Fetishes—male on male sexual encounters (not something I had previously been interested in)." Or enhance things even if it's in secret, as Lisa M comments: "Actually has enhanced my sexuality, even though I'm a straight female. No one knows I read fan fic, except writers who I have left comments for . . . and you."

It can also be a counter to previous heteronormative or restrictive approaches to sexuality: "Fanfic has definitely made me explore my sexuality more in my 40s! I think I would've been a lot more explorative in my younger years. It is for a repressive Catholic upbringing. I'm in a wonderful heterosexual marriage but looking back wish I would've taken more sexual risks" (Youvegotanartistry).

It is a complex area and one that we cannot—and should not—police. Many queer women write exclusively queer men in fanfiction because fanfic and female sexuality are closely tied as those safe spaces for exploration away from the male gaze or freedom from patriarchal notions of what it means to be a queer woman as much as a straight one. Of course, straight women are writing erotic fanfiction, which for the most part, can be viewed as equally a healthy expression of female sexuality away from the male gaze. But do the waters muddy in an already queer story? Is it appropriation or fetishization for straight women to write sexually explicit stories about David and Patrick or to enjoy reading them?

Fetishizing Queer Experience

Schitt's Creek is a mainstream show that is also queer. It's a show with a special place in queer audiences' hearts for its portrayal of queer characters, but it also has a broader appeal to straight audiences. As argued elsewhere, the combination of these two is the show's real power: it demonstrates that you can resonate strongly with queer audiences while bringing these stories to straight viewers and having them take them to heart—the TV dream and the queer narrative dream. However, when fanfic has been a refuge for queer writers and readers, is this more than feeling like taking something away from their space? And where is that balance?

Many responded that it had had a positive impact on their sexual self-expression: "Never thought I would be turned on by reading about people having sex, but I love it. I love the descriptions of intimacy. I have no idea why gay male sex does it??" (Heather Rice).

Of course, some elements could be perceived as "problematic"; one fan inadvertently raised this: "Seriously, I thought I was the only woman in the world obsessing over D&P. not. Beautiful people—women mostly of a certain age . . . what is this about?" (Tanja Kovac).

There is nothing inherently wrong with what Tanja and others engage in or the community around them. However, there is an uncomfortable conversation about the fetishizing queer experience that needs to be worked out.

It can feel like objectification or othering by proxy. That fetishization feeling can feel like it's undoing some of the allyship *Schitt's Creek* fans profess, too, in this instance. Because in becoming a sexual object to people, queer fans feel othered. It also feels like having something theirs taken "back" by straight people. The idea that we are only permitted the stories if they cater to straight tastes and serve a straight audience is difficult to wrestle with. This is an area filled with blurred lines. Nobody is suggesting the majority of straight fans enjoying and being turned on by queer fanfiction are doing it with malicious intent or for any reason other than personal gratification (in a very literal sense). Nor would most queer fans want to take that away from them. The problem comes when straight fans try and dictate queer stories to their tastes and sexual or romantic gratification against the grain of what queer fans would wish.

While it would be hypocritical to ask nobody to sexualize David and Patrick—and indeed, many a queer fan also enjoys explicit fics—there is occasionally a line crossed where the characters, and by association with their queerness, become fetish objects. There is a subtle but important difference between finding a man who happens to be gay attractive or finding him attractive because of it and/or deriving sexual satisfaction from a simple sex scene versus because it's a gay sex scene. Again, there's nothing inherently wrong with being turned on by that, but there should be an awareness from cis/het fans of the impact that can have on queer fans. In this and other fandoms, there's a clear difference between the show being accessible to all, queer people creating a viewer's want to welcome straight audiences, the length of fan labor, and the impact of straight audiences there. There is a sense with a queer-led show like *Schitt's Creek* that straight fans and fanfic writers are "guests" in a queer space, and there are lines of respect to be observed.

This also feeds into a more significant issue of the "infantilization" of gay men, specifically by queer women. They are often seen in internet parlance as "cuties" or "precious babies" or similar terms. This reduces gay men to the playthings of straight women as objects in another way, taking their agency as humans or as characters and again othering them. This can sometimes feel more difficult for queer fans, as with sexualization, the desire for sexual gratification, and even the separation of kinks and turn-ons to real life is easier to grapple with. But the idea of gay characters only being there to be cute or entertaining for straight women is an "othering" feeling.

In the case of *Schitt's Creek*, this feels more pronounced than in other "queered" media because it feels like taking something away that has been given. David and Patrick felt like a gift to so many queer fans, and that's why the fetishization can sometimes feel like some of the good work the show does is being undone. It can also feel like invalidating the allyship claimed by fans who, on the one hand, say they are supporting LGBTQ+ rights and, on the other, engage in problematic behaviors. Most, if not all, do not realize that they are engaging in such behaviors. While some may respond with hostility if challenged, it is perhaps an ongoing education challenge for queer fans. Many factors at play make people write fiction, from attachment to characters to working through their issues. But also, the gravitational pull of fiction writers toward gay male stories is essential.

One fan in interviews raised this too: "I may be mistaken about this, but I believe the demographic of fic writers tends to skew towards straight cis women. I keep that in mind when I'm reading and don't assume that a lived experience inspires the exploration of these issues in any particular fic. But many writers share personal insights in their notes; in cases where they're relevant to queer issues explored in a fic, I think I would read the Fic through a different lens" (Siobhán).

Many are aware of it, but many more might not be. Is this a disproportionate element of straight female writers reading and writing David and Patrick fanfiction? Yes. This is not, as the previous discussion indicates, a phenomenon unique to *Schitt's Creek* fanfiction, but the show and its progressive storytelling make this an interesting point to reflect on. In the world of queer fanfiction, it can sometimes feel to queer audiences that the dominance of straight (predominantly white, mostly female) writers and readers do, in a way, encroach on queer spaces or that they may write stories that poorly reflect on the queer experience as well. While the debate is nuanced and naturally fueled by emotion in the show itself, there are interesting questions. It's also not always about "sex" in the act itself put a positive impact in being more sex-positive in general: "It's helped me to talk about sex with my husband and also my kids" (Obsessedwithdavrick).

This shift to sex positivity seems in line with the "queering" notions of the show as the queer relationship itself, and really as David would say, should be celebrated. As should the space that fanfiction gives queer readers and writers.

Queer Joy and Finding Queer Identities in Fic

This relates to the importance of queer expression, something fanfiction has long been a refuge for. "Sometimes, the online space is the only place they [queer people] can be out," says Kristina Busse (2017), founding coeditor of Transformative Works and Cultures. "They are still negotiating what they want to be called—like what their pronouns are—and coming out as trans online allows them to explore that identity." Your story resonates with readers, they offer feedback and commentary, and you discover there are people like you.

First, for many queer fans, fic reading helped them in their journey. Interestingly, a few fans aligned *Schitt's Creek* with asexual spectrum identity—this is not discussed in canon, but one that the chance to explore queer identities on the page helped them find:

- "Absolutely. I have changed the way that I think about gender and my place on that continuum. I've learned what asexuality and aromantic mean (having never heard the latter word until the past year)" (LeeAnn Z).
- "Yes. I started reading it when I figured out I'm demisexual. It took me a while to figure out why I enjoy reading explicit fics when I have zero interest in those activities myself. I finally realized that it's not the physical aspects but the emotional connection they represent" (Anna).
- "Now, I've identified as asexual for 5+ years, but there's only so many times I can read about Patrick not being sexually or romantically attracted to women before I started to think that this is how I feel about everyone. I adore David and Patrick and their relationship and love for each other. However, even when reading the few wonderful fics where David or Patrick are on the asexual spectrum, I still don't understand their attraction for each other in a way that matches my own experiences. So, *Schitt's Creek* fanfic has helped me start a journey towards exploring aromanticism and whether or not that matches my own experiences" (Rebecca Humphreys-Lamford).

This is worth discussing, particularly regarding the discussion earlier in this book of Patrick's demisexuality. While not canon, even within a small sample, several fans aligned asexuality with their experience in the fandom. While some fans react angrily to any association of Patrick with this identity, it meant a great deal to these fans. They illustrated fanfiction's power to give voice to things not in canon for queer fans, even in the queerest of texts.

Demi! Patrick (as the AO3 labels denote him) is a small but essential piece of queer representation and goes back to the historical reasons for queer fic, giving voice to what isn't there. Asexual representation is virtually non-existent in media, and while the community has grown more visible in recent years, the representation has not caught up. Therefore, asexual people often interpret characters as asexual even if not explicitly labeled. Data in *Star Trek* is an obvious example. Others are less easy to spot and rely on fans interpreting signs of their asexual orientation, much like other queer identities have had to do for years. A handful of fics have claimed Patrick under the explanation (as explored earlier in the book) that his attraction depends on a relationship with a person and attachment, which is a powerful piece of fan-created representation for those fans on the asexual spectrum who are able to write a favorite character sharing their experience and identity.

As discussed previously, this doesn't take away Patrick's love for or attraction to David or his "gayness." His demisexuality is an "add," if you will. But a small corner of fandom found an issue with this and pushed back firmly against these fics and those discussing this part of his character. Why, in particular, does this canon interpretation irk some fans so much? Unfortunately, to some degree, it overlaps with the problematic corner of fetishization. If Patrick is there to fulfill only a sexual fantasy, his potential asexuality is interpreted as a threat to that. The other side, too, is that gay men, for some, fall into the category of acceptable or good queers. But others, like asexuals, threaten the established order of things, don't mimic heteronormative society, or can't be either object of lust or treated as cute playthings. This becomes particularly powerful when thinking about fanfiction, when readers encounter something that doesn't play into their particular vision of Patrick. It doesn't threaten a fan's interpretation of the character or their enjoyment of fic more than a specific kink or alternate universe they dislike; it's perfectly possible to scroll by and not read. Equally, in fanfiction, Patrick being into BDSM or running a coffee shop doesn't threaten canon Patrick, and fans aren't angry about that. So what's the difference?

The difference is an old-fashioned dose of homophobia—or in this case, specifically, acephobia. This a sign that not all is erased or magically fixed by the world of *Schitt's Creek*; much may be improved by it, tolerances and horizons widened, but there is still a way to go. But the fact that ace-spectrum fans can find themselves and write themselves into the story also proves the power of fic for queer fans and that the foundation of a queer relationship allowed a group who feels rarely seen to see themselves.

Patrick as a character is often the most powerful for fans in fic. His coming out as a "grown-up," as discussed in chapter 11, is a profound, powerful, and important TV moment. Therefore, it's understandable that this is a powerful element for fans to explore in fic.

More broadly, Patrick's coming out and the chance to explore it in fiction is hugely vital to queer fans. Again, looping back to the analysis of Patrick's character, this was tremendously impactful beyond the show itself. Ashley, in their interview, said, "Yes! Patrick's coming out as an adult and the idea that he didn't come out earlier because he felt pressured to live up to others' expectations has resonated with me." More broadly, too, Ashley talked about the impact on the fan community and feeling welcomed allowed them to embrace their own identity. They go on: "I've been able to slowly embrace the label of pansexual as I feel that it's the most accurate way to describe my true self. I wouldn't have made it to this place without fanfic." There is a sense of safe spaces to explore ideas in the world of fanfiction, as well as a supportive fan community, which has helped many queer fans. Having this off the back of a show that is a queer safe space and which centers a safe and happy queer relationship has no doubt allowed these stories to flourish in the fanfic community. Because fans aren't trying to "fix" the show itself, they can play with things they wouldn't see on screen. So while this can be authors that depart from canon or extremes (yes, BDSM Patrick again, or tentacle fic, or a David who works for Rose Video, etc.), what it usually means is situations that are too mundane for a little extreme or just wouldn't fit the tone and style of the show, while still honoring the characters and their solid established relationship.

Catharsis through Stories

Beyond the queer narratives, fic is a safe space for fans to read or write about things that have affected them, using the characters they love. For some, this could be the general mental health concern a lot of fics tend to have—in exploring David and Patrick's mental health, anxiety, depression, etc., often feature, and many fans find that cathartic: "I especially identify with Patrick when he's struggling with mental health. I am also a hypercapable person that has a hard time asking for help" (Margaret). "I have some mild mental health issues, but my SO has more severe diagnoses. I am very drawn to fics where D or P are helping the other navigate mental illness through the lens of being a caring spouse" (Coffee_and_glitter).

For others, they found specific fics or themes within David and Patrick's stories which helped them work through their struggles. One fan talks about fic writers' attitude to David and Patrick not having children as supporting her understanding of what family meant: "Seeing the ep/reading fics dealing with D/P not wanting children has helped me process my infertility issues. Seeing a couple choose to be childfree but acknowledging it as a choice has helped me and my husband . . . realizing that whatever choice we make is the correct one and that we can have a fulfilling life on either path" (MeadowHarvest).

This is a lovely, if bittersweet, example of the fandom around the show and the stories created in it helping people with real-life struggles as much as the show itself. It also shows that continuing to live in a world of the show that fanfic is driven by also continues the ethos of the show, in helping people, offering a "lead by example" and altogether "good" way of being. The stories, when picking up specific themes or issues but seeing them through beloved characters' eyes, can be helpful to fans. Two other fans reference a specific fic: "In Case You Don't Live Forever" (by SoonerorLater), which deals with the (canon-divergent) death of Patrick's father and how it helped them in their grief:

- Yes. I've never said this, but parts of Patrick's (and Clint's) story in ICYDLF [In Case You Don't Live Forever] echo my own life. My dad passed away 29 (holy cow!!) years ago from the same illness. I was 21. I never knew my dad as an adult, he never knew me as one, and I related to Patrick in that regard, him not having the opportunity to have a relationship with his dad as he is. It's such a loss. (BWG71)
- One particular fic about Patrick's Dad getting cancer and dying from said cancer. Helped me a lot with my own personal hang-ups about death and dying. The Fic sat so long in my to-read list because I spent so long worried that the story would trigger me. I was right. It was incredibly triggering, but I kept reading, and I related to Patrick a lot. I ended up reading the sequel where Patrick gets that same cancer, and honestly, I cried the most in my life with both fics, but they were very cathartic and helped open up the door for a lot of dialogue with my therapist. (Bexx)

This can also work from a writer's point of view, using these characters as catharsis. The writer of the fic, SoonerorLater, said, "I based part of Patrick's experience on my own—as an only child, losing a parent hits differently, and I wanted to write that story. But it was an imagined alternate reality where I had a loving partner and an extended chosen family like Patrick does." For the author, it was a safe space to process and write that story: "I've never been brave enough to tell that story honestly before, but it became a space I could through Patrick say the things I needed to."

Or in another example, author Magnolia8727 said of their fic "I Climbed a Mountain, and I Turned Around": "There are scenes that were ripped from real life in there, especially the scene in the bedroom where Patrick tells David, 'I love you, but I'm not in love with you. I have feelings for someone else,' which is exactly what my wife said to me."

For them, the fic was an act of personal catharsis, working through that reality with a different outcome through the eyes of characters they love: "The fic helped me work out a lot of my feelings, have more empathy for my wife's position, and let me write a happy ending even though we don't have one in real life yet."

Community

There was, for fans, a sense of community among fic writers. Busse (2017, p. 47) argues that fanfiction is a fragment of a broader fandom discourse. She writes that "much of the text's meaning can be tied in with a specific place, time, and community" (Busse, 2017, p. 53), underlining the importance of the context in which the authors write their stories as it can influence the stories they tell. Busse's argument is exemplified by the development of fanfiction in the fandom after its third season, once the relationship between David and Patrick became canon. It is a point at which the fan community also became much more focused and engaged with this ship and by association, the fanfiction around it. Fans feel their fanfiction community is a vital part of their fandom experience. For both readers connecting with like-minded people and the authors whose work they enjoy, "Being a part of the [fanfiction] Book Club on Facebook has added a component of enjoyment to the whole thing. And even on Twitter, people will mention different SC fics and I'll drop into those conversations. So, I think, yes. That all contributes to the sense of community" (Michelle Penny).

Or as a reader, similar to being a fan of books, there is a feeling of being part of a shared excitement around fic authors too: "Absolutely. I love the community feel of fic reading. There are so many great authors that I feel like I've gotten to 'know' over the years, and I love how supportive and encouraging the fans are in the comments. As someone new to fandom, that sense of community isn't something I expected to find and has really enhanced my experience" (Anon).

There's also a certain amount of fun in the engagement that's important to many: "There's fic fests which bring the community together, whether you're writing for the fest or doing fic bingo for what you've read. If you can't find a fic you've previously read can ask several people on Tumblr and you'll have a reply within a few hours. It's such a friendly community too!" (Rebecca Humphreys-Lamford).

Since writing and reading is a solitary occupation, it speaks to a more extensive community feel within the fandom. People find they can connect, talk, and even find friendships around reading and writing fanfiction.

Allyship and Education

We've seen how queer fans value the show and how engaging with fanfiction supports that. For queer fans, this can be similar to what Dan Levy did in making the show, taking ownership of who they are and their stories. Fanfic can be an essential part of that both in reading and writing, as Lemon explains: "*Schitt's Creek* fic has taught me a lot about what it means to be queer. It's helped me think about sex differently and how the world oppresses everybody for gender and sexuality. It's made me world a little bigger and helped me take up more space in it (which is saying something, I take up a lot of space already!)."

Despite these potentially problematic elements in fanfiction, much like the show, a part of education and allyship is wrapped up in fic for some fans. Immersing themselves in stories about queer leads expands this understanding as they read or write the world from that perspective and, hopefully, understand a little of how the world might feel for queer people. Mostly, it's a simple fact of exposure to queer stories in a world dominated by straight ones, which helps. It's taking the seed of the show and letting it grow. A selection of allies explained how their reading and writing fic helped their understanding and allyship with the LGBTQ+ community. For Liz, it feels like education about the good and bad in other queer representations:

> I think it's helped me understand my privilege and led me to realize JUST how poorly LGBTQ+ representation is handled in books and TV. I just read a book where a female character came out as gay, and the differences between SC/SC fanfic and how her story was handled were jarring. Same with another book. The characters weren't allowed just to be gay. It had to be A Whole Thing. I always knew the representation was lacking but seeing how it can be otherwise made it clearer.

For fans, it's the understanding they gain through fandom. Specifically, fic plays as vital a role in their allyship experience as the show. Despite potentially problematic elements in both fic and fandom, these messages of tolerance, acceptance, and seeing the world through another lens shine through.

Conclusion
Happy Ending

All good things have to end, and Dan Levy decided to end *Schitt's Creek* on a high. And what a high it ended up being. First, Levy knew the last season would be the last well ahead of time, a luxury few showrunners get, so he ended it firmly on his terms. They could no doubt have taken the money and run for two, three, or more seasons. Other showrunners might have done that, but Dan and Eugene kept the show true to the plot arc they'd set out to create. They had previously thought season 5 might be the end, and when it wasn't, they could fully give themselves the space to end it on their terms.

"What I wanted for our series finale was just a great [expletive] episode of TV," he said. "I think that's all people want. They don't need a huge fireworks display. They just want to know that the characters are going to be OK."

And they were. The show ended with an "everything will be okay" feeling, and that's what it turns out people needed at that moment, with the world about to fall apart. But it also was what the viewers, the fans needed. The happy ending was political, yes, but it was also what mattered most about the show in the end.

The important thing about Daniel and Patrick's relationship is that it is treated with the same ease as straight romances have been treated on television for decades. It feels subversive and rebellious and, well, very queer because it is. To have it so uneventfully peacefully queer feels like a true rebellion against the plethora of gay love stories rooted in death, sadness, trauma, or abuse. As Dan Levy said to *Esquire*: "To be able to present a love story that's without fear of consequence was something that I wanted from the very beginning," Levy said before pausing to collect his thoughts. "Something that I never wanted to compromise on" (Kirkland, April 10, 2019).

And compromise he didn't—the final episode's ending was a perfect punctuation to David and Patrick's love story. Rarely for TV, particularly queer TV, the ending satisfied fans, and there was little complaint about how Levy left the Roses. But in particular, giving David that happy ending was an act of catharsis and a political statement. It is a political act in itself but also one of solidarity with the community. As Dan Levy describes, giving David his own happy ending was a form of catharsis: "I wanted him to live in that safe space where he can let his guard down and be vulnerable and be loving and warm," Levy says. But even though he hasn't found his relationship version of a happy ending, he's found fulfillment that very well may open himself up to whatever the future brings. "When I was developing David as a character, I thought back to a time in my life that I've long since moved past in terms of personal growth and self-worth. We had a shared world—a past where you give yourself away to people and overlook your own needs to keep others in the mix" (Dresden, February 12, 2018).

It's important that the final episode felt like a celebration—it centers on David and Patrick's wedding, and it feels like a true celebration. Unlike many TV weddings, there is little drama around their wedding. There is *drama* in the sense it's David Rose's wedding, but there is never any danger it will really go wrong. The biggest obstacle to them getting married is rain (and, okay, an ill-advised massage) but the audience never for a second doubts that they will make it down the aisle and have their "happy ending." Instead, the episode becomes a celebration of their love, the love of their family—of all kinds—and the love of the town.

It's a real rebellion to have a happy ending instead of always seeing queer love as a gateway to trauma. Are David and Patrick the solution to that? To decades of missing stories? No. But they're an important step on that road, perhaps even a fork in that road, where the sign pointing to Schitt's Creek (qualifier, "She's his sister") offers the path to a better life, just like it did for the Roses.

"Why doesn't this film/TV show represent everyone?" is the wrong question. "Why isn't there enough representation?" is the right question.

And that's really where the legacy of *Schitt's Creek* leaves us. David and Patrick aren't the definitive couple for all time—though they'll remain that for many fans, they are another step along the road. Like other stories, queer and otherwise, eventually, they'll be "of their time" but no less pivotal for it. Because David and Patrick exist, because they got that happy ending, it opens the door to more queer stories and more happy endings. Is it a really easy life lesson then—if you make spaces where everyone, including queer people, can be their authentic selves, then this filtered through and lets everyone be their best selves. For queer viewers, it's a chance to see their stories told as normal stories, which, we already know, they are, but so often have to be filtered through the impact of others' prejudices. More importantly, they get to see a happy, relatively carefree version of a gay love story, something rarely seen in cultural portrayals. Usually, any gay love story is filtered through the lens of overcoming external prejudice.

The town as a safe space, much like queer safe spaces, works as an allegory because queer spaces mean different things to different people. For some, it's a place they need when growing up, to help them figure out who they are and what they need, like Alexis. For others, like David, it's about realizing trying to fit in with other places and people didn't work for a reason, and finding your place in the world matters. It's not *just* that David and Patrick can have a big gay wedding in the town hall, though that is vital. But it's that Moira can walk down the street being Moira. Alexis can be supported as a high school student. Johnny, the fallen-from-grace businessman, can be picked up again and supported. And that Roland can . . . be Roland. These are inherently queer ideas that the town and the show enable.

The show came at the right time to find success at the end of its run: the impact of the 2020 lockdowns and a need for perhaps proof that there was good in the world made the show a place people could escape. As the world started to look increasingly dark for queer people once more, it's become a beacon of hope that there can be good, that we can choose to live as the townsfolk of Schitt's Creek do, without prejudice. And as the bad news, the worrying times for queer communities continue, we might also remember David and Patrick and their happy ending, and feel hope that we all might find one too.

Finding My Happy Ending

This show has had a series of happy endings for me as it gave me new understanding of what it is to be a queer person, but also the stories I'd missed out on growing up. It's a happy ending to a queer story, that thing that thirty-something queer people didn't grow up with. And that's where my professional life begins to intersect with my personal life and why this show hit so hard. We grew up with legislation that meant we couldn't discuss being queer in school. In the wake of AIDS, we grew up with maybe two famous queer people to look up to. So that's why we needed Dan Levy and his show, for what's inside the show and what's outside.

Because, for the first time on TV, queerness felt . . . normal? But also, there were versions of normal versions of myself in that show that I hadn't thought about or looked at until now. This feels like a coming-of-age story for me, even in my thirties.

The first time around, David's "the wine, not the label" made me feel seen, like it did many pan/bisexual people who lacked easy explainers or the kind of fun happy representation David Rose offers. After thirty-something years of trying to explain what pansexual meant to people and even being told it didn't exist, here he was existing, on TV with nobody batting an eye, and with a handy little way to explain it using wine. But despite all this, in a really complicated way (as such things are), a little while after rejoicing in David's "the wine not the label" moment, something shifted in hearing Patrick talk about not knowing what right felt like. The revelation that maybe I hadn't realized some things about myself was startling but important. This is why we need more queer stories: maybe I'd been resting on the narratives I had clutched at as a teenager, and it took someone else to explain something differently, to reflect it back on myself.

Patrick was beautiful to me, figuring out his identity later in life because not everyone's coming out story happens in high school, and not everyone finds great love in their twenties. For us, like Patrick, who waited to figure out what "right" feels like, or David, who hasn't found our "Mariah Carey," a love story is important. I love that there are so many queer stories for young people now, but David and Patrick were my age, and we feel like a generation who lost out on many stories, specifically happy stories.

David and Patrick's queer love story was hugely formative for me because it was queer. It's not gay because David's pansexual identity is a huge part of who he is and was never erased by his romantic or sexual relationships. It seems a tiny distinction, but as a pansexual woman, that was huge too. I didn't realize how much I needed a David Rose on TV until I had one. I'm the same age as David/Dan, and I had never heard a character articulate my sexuality as I understood it so clearly. Yes, "the wine, not the label" has become a T-shirt-worthy catchphrase, but it's one I wish I'd had twenty years ago if it made people understand me a little more. Beyond that, though, David Rose helped me understand myself—by being a pansexual character just allowed to exist, whose identity was never questioned or, more importantly, never erased, it was beautiful to see.

My journey with Patrick didn't end there. The "I spent my whole life not knowing what right was supposed to feel like" made me start to evaluate my life and my identity, and led me to find a new one. I found myself writing fanfiction about Patrick that someone identified as a demisexual depiction of Patrick. Through talking about that fic, through talking through that reading of Patrick, I came to the realization I was asexual. It doesn't matter that Patrick himself isn't in canon asexual. What matters is that a reading of him as such, that a conversation based on that conversation led me to a path that changed my understanding of my sexuality. That is why the representation of all kinds matters. I was finally able to understand what right felt like just like Patrick. I had my coming out as a grown-up, like Patrick. For me, Patrick Brewer became the queer character who finally made me feel right.

Dan Levy created in his show a safe space for queer identities. It doesn't matter whether my own was directly represented or not, but by showing a welcoming world where queer identities could exist, his show allowed mine to flourish. Lots of thirty-somethings needed to see a gay man, as a writer and showrunner, owning his queer stories and fighting for them. Yes, he's following in the footsteps of others who had gone before, but more importantly, he's paving the way for others to come after. Seeing him unapologetically be out and proud talking about his show is vital. The sheer hope in that is so powerful, especially for anyone who didn't grow up with that.

I needed a "TV dad," and I found one in Johnny Rose. I didn't know how much the queer child in me, and even the queer grown-up, needed Johnny Rose (and Eugene Levy) to tell me it was all okay. As one of those queer kids who needed Johnny Rose and didn't realize it, I will be forever grateful for what he brought. Both the joy of imagining having a dad like him—just embarrassing and making dad jokes—but also a guy who is capable, calm, and, above all, there for his family. It might seem strange to wish for, but to also wish for a dad who loved his wife like Johnny loves Moira, to have that level of love and respect to look up to. And a reminder that it doesn't need to be fairytale-like to happen. But I also needed TV mom, who I found in Moira Rose, to encourage me to be myself, and the rest of the world be damned (though she'd put it more eloquently, or at least more incomprehensibly). I think, too, I needed a TV "big brother"—David Rose—to show me a happy ending is still possible, no matter how burned by life you get. While I might not have got Patrick's coming out experience in real life, or David's even, through the show, I get to imagine a world where Johnny Rose or Clint Brewer is the kind of dad life gave me. It might not be true and make me sad, but it also gives me hope. It reminds me those dads do exist, that Eugene Levy exists in real life and talks so eloquently about supporting his gay son that he helped his son create this story, which gives hope to all of us who don't have a Eugene in our lives.

This show changed me; it saved me a little. I know, without a doubt, this show got me through the toughest of times. I know people mock it, saying it's only TV, to which I say, part of me hopes you never needed those stories to feel seen that badly, but part of me hopes you do experience that one day because finding something that speaks to you, whatever it is, always changes things. This little show told me it was okay to be who I am, to be burned and bruised by life, to be the one who doesn't quite fit in or hasn't found their path or person yet.

References

Books

Bredin, Marian, Scott Henderson, and Sarah A. Matheson (eds.). *Canadian Television: Text and Context.* Waterloo, Canada: Wilfred Laurier University Press, 2011.

Busse, Kristina. *Framing Fan Fiction: Literary and Social Practices in Fan Fiction Communities.* Iowa City: University of Iowa Press, 2017.

Czach, Liz. Television, Film and the Canadian Star System. In Marian Bredin, Scott Henderson, and Sarah A. Matheson (eds.). *Canadian Television: Text and Context.* Waterloo, Canada: Wilfred Laurier University Press, 2011.

Isherwood, Christopher. *Sally Bowles.* London: New Directions, 1937.

Isherwood, Christopher. *Goodbye to Berlin.* London: Hogarth Press, 1939.

Isherwood, Christopher. *The Berlin Stories.* London: New Directions, 1945.

Isherwood, Christopher. *The World in the Evening.* London: Metheuen, 1954.

Isherwood, Christopher. *Christopher and His Kind.* New York: Farrar, Strauss and Giroux, 1979.

Jenkins, Henry. *Textual Poachers: Television Fans and Participatory Culture.* London: Routledge, 1993.

Prince, Harold. *Sense of Occasion.* Milwaukee, WI: Applause Theatre & Cinema Books, 2017.

Sunshine, Linda. *Cabaret.* New York: Newmarket Press, 1999.

Taras, David, and Christopher Waddell. *The End of the CBC?* Toronto: University of Toronto Press, 2020.

Waugh, Evelyn. *Brideshead Revisited.* London: Champman and Hall, 1945.

Articles

Adalain, Jeff, The Unlikely Rise of *Schitt's Creek, Vulture*, April 7 2020.

Artiva, David, Comedy Scion Daniel Levy Is the Schitt, *The Advocate*, January 10 2019.

Arthur, Kate, Daniel Levy Looks Back on the Evolution of Schitt's Creek*, Variety*, April 4 2020.

Arthur, Kate, 'Schitt's Creek': After Six Incomparable Seasons, the Roses Are Ready to Say Goodbye, *Variety*, 2020.

Conway, Jeff, Dan Levy Is Creating A More 'Visible' World, *Forbes*, November 20 2020.

Davies, Dan, Mr. Dan Levy On Why *Schitt's Creek* Is The Show We Really, Really Needed, *Mr Porter*, December 15, 2020.

Dibden, Emma, The Definitive History of Schitt's Creek's 'A Little Bit Alexis,' *Elle*, September 21, 2020.

Dresden, Hilton, BlackBook Interview: Daniel Levy's 'Schitt's Creek' Depicts A Fallen Kardashian-Like Family, *Out Magazine*, February 13, 2018.

Fraiman, Michel, Schitt's Creek Is Classic Jewish Fish-out-of-Water Tale*, The Canadian Jewish News*, January 25, 2017

Gray, Margaret, 50 Years of 'Cabaret': How the 1966 Musical Keeps Sharpening Its Edges for Modern Times, *LA Times*, July 20, 2016.

Kirkland, Justin, For Dan Levy, the End Is Just the Beginning, *Esquire*, April 10, 2019.

Kutas, Danielle, 11 Very Jewish moments you may have missed on Schitt's Creek, *Bustle*, December 10, 2020.

Lamagna, Lauren, 'Schitt's Creek' Star Annie Murphy Is More Than Just a Little Bit Alexis, *Backstage*, September 15, 2020.

Liszewski, Bridget, Schitt's Creek's Dan Levy on Exploring David's First Functional Relationship, January 9, 2018.

Lloyd, Robert, Review: Canadian 'Creek' Overflows with Good Humor*, Los Angeles Times,* February 11, 2015.

Ivie, Devon, Schitt's Creek Is a Master Class in Aspirational Fashion, *Vulture*, March 28, 2018.

Ivie, Devon, Annie Murphy Can't Help But Bring Her Schitt's Creek Vocal Fry Home With Her, *Vulture*, April 11, 2018.

Miller, Gerri, Eugene & Daniel Levy's Real-Life & Schitt's Creek Interfaith Family, *18 Doors*, 2020.

Peele, Anna, Thank God For Dan Levy*, Bustle*, December 18, 2020.

Rothenberg, Celia E, 'Schitt's Creek' Holiday Special: For Jews like Johnny Rose, the Menorah Is Still Polished and Lit Even in Diaspora. *The Conversation*, November 28, 2021.

Rothenberg, Celia E,'Schitt's Creek': Where 'Jews of no Religion,' Facing Exile, Find Redemption, *Brighter World*, June 23, 2021.

Sciallo, Andrew, What You Can Learn From Dan Levy's Journey to 'Schitt's Creek,' *Backstage*, May 21, 2020.

Stern, Marissa, Go Up 'Schitt's Creek' Without a Paddle. *The Jewish Exponent*, February 14, 2018.

Toronto Film and Television Office, Film and Television Industry Review, 2011.

Waugh, Evelyn. Brideshead Revisited. London: Champman and Hall, 1945.

Wong, Curtis M., Dan Levy Of 'Schitt's Creek' Once Feared Having To Keep Sexuality A Secret For Life, *Huffington Post*, October 1, 2019.

Wong, Tony, How Eugene Levy Convinced CBC to Name His Show "Schitt's Creek," *Toronto Star*, January 12, 2015.

Theatre

Cabaret, music and lyrics by John Kander, lyrics by Fred Ebb, and book by Joe Masteroff, 1966.

I am Camera, play by John Druden, 1955.

The Drowsy Chaperone, music by Lisa Lambert and Greg Morrison, book by Bob Martin and Don McKellar, 1998.

Kiss Me Kate, music and lyrics by Cole Porter, 1948.

Video

LA Times. "*Schitt's Creek*" Show Runner Dan Levy on Creating a "Kinder" World Than Our Own. June 1, 2020.

Entertainment Weekly. The Double Wedding That Wasn't and More Untold *Schitt's Creek*. YouTube, April 9, 2020.

Entertainment Weekly. Dan Levy and Noah Reid on David and Patrick's Honeymoon. YouTube, April 9, 2020.

Entertainment Weekly. *Schitt's Creek* Series Finale; Dan Levy and Noah Reid. YouTube, April 9, 2020.

Websites

Archive of Our Own: *Schitt's Creek* Tag: https://archiveofourown.org/tags/Schitt's%20Creek/works

Mama Bears Facebook Group: https://www.facebook.com/293910154285181/posts/we-keep-hearing-from-the-moms-who-signed-the-letter-saying-how-proud-they-are-to/1131755323833989/

MostlyintheMorning Tumblr fic round up 2021: https://mostlyinthemorning.tumblr.com/post/672206824497463296/its-january-1-and-we-all-know-what-that-means

Order of Canada website, 2023.

Television Episodes/Series

Best Wishes, Warmest Regards, directed by Amy Segal, Netflix, 2020.

Buffy the Vampire Slayer, season 6, episode 7, directed and written by Josh Whedon, 2001.

How I Met Your Mother, created by Carter Bays and Craig Thomas, 2005–2014.

*M*A*S*H*, created by Larry Gelbert and Gene Reynolds, 1972–1983.

Riverdale, created by Roberto Aguirre-Sacasa, 2017.

Schitt's Creek Episodes Cited

"A Whisper of Desire," season 5, episode 7, directed by Jordan Canning, written by Michael Short.

"Asbestos Fest," season 4, episode 3, directed by Bruce McCulloch, written by Monica Heisey.

"Baby Sprinkle," season 4, episode 10, directed by Bruce McCulloch, written by Rupinder Gill.

"Bad Parents," season 1, episode 4, directed by Jerry Ciccoritti, written by Kevin White.

"Bob's Bagels," season 2, episode 5, directed by Paul Fox, written by Chris Pozzebon and Daniel Levy.

"Drip, The," season 1, episode 2, directed by Jerry Ciccoritti, written by Chris Pozzebon.

"Driving Test," season 3, episode 4, directed by Paul Fox, written by Michael Short.

"Estate Sale," season 2, episode 4, directed by Jerry Ciccoritti, written by Teresa Pavlinek.

"Happy Ending," season 6, episode 14, directed by Andrew Cividino and Daniel Levy, written by Daniel Levy.

"Hospies, The," season 5, episode 8, directed by Jordan Canning, written by Rupinder Gill.

"Life Is a Cabaret," season 5, episode 14, directed by Daniel Levy and Andrew Cividino, written by Daniel Levy.

"Little Sister," season 1, episode 11, directed by Paul Fox, written by Michael Short.

"Meet the Parents," season 5, episode 11, directed by Jordan Canning, written by Daniel Levy.

"Moria Rosé," season 6, episode 7, directed by Jordan Canning, written by David West Read.

"Motel Review," season 3, episode 8, directed by Paul Fox, written by Kevin White.

"Olive Branch, The," season 4, episode 9, directed by Bruce McCulloch, written by Rupinder Gill.

"Open Mic," season 4, episode 6, directed by Bruce McCulloch, written by Daniel Levy and Rebecca Kohler.

"Our Cup Runneth Over," season 1, episode 1, directed by Jerry Ciccoritti, written by Daniel Levy.

"Pitch, The," season 6, episode 12, directed by Andrew Cividino, written by Daniel Levy.

"Premiere, The," season 6, season 5, directed by Andrew Cividino, written by David West Read.

"RIP Moira Rose," season 4, episode 5, directed by Bruce McCulloch, written by Rupinder Gill.

"Sebastian Raine," episode 3, episode 10, directed by T. W. Peacocke, written by Kevin White.

"Smoke Signals," season 6, episode 1, directed by Daniel Levy, written by Daniel Levy.

"Start Spreading the News," season 6, episode 13, directed by Jordan Canning, written by Daniel Levy.

"Town for Sale," season 1, episode 13, directed by Jerry Ciccoritti, teleplay by Kevin White, story by Daniel Levy.

"Wingman, The," season 6, episode 6, directed by Donna Croce, written by David West Read.

Index